THE
NEBRASKA
SANDHILLS

North Loup River.

THE NEBRASKA SANDHILLS

Edited by
Monica M. Norby
Judy Diamond
Aaron Sutherlen
Sherilyn C. Fritz
Kim Hachiya
Douglas A. Norby
Michael Forsberg

BISON BOOKS

University of Nebraska Press
Lincoln

The University of Nebraska Press is part of a land-grant institution with campuses and programs on the past, present, and future homelands of the Pawnee, Ponca, Otoe-Missouria, Omaha, Dakota, Lakota, Kaw, Cheyenne, and Arapaho Peoples, as well as those of the relocated Ho-Chunk, Sac and Fox, and Iowa Peoples.

This book was made possible by the University of Nebraska–Lincoln Institute of Agriculture and Natural Resources.

Except where noted, all photos are courtesy Nebraska Game and Parks Commission. Used with permission.

∞

Library of Congress Control Number: 2023027046

This book is typeset in Avenir

Book design by Aaron Sutherlen

Dedicated to all persons, past and present, who have lived and traveled the Nebraska Sandhills. Our hope for the region's future rests with those who respect its unique land and spirit.

The authors humbly and specifically acknowledge that the Nebraska Sandhills are situated within the ancestral and current homelands of a number of Indigenous nations, including but not limited to the Pawnee, Ponca, Omaha, Dakota, Lakota, Nakota, Arapaho, and Cheyenne Nations.

Donors

In addition to support from the Office of the Vice Chancellor for the Institute of Agriculture and Natural Resources, donors and underwriters helped realize publication of *The Nebraska Sandhills*. Thank you to all who made this book possible.

Trumpeter Swan / $10,000+
Agriculture Builders of Nebraska
Rhonda Seacrest
Joe and Chris Stone

Blanding's Turtle / $5,000–$9,999
University of Nebraska Center for Grasslands Studies

Bobolink / $1,000–$4,999
Arrow Seed Company Inc. (Jim and Deb Girardin)
Tom Farrell
Dale A. Grosbach
George B. Hinman
Donna and Don Hutchens
Michael and Julie Jacobson
Cristy H. Klaver
In memory of Wilber and Doris Kuenning
Angenette and Robert Meaney
Shovel Dot Ranch (Homer, Darla, Chad, and Tricia Buell)
Wagonhammer Ranch (Jay and Susie Wolf)
Art and Chris Zygielbaum

Prairie Sage / $500–$999
William C. Banks
Richard D. Berkland
Kenneth and Susan Cassman
Cooksley Ranch (George and Barbara Cooksley)
Neal A. and Bonnie S. Kanel
Martin A. Massengale
O-L-O Ranch (Al and Dottie Davis)
Sandy Scofield and Bob Wickersham
Kathleen J. Wittler

Up to $499
Susan E. Ahlschwede
Seif Mahagoub Balul
Margaret A. Bartle
Ann K. Bruntz
Daryl A. Cisney
Steven E. Den
Katherine A. Endacott
Sherilyn C. Fritz
James W. Goeke
Kim H. Hachiya and Thomas L. White
Robert F. Hachiya
Mary Manton Herres
Nila K. Jacobson
Sandra S. Krueger
Sara H. LeRoy-Toren
Brandon D. Lesoing
Edward J. Love
Karen M. Morin
Joleen A. Ness
Hon. Kathie L. Olsen
Roric and Deb Paulman
Lynn Riedel
In honor of John and Mary Schuele
Deborah A. Shanahan
J. Richard Shoemaker
Frank J. Sibert
Megan M. Volpp
Kent and Lisa Wagener
David Weber
Marcia A. White
Jens and Alison (Wimmer) Schmieder

Contents

White-tailed doe and fawn in Dawes County.

Foreword

Michael J. Boehm

When I first encountered the Sandhills after moving to Nebraska the better part of a decade ago, I immediately wished that as a kid I had received a postcard from Valentine or Mullen or Callaway or any of the ranch communities I have been privileged to visit and have come to love. It felt like the center of the world, and I wished I would have realized the magic of this region sooner.

As it was, I had just passed the midcentury mark when I first set off for the Sandhills on a frigid December morning. The shift in landscape on that drive was subtle at first, starting in a place that reminded me of Ohio and Indiana before the trees became fewer, the center pivots more uniform, and the air more crisp and less humid. And as I crossed the Kingsley Dam, the fog from Lake McConaughy lifting, I realized that I was enveloped by Nebraska's famous sea of grass, a place unlike anywhere I had ever visited—majestic, mysterious, and incredible, even on a frigid winter day.

The Sandhills are a vast landscape; the region comprises more than 19,300 square miles. Yet the Nebraskans who live in this working agricultural landscape form a tight-knit community, drawn together by the region's beauty, the breadth and reach of the cattle industry, and the joys and challenges of living in one of the least populated places and most diverse ecosystems in the world.

Sandhills communities are surrounded by rolling sand dunes stabilized by grass and intersected by winding rivers atop one of the world's largest freshwater aquifers, the Ogallala—or High Plains—Aquifer. The Nebraska Sandhills are part of the expansive Great Plains of North America on par with the Pampas of South America, the Steppes of Central Eurasia, and the Savannas of Africa.

Nebraska's Sandhills livestock—bison, horses, and sheep, but mostly cattle—graze these grass-covered dunes that also support a vast array of plant, animal, and microbial life. Cattle form the backbone of the region and the state's largest industry, which of course is agriculture. Nebraska is the Beef State, and the Sandhills are Cattle Country.

But the region is so much more, and *The Nebraska Sandhills* captures its breadth and complexity. Chapters explore the geology, ecology, climate, and vast water resources of the Sandhills. *The Nebraska Sandhills* celebrates the uniqueness of the life the region nurtures, including blowout penstemon, an endangered flowering plant once thought to be extinct that thrives in loose sandy pockets of Earth the wind has made uninhabitable to other plants. It details the rich cultural heritage of the Native Americans who have lived in harmony with this vast and life-sustaining landscape since long before there was a Nebraska. It chronicles the arrival of the homesteaders, immigrants, and cowboys who followed, and it provides a glimpse into the lives of some of the Nebraskans who live there today. One essay in this book captures the unique rhythm of life on a working ranch through all four seasons. Another looks at a quite different aspect of the Sandhills—the tourism generated by the region's remote, pristine, world-class golf courses.

This book, I hope, is the postcard I never received, a collection of all the reasons this unique area is worth visiting, worth understanding, and worth conserving for future generations. In 2022 we celebrated the College of Agricultural Sciences and Natural Resources' 150 years of impact. And 2023 marked the fiftieth anniversary of the founding of the Institute of Agriculture and Natural Resources (IANR) at the University of Nebraska–Lincoln. *The Nebraska Sandhills* is a postcard from IANR to you, the reader, in celebration of these important milestones and in celebration of this special place that feels like the center of the world.

Michael J. Boehm is University of Nebraska vice president and Harlan Vice Chancellor for the Institute of Agriculture and Natural Resources at the University of Nebraska–Lincoln.

Shell Lake Wildlife Management Area, Cherry County.

Introduction to the Nebraska Sandhills

Mary Harner

Like me, many authors who contributed to *The Nebraska Sandhills* are not of the place but came to the region through their work, studies, or a personal connection. And like me, they discovered that being in the Sandhills was life changing. They returned to learn about the natural and cultural resources, experience the beauty and solitude, and come to know people whose homes and livelihoods are within the prairie and undulating hills. In these pages, more than sixty contributors share insights about the land, water, climate, grasslands, sense of place, ranching, wildlife, and future of the Sandhills. Their writings build upon *An Atlas of the Sand Hills*, first published in 1989 and edited by Ann Bleed and Charles Flowerday.

The Sandhills cover about a quarter of the state of Nebraska, but they are distant from where most Nebraskans live. One of the Sandhills' most noticeable aspects is the darkness of the skies, an indicator of its remoteness. In fact, the outline of the Sandhills is visible on maps of the darkest areas of North America. Here star-filled skies, unobstructed views of the horizon, and places free of sounds made by people—notably traffic—offer a sense of wildness that is rare in so much of the world.

My first in-depth experience in the Sandhills—and its brilliant night sky—was at Crescent Lake National Wildlife Refuge, north of Oshkosh, Nebraska. There I assisted with a study of how kangaroo rats, a nocturnal mammal, distribute seeds in the prairie sand. That research trip, like many others to the Sandhills, involved colleagues from multiple University of Nebraska campuses and others. The fieldwork provided a way to observe and discover in the outdoor laboratory that the Sandhills offer. Even more, it sparked my curiosity to learn more about the region and a sense of responsibility to increase awareness about the place to students and others.

I first turned to *An Atlas of the Sand Hills* for information, and I have continued to use and share that publication as I have conducted research throughout the region. *An Atlas of the Sand Hills* was written as a reference book, a field guide of sorts, that was supported by scientific research and detailed descriptions that included maps, charts, and other graphics. Bleed and Flowerday said its intent was to provide readers "a better understanding and deeper appreciation of this distinctive area of Nebraska."

As a researcher who studies rivers and wetlands, I was drawn to chapters about groundwater, streams, lakes, and wetlands within this semiarid region. Decades later, the variability of the aquatic systems in the Sandhills and how water moves through this landscape continue to amaze and perplex researchers, residents, and others. For example, a lake present one month may become a dry sand bed the next; a county road may turn into a flowing stream overnight; a meadow may flood even in the midst of a drought. There remains much to learn about what this hydrologic variability and complexity mean to various organisms, including people, who rely upon and manage this ever-changing resource.

Since 2011 Platte Basin Timelapse (PBT) has documented the Sandhills through the placement of cameras that take hourly images of different landscapes and water features, including lakes, streams, and stock tanks. This visual record allows viewers to perceive change across time in ways not possible through direct observation and serves as a source of data for ecohydrological research. With a storytelling approach, PBT partners are creating context around these images and through interviews with residents, land managers, and researchers. And, importantly, they are building a community of students, early-career professionals, and others with skills to document and convey complexities of water and other natural resource topics in the Sandhills and well beyond.

In the introduction to *An Atlas of the Sand Hills*, Bleed and Flowerday described how, "yet in spite of this expertise, nearly all were quick to point out that there are still many unanswered questions about the Sand Hills. In a real sense, as the region was once a frontier for settlers, it is still a frontier for scientists." In the intervening thirty-plus years, people have continued scientific research, exploring other ways of coming to know the Sandhills and advancing knowledge of this unique place.

It is in the spirit of storytelling that authors have contributed to the following pages, seeking to share understanding and appreciation for this place and why its conservation matters. The original atlas highlighted various intersections, such as plant communities from different parts of North America that converge in the Sandhills, and opposites, such as wet versus dry and homogeneous yet varied, that occur in the region. This new book continues those themes and further empha-sizes how the land, water, climate, land use, and people are *interconnected* and *interdependent*. Attention to the roles of people in the Sandhills also extends through this book.

The Nebraska Sandhills editors' goals are to engage readers to think about this unique landscape, its future, and what it means for Nebraskans. It presents the work of scientists, historians, archaeologists, Indigenous scholars, journalists, and residents. Many have a personal stake in the region's future. In fact, all Nebraskans have a stake in the future of this landscape that supports much of the state's economy and biodiversity, as well as the health and well-being of its people.

Mary Harner is a professor of communication and biology at the University of Nebraska at Kearney.

Country road near Brownlee, Cherry County.

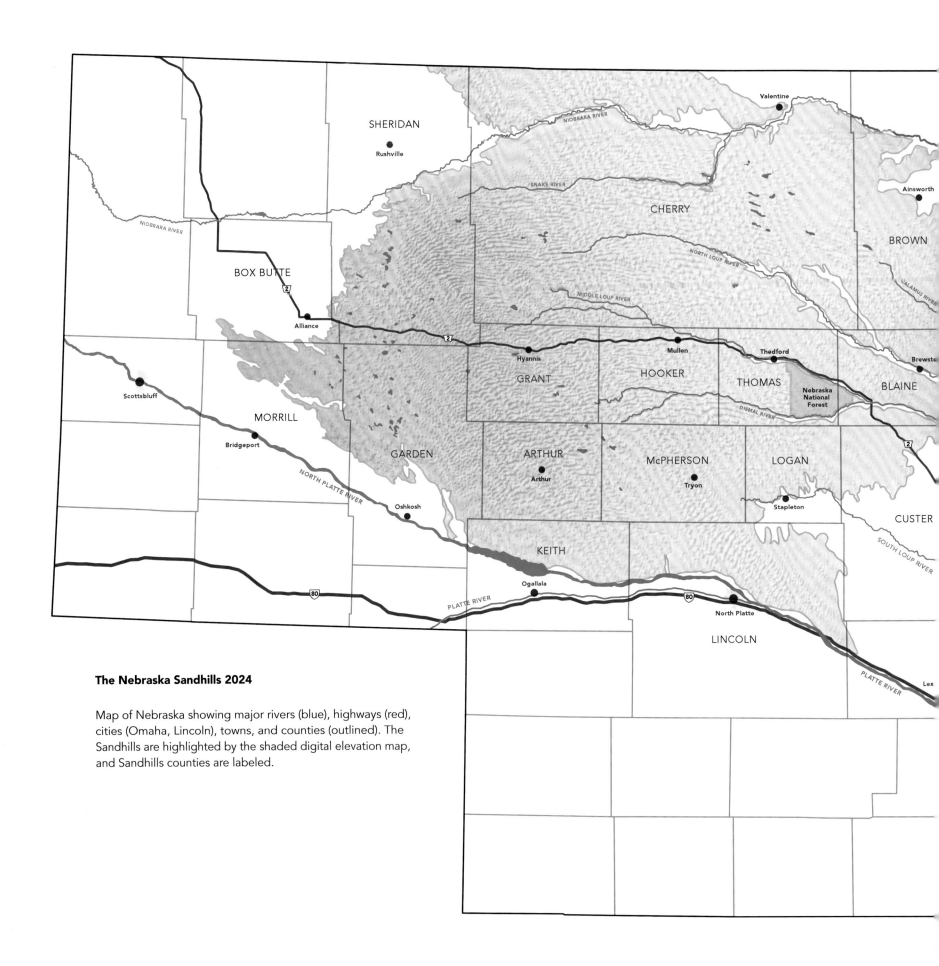

The Nebraska Sandhills 2024

Map of Nebraska showing major rivers (blue), highways (red), cities (Omaha, Lincoln), towns, and counties (outlined). The Sandhills are highlighted by the shaded digital elevation map, and Sandhills counties are labeled.

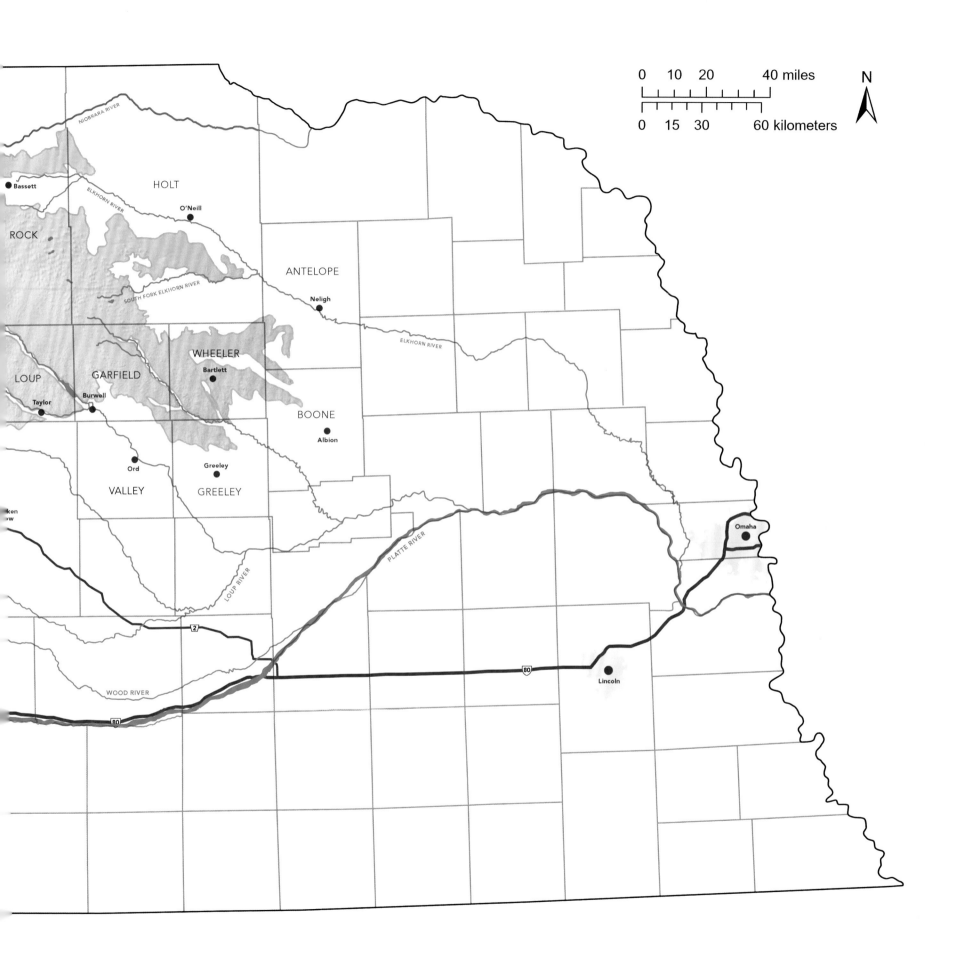

A Kingdom of Grass: The Nebraska Sandhills

Michael Forsberg

As to scenery, while I know that the standard claim is that Yosemite, Niagara Falls, the Upper Yellowstone and the like afford the greatest natural shows, I am not so sure but the prairies and plains, while less stunning at first sight, last longer, fill the esthetic sense fuller, precede all the rest, and make North America's characteristic landscape.

—Walt Whitman, *Specimen Days* (1879)

Walt Whitman probably never visited the Nebraska Sandhills, but if he had, I can only imagine what he might have thought, leaning into the wind atop a three-hundred-foot-high dune covered in a thick hide of sand bluestem and Indian grass, listening to the whistle of an upland sandpiper or watching a kettle of cranes contemplating their descent above a lonely prairie lake.

The Nebraska Sandhills is an iconic grassland landscape, cradles a diversity of prairie wildlife, and sits squarely in the middle of our nation, yet until recently few outside the region even knew its name. In 2011 this sparsely populated region was thrust onto the national stage when the proposed Keystone XL pipeline route that would carry tar sands oil from Alberta to Texas made the evening news. The route was set to cross the eastern flank of the Sandhills but met fierce resistance from ranchers and environmental activists. After months of intense debate, industry shrugged, the route was redrawn farther to the east, and the project eventually halted, tabled by Washington.

Like a rumpled wool blanket, the Sandhills spreads out over 19,300 square miles of north-central Nebraska and is the largest stabilized dune field in the Western Hemisphere. It is also the largest intact mixed-grass prairie left on the continent and covers the deepest part of the Ogallala Aquifer—the holy grail of the High Plains.

Here, when rains fall and snows melt, water soaks into the hills like a sponge, percolating through sandy soils to feed lush grassy valleys between the dunes, recharging the aquifer that in turn infuses countless wetlands, lakes, and streams.

During its brief geologic history, the Sandhills was a place of shifting sands, shaped by periods of prolonged droughts, pulses of bison, and Plains Indian tribes, like the Pawnee and Sioux, who used it for communal hunting grounds. Since Euro-American settlement, a strong cattle ranching tradition and careful land stewardship have kept the fragile soil in place, creating perhaps some of the best-managed grazing land in the world, and nearly all of it in private ownership. Though the human culture has changed, the integrity of grass has in large measure remained.

Despite its natural bounty, few people outside this geography have ever seen golden late-day light rake across wine-colored hills in October or heard the booming of prairie-chickens on frost-covered dancing grounds during an April dawn. Nor have they witnessed waterfalls that tumble over prairie ledges or through hidden forested canyons, or floated Sandhills rivers that carve their signatures in the landscape with names like the Niobrara, Dismal, and Snake.

In the depths of winter, powerful springs form pockets of open water and shelter wintering flocks of trumpeter swans, Canada geese, and mergansers. On summer days, shallow lakes reflect massive cloud towers and nesting colonies of grebes. In the prairie uplands grassland birds, like meadowlarks and long-billed curlews, make their ground nests, and windmill stock tanks harbor nurseries of amphibians, including tiger salamanders and leopard frogs. At night a party of stars gather in one of the darkest skies left in the Lower 48.

Our world's temperate grasslands have cradled civilizations for millennia. With rich soils and gentle topography, they are our world's breadbaskets and increasingly our energy pumps. Intact, they sequester massive amounts of carbon, filter our water, control soil erosion, and hold reservoirs of pollinators and biodiversity. But today they are considered the most altered and least protected biome on Earth, a victim of their natural wealth and overlooked for their beauty.

In North America's Great Plains, roughly half of our grasslands are converted to agriculture. According to the World Wildlife Fund Plowprint Report, since 2009, 53 million more acres of Great Plains grasslands (roughly the size of Kansas) have been plowed up, encouraged by a complex soup of agricultural policies, commodity pricing, and Farm Bill politics that somehow still encourage and subsidize conversion of grassland, even on marginal lands. The Nebraska Sandhills are not immune.

A few years ago, against the backdrop of severe drought, the march of conversion from grassland to cornfield continued even within the Sandhills perimeter. To its west, rumors circulate that a thirsty Denver and its sprawling population along the Front Range is carefully eyeballing the wealth of water that lies beneath the Sandhillers' feet. Now, once-dormant pipeline proposals may be revisited, and future Farm Bills will set agriculture policies. The future of these grasslands is uncertain.

So for now the Sandhills and its fragile kingdom of grass remain intact. The magic of water still spills forth from hidden contours in the sand, the valleys are still green and alive with birdsong, and the Sandhills prairie and its citizenry remain resilient. It is time to pull the curtain back on this unique landscape in the heart of the Great Plains so it can serve as an emblem of beauty, diversity, and hope for all native grasslands that still remain.

Michael Forsberg is a conservation photographer and research assistant professor in the School of Natural Resources at the University of Nebraska–Lincoln. He is a co-founder of Platte Basin Timelapse.

An Abandoned Stone Schoolhouse in the Nebraska Sandhills

Ted Kooser

These square stone walls are of sand too:
blocks of cut sandstone, stone yet sand

like all sands, always ready to go,
always showing their glittering sails.

Someday, with the work of the wind,
this will all be gone—the hollow school,

its hollow in the changing hills,
the fallen door with its shiny black knob.

Touch the wall with your fingertips,
and a hundred thousand years brush away

just like that, exposing no more
than a faint stain the color of coffee.

Put your palm flat on these stones.
Something is happening under the surface:

even in sunlight, the stone feels cool,
as if water were trickling inside,

flowing through darkness—a silent,
shadowy river, cleaning itself

as it eases along through the sand,
rubbing away at our names and our voices.

"An Abandoned Stone Schoolhouse in the Nebraska Sandhills" from *Weather Central* by Ted Kooser, © 1994. Reprinted by permission of the University of Pittsburgh Press.

Ted Kooser is the former Poet Laureate Consultant in Poetry to the Library of Congress, serving from 2004 to 2006. He is Presidential Professor Emeritus at the University of Nebraska, where he taught poetry writing.

Cattle gathered at an abandoned homestead south of Harrison.

A SENSE OF PLACE

Prairie and windmill in evening light, Valentine National Wildlife Refuge, Cherry County. Photograph by Michael Forsberg. Used with permission.

Tantalizing Clues as to Indigenous Peoples' Lives in the Sandhills

John R. "Rob" Bozell and Courtney L.C. Ziska

Humans are no strangers to the Sandhills. Long before cowboys drove their cattle to graze on its grasses and before Kinkaiders settled the area, people were here. Indigenous groups have continuously used the area for at least thirteen thousand years, hunting its game, gathering its plants, and drinking its water. They experienced the region's winds and temperature swings. They endured its storms and its droughts.

We know the experiences of these early Great Plains inhabitants through the material traces they left behind. These items and places are tangible reminders of living communities both past and present, evidence of which has been found by researchers and residents alike. Archaeologists have been probing the region for nearly a century in search of evidence of these people and their day-to-day lives to develop a better understanding of ancient habitation of the area. Increasing our understanding of these groups can be complicated, however, as much of their story lies in abandoned places and in artifacts hidden beneath the sand in thick dune fields and dense grass. The complex geologic and vegetational history of the Sandhills is a mixed blessing for archaeologists. With ancient land surfaces quickly covered by blowing sand, the places occupied by the area's earliest inhabitants may be extraordinarily well-preserved yet equally difficult to find and study. Many of the earliest traces of these groups have only been found by chance occurrence on the modern surface, exposed through erosion in blowouts or along roadcuts.

Little is known of the earliest people to enter the Sandhills region. Objects from this period have been isolated finds, which simply demonstrates that people were in fact here. The oldest artifacts found are Clovis spear points used to hunt mammoths and other now-extinct animals over thirteen thousand years ago. Over the course of the next ten thousand years, human occupation of the region continued, although it certainly ebbed and flowed as climatic and environmental conditions changed. A variety of later spear point styles dating from twelve thousand to two thousand years old have been found throughout the region and provide evidence that a myriad of ancient hunting-gathering Indigenous populations frequently lived and hunted in all areas of the Sandhills, with bison having become the predominant species on the plains. Additional information about the lives of these early inhabitants can only be gleaned from nearby sites. Other than a few burials on a remote McPherson County lakeshore and a small campsite in Sheridan County, no intact archaeological sites dating to this period have been discovered in the Sandhills. Materials found at these neighboring sites suggest that in addition to bison, these central plains peoples were hunting a wide variety of smaller game, collecting plant foods, and were involved in sophisticated long-distance trade networks.

Then, about two thousand years ago, things began to change. The number of intact habitation sites increased significantly, suggesting population growth. While this

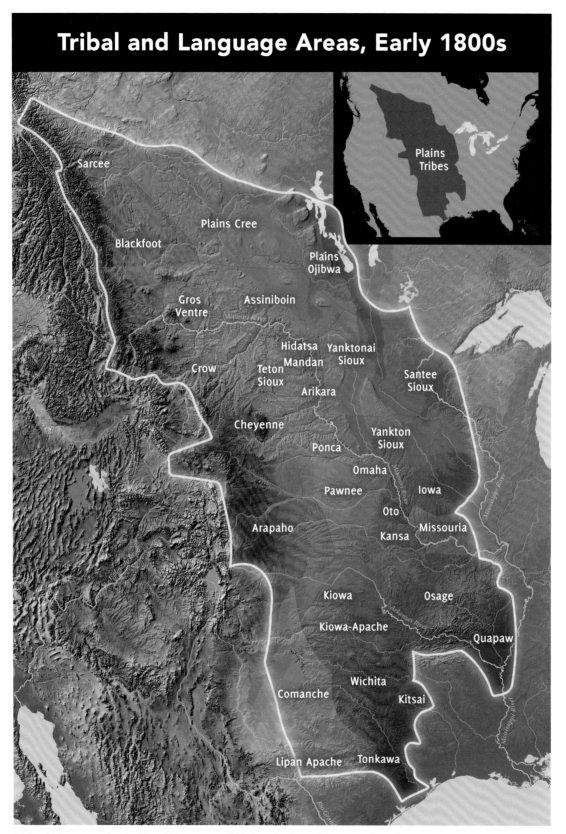

Tribal and Language Areas, Early 1800s

Plains Tribes

Sarcee

Plains Cree

Blackfoot

Plains Ojibwa

Gros Ventre

Assiniboin

Missouri River

Hidatsa

Yanktonai Sioux

Mandan

Teton Sioux

Crow

Santee Sioux

Arikara

Cheyenne

Yankton Sioux

Ponca

Omaha

Missouri River

Pawnee

Iowa

Oto

Arapaho

Missouria

Kansa

Mississippi River

Kiowa

Osage

Kiowa-Apache

Arkansas River

Quapaw

Wichita

Comanche

Kitsai

Lipan Apache

Tonkawa

Rio Grande

Mississippi River

Plains Tribe map. Angie Fox / University of Nebraska State Museum. Based on "Native American Tribal and Language Areas during the Early 1800s" in *Handbook of North American Indians*, Vol. 1. (Smithsonian Institution, 2001).

Death of Crazy Horse at Fort Robinson, depicted as ledger art by Amos Bad Heart Bull (Wanbli Waphanha), an Oglala Lakota witness to the event.

increase may be more apparent than real, with earlier sites more obscured from discovery by overlying sand dunes, this period of remarkable change is further defined by new technologies and cultural practices. Groups were becoming more sedentary, constructing small, semipermanent villages with storage systems to support longer-term occupations. These people, influenced by the Woodland Tradition of the Midwest, were the first Indigenous people to make pottery and experiment with horticulture. Deer, bison, turtle, bird, beaver, rabbit, domestic dog, and many wild plants were all food sources being consumed at small habitations found along Sandhills lakes and the Middle Loup River.

An even greater influx of people and ideas began a thousand years ago. These immigrants came from the south and were the distant ancestors of the Pawnee, Arikara, and Wichita, the first people who can be directly associated with named tribes. They lived across most of Nebraska, northern Kansas, and western Iowa, and they regularly ranged into the eastern and central Sandhills. Places like the McIntosh site in Brown County provide a glimpse into the daily lives of these people, as they occupied a small village along a Sandhills lakeshore. Here they resided, hunting and fishing over fifty bird, fish, turtle, and mammal species, gathering wild plants like chokecherries and plums, and growing domestic plants of their own, including squash and corn. The remains of their meals, their pottery, and a broad variety of stone and bone tools have been found hundreds of years later in the many storage and trash pits located across the site.

Due to climatic deterioration and related social pressures, human population in much of Nebraska dwindled significantly in the 1400s and 1500s. However, by the mid-1600s, Apaches had begun to travel and settle across the vast areas of western Nebraska and the Sandhills, occupying the region during their long migration from the subarctic to the Southwest. These hunters focused primarily on the area's bison herds, but deer, pronghorn, turtle, small mammals, and mussels were also captured and eaten. Plains Apache horticulture and plant gathering was limited, but charred remains of squash, gourd, corn, plums, chokecherries, hackberries, and black walnuts have been recovered. Hundreds of places are known to have been visited or occupied by the Apache in the Sandhills, with the best known being Humphrey, a small village along the Middle Loup River.

To the east, the Pawnee, operating out of large earth-lodge towns in the lower Platte River and Loup River basins, conducted bison hunting forays into the eastern and central Sandhills. This may have led to competition for hunting territory, perhaps explaining Apache abandonment of the area by the 1700s. Other tribes such as the Lakota, Cheyenne, Arapahoe, Crow, Comanche, and Kiowa also hunted and traveled through the Sandhills,

though they left virtually no archaeological signature. Interactions among these tribes and their use of the Sandhills continued much the same up until the development of the area for cattle ranching and subsequent European settlement.

We really have only just begun to understand the relationship between ancient people and this remarkable landscape. The story is not an easy one to tell, in that so many of the details remain unknown. While it is tempting to assume the Sandhills only provided Indigenous groups with an abundance of bison hunting territory, the reality is far more complex. The Sandhills offered a vast array of fish, birds, mammals, and reptiles for food, tools, and ornaments. Stream floodplains, lakeshores, and marshes, supplied by the groundwater

In 2005 Ronnie O'Brien planted the last twenty-five kernels of Pawnee corn in the Echo-Hawk family's possession, renewing Eagle corn, pictured here.

reservoir, provided opportunities for productive wild plant collecting and horticulture, possibly persisting even in times of drought. With its enormous size and so many remote places, the region provided an excellent opportunity to avoid conflict and hostility with other groups. In this sense, the Sandhills might have served as a refuge of sorts. Of course, the opportunities presented by the Sandhills were no doubt matched by a number of challenges. Even with today's technology and modern transportation and communication networks, life in the Sandhills can be difficult and isolating.

Sandhills archaeology is much more than a collection of beautiful spear points and ceramic vessels. It is an ongoing quest to understand how people adapted to this vast and unique region through time and space. The region remains ripe for exciting and productive archaeological research, with its ancient surfaces preserved deep under sand. However, as more sites are exposed as a result of continued erosion or discovered ahead of development, it is important to remember that such places are finite and truly nonrenewable resources. As opportunities to explore these places arise, we must weigh preservation with unlocking the secrets they hold and continue to emphasize a multidisciplinary approach. Only by taking into consideration studies involving geology, the past climate, and the past environment can archaeology help us to understand how the earliest central plains inhabitants experienced the Sandhills thousands of years ago.

John R. "Rob" Bozell retired as Nebraska State Archaeologist in 2021 and remains active in archaeological research and consulting.

Courtney L.C. Ziska is an archaeologist and national environmental policy act specialist at the Nebraska Department of Transportation.

People gathered around a drum at a powwow at Fort Robinson State Park.

Humphrey Site Reveals Apaches' Presence

John R. "Rob" Bozell and Courtney L.C. Ziska

The Humphrey site near Mullen is one of the premiere archaeological properties that has helped tell the complex story of the Plains Apache people and what life in the Sandhills was like hundreds of years ago. Named after a local amateur archaeologist who first reported the site in the 1940s, the property was reinvestigated in 2017-2018. Using ground-penetrating radar and other geophysical prospecting methods, archaeologists located several buried house ruins at the site. Excavation of these structures revealed details related to settlement, architecture, diet, trade, and conflict in the Sandhills.

Humphrey was occupied repeatedly by one or more Apache groups in the 1600s. The site was not just a campsite. The people who lived there built semi-permanent houses made from local cedar and juniper trees, which may have resembled southwestern-style Navajo or Apache hogans and wickiups. They were apparently food secure, selectively hunting bison, deer, antelope, birds, and turtles. They gathered local edibles, including chokecherries and grapes, and probably even established corn gardens. While corn varieties had been on the central Great Plains for hundreds of years by this time, having originated in central Mexico, raising corn in the Sandhills without irrigation is a feat in a climate similar to today's.

The Plains Apache made dozens of clay pots for storage and cooking and had a diverse assortment of stone tools and weapons. The Sandhills has no outcrops of stone needed to make arrow points, knives, and scrapers, requiring trade networks or long distance travel to source areas located at least 150 to 200 miles away. At least one material, obsidian, originated as far away as New Mexico. No horse bones were identified during excavation, suggesting that travel would have been conducted on foot. Dogs were kept as domestic animals and may have hauled materials and supplies.

Humphrey represents the most northeasterly incursion of Plains Apaches into Nebraska. Evidence of European contact is limited to a single metal bead and two animal bones with metal tool cut marks. This area was traditional Pawnee hunting territory from the 1600s and shared perhaps with the Omaha and Ponca after 1700. Oral traditions by these three eastern Nebraska tribes refer to an awareness of and conflicts in the Sandhills with the "Padouca" which likely refers to Apaches. This conflict might explain why the Apaches ended up abandoning their homes on the Middle Loup River around 1700 CE, leaving behind only the archaeological site as we know it today.

The Turtle at the End of the World

Roger Echo-Hawk

Esoteric visionary experience once shaped the Pawnee worldbuilding project. Dreams and visions descended from hidden mechanisms of the cosmic order, floating down from celestial realms of the deities of the heavens to define what it meant to be Pawnee, the truths of history and culture.

When François Marie Perrin du Lac wrote a memoir of his 1801–1803 journeys across the United States, he mentioned a visit to a Chaui Pawnee city. He included a fascinating map. Along the edges of the upper waters of the Many Wild Potatoes River, a curious note appeared, translated as "Great Desert of quicksand where there is no wood, no earth, no stone, no water, no animals except small turtles of various colors."

Scholars agree that Perrin du Lac fabricated his account of visiting Pawneeland in 1802 borrowing from other fur traders headquartered in St Louis. It seems that he visited St. Louis in 1802, he found various records there, he talked to some fur traders, and may even have met a Pawnee or two. Perhaps he did take a trip up the Mysterious River. But he most likely just invented that journey to Pawneeland. And as he pictured what he would have seen there, he decided to include a desert filled with turtles.

Turtles do exist in the Nebraska Sandhills. Very pretty creatures—Americans call them ornate box turtles. The Pawnees have several terms for turtles, but the most likely Pawnee name for the ornate box turtle is a Skidi Pawnee word: caaskíwiktu', or "sand turtle."

A turtle headed for water left evidence in the sand at a Garfield County lake. Photograph by Michael Forsberg. Used with permission.

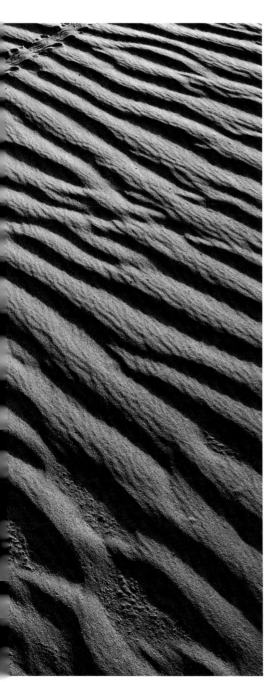

I make these comments on turtles with a slight disquiet. Long ago I dreamed that I found my way to the edge of a lake, and as I stood on a bluff above the water, I slowly noticed that I was surrounded. Dark, unsettling holes. And turtles. Many turtles dwelt there. I watched as they slipped in and out of the water, disappearing on unknown errands. I watched for a time, glad that they took no notice of me. Ever since, turtles seem creatures of a solemn antiquity. Masterful. Capable of inexplicable magic. Keepers of dread secrets long lost from our sunlit world. And I dare not inquire.

My dreaming can be read many ways in Pawneeland today. But it wasn't so long ago that Pawnees centered the magic of dream imagery in civic life and ceremonial storytelling. This mystical Pawnee dream-world has wafted away, displaced, thoroughly Americanized by alternate cultural protocols. During the decades around 1900, the ancient surrealism of dream worldbuilding evaporated from the essences of Pawnee cultural identity. And when the Pawnees of that time realized their world was vanishing, concerned tradition-keepers took action. They helped to create a vast written literature of oral traditions, precious glimpses of the inner realms of Pawneeland.

Around 1905 Little Chief was the leading Chaui resaru, a community leader with celestial blessings. He related a story that was usually told during the Chaui Bear Dance. When a man named Smoking With The Bear was a youth, he got lost while hunting a káwahki—a magpie. And he dreamed of a magic turtle "covered with mud. Fire came from his mouth and eyes." The turtle told him: "I am the fireplace of the animal lodges." The youth awakened and "he saw in the pond sparks of fire."

Some Pawnee doctors constructed a special turtle sculpture in their rites. In 1914 Skidi scholar James R. Murie wrote that preparation of the ritual lodge for the annual doctor ceremonial included a special fireplace: "The fireplace is cleared out and a large turtle modeled there, his head toward the altar. A new fireplace is then made on his back."

In 1905 Kiwikurawaruksti or Mysterious Buffalo Bull was a prominent Skidi ceremonialist; he told of how the great ghost divinity, Pahukatawa, predicted a meteor shower. One particular star would fall to earth, "the shape of a turtle and will have many colors." And one night in 1833 the stars fell, and they "flew around like birds." Several years later two men found a meteorite in "the shape of a turtle," and the Skidi priests decided to keep it with the Morning Star Bundle.

And one day in April 1905 Mysterious Buffalo Bull spoke to James R. Murie about the dedication of a ceremonial earthlodge: "You see our fire place. It is the Morning Star that is where our sun come from. It is also the picture of a turtle when really it is the Morning Star. You see the head of the turtle is towards the east. That is where the gods [do] their thinking in the East. While in the west is where all things are created and you see the hind end of the turtle is in the West. The four legs are the four world quarter gods uphold the Heavens."

In Pawneeland the caaskíwiktu' is filled with fire, a meditative keeper of celestial magic and obscure intentions.

Waters of Merritt Reservoir in Cherry County reflect the Milky Way and a passing thunderstorm. Photograph by Michael Forsberg. Used with permission.

Surrealism can grant us glimpses of mysterious truths. We value unexpected juxtapositions that bestow new insights. But this functional surrealism differs from fictional inventions—Perrin du Lac gave himself permission to imagine a realm of colorful turtles in the Sandhills of Pawneeland, and we can readily distinguish his invented Pawnee turtles from Pawnee mythological dream turtles.

Culture can be manufactured from dreams, but history is not a dream. And making sense of dreams is not the same as fabricating the past. We need to know what really happened; lies do not help. In this true story, dream and visionary experience once shaped the psychedelic mythmaking of Pawneeland. That world has faded, but perhaps we can nevertheless suggest that caaskíwiktu' still lingers at the edge of our dreaming, filled with fire.

And in 1875 before the Skidi left their ancient homeland, removing to Oklahoma, Lone Chief and several men rode off on a secret errand, bearing the Morning Star meteorite turtle. They set this turtle from the stars "on a high, sandy hill in the western part of Nebraska." We can guess that they wished to make it possible for the turtle to return to the stars. This turtle, foretold in a vision, had one more dreamlike journey to make.

And we could say that this final mystical journey of the meteorite turtle marked a symbolic end to Pawnee dream-culture. Lone Chief and his men rode down from that sandy hill, then returned to Wild Licorice Creek. When the Skidi departed from the Pawnee homeland, they forever left behind their surreal project of dream worldbuilding.

Roger Echo-Hawk is a writer and artist who studies Pawnee history.

Skidi Pawnee Mythic Journey

Roger Echo-Hawk

In a 1904 Skidi Pawnee story told by Newly Made Leader Woman or Clara Yellow Sun, a young woman ran off with a man who turned out to be a dreaded outcast, a kitsahuruksu. She probably heard this story from her father, a famous Skidi doctor named Scabby Bull. In the story, the Scalped Man held the poor woman captive. When she got pregnant, he brought her a cradleboard. And after her contractions began, she made ready to give birth, and the Scalped Man stepped to a dark corner of the cavern, promising to summon a midwife. An opening appeared. A large turtle crawled out of the river. It placed its paws on the woman, and she "gave birth without pain, and the turtle went back into the water." This association of turtles with childbirth is rooted in mythological storytelling.

One of the greatest of Skidi priests was Scout Roaming the World, and about 1905 he told a fascinating version of a Skidi cosmogonic narrative. In the story, Morning Star carried Sun as a "ball of fire" and he wielded that fire to vanquish a series of obstacles. On this quest he achieved various tasks, including "the bringing of the baby-board which is guarded by turtles in the form of hot fire." This mythic journey gave rise to the form of the cosmos. And the folk of Pawneeland sought to reflect in ceremony the wishes of the heavenly realm, the celestial intentions that gave rise to humankind.

Cheyenne Sanctuary
The Northern Cheyennes' Exodus, Mari Sandoz, and Lost Chokecherry Lake

Emily Levine

The Indigenous people of the central plains understood the Sandhills to be an enormous larder of bison as well as deer, elk, and pronghorn. They knew the Nebraska Sand hills and were not afraid of them; they knew how to travel through them; they knew where the springs and sweet water were, which lakes were alkali, and which were not.

White men, *vé'ho'e* to the Cheyenne, held quite a different view. The first written description of the Sandhills is on a published map attributed to James McKay, the leader of an Upper Missouri Company fur-trading expedition in the 1790s. He wrote of the region, "Great deserts of drifting sand without trees, soil, rocks, water, or animals of any kind." Army lieutenant G.K. Warren was the first to traverse the Sandhills north to south and recorded an even dimmer view in 1855, grumbling that "the scenery is exceedingly solitary, silent, and desolate, and depressing to one's spirit" and he hated having to constantly climb "up one side and down the other" of the dunes while his animals sank deeper and deeper in the sand. Unlike the Indigenous peoples, he did not know how to travel through the Sandhills, how to navigate their passage. Warren was, however, prescient in his observation that the "character of the country is well calculated to cover a stealthy approach or retreat, and if one keeps as much as possible to the hollows he may even fire his rifle within a quarter-mile of an enemy's camp without the faintest sound reaching it. Two parties may pass close without being aware of each other's presence, and I consider it hopeless to attempt to capture any who sought refuge in the Sand Hills."

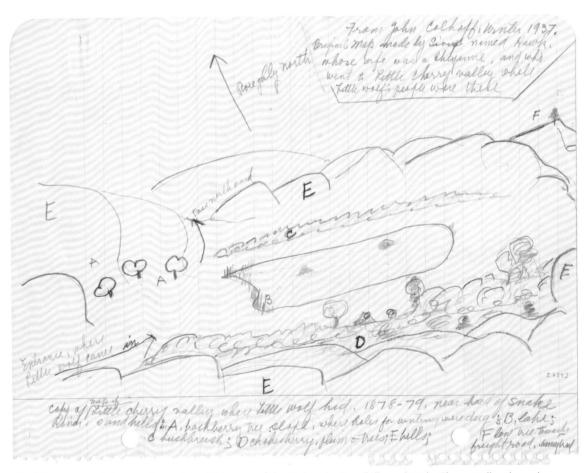

Mari Sandoz hand-drew and annotated this map of the Nebraska Sandhills and Little Cherry Valley, based on an original by Hawk, a Lakota, who made it in 1878. Used with permission. McIntosh & Otis, Inc.

On the night of September 7, 1878, more than 350 Northern Cheyenne—92 men, 120 women, and 141 children—left their reservation, led by two of their Old Man Chiefs, Morning Star (Dull Knife) and the Sweet Medicine Chief and bundle carrier Little Wolf. They were leaving the hated Oklahoma reservation to which they had been sent after their final defeat and surrender following the Little Big Horn fight. It was a place where the heat, starvation due to insufficient rations, and rampant diseases addressed with wholly inadequate medical care had killed scores; the Cheyenne were heading north to their Wyoming homeland. Military telegrams flew, troops were mustered, and the pursuit began. The story has been told many times of the Cheyenne "exodus," "odyssey," the "trek north," though rarely satisfactorily and never completely.

As the Cheyenne moved into Nebraska, a series of Keystone Cops–type military failures plagued the U.S. Army as thousands of troops were mobilized from Fort Reno, in present-day Oklahoma, to Fort Robinson, yet the Indians continually slipped away. Sometime after crossing the Platte forks in Nebraska, Morning Star and Little Wolf parted ways. Morning Star wanted to go to their friend Red Cloud's agency in the northwest corner of the state, while Little Wolf wanted to continue home. At this point, every account of the exodus follows Morning Star's people, who, much to their dismay, discovered that Red Cloud's agency had been moved and all that remained at Fort Robinson were soldiers. The horrors of their forced starvation while being held prisoner in the barracks, the bloody desperate breakout escape into the snow and bitter cold, and the final decimation in the "pit" at Hat Creek are well-documented.

Yet the story of Little Wolf and his followers is barely told, usually something along the lines of "Little Wolf continued north" or, if we're lucky, "they wintered in the Sandhills," and then a yawning ellipsis leading to "they

surrendered to Lieut. Clark in Montana." Why? Because the Cheyenne disappeared into the Sandhills, and try as they might—more troops, more scouting, more telegrams flashing across the frozen wires—the army never found them that winter.

Little Wolf led his people north from the Platte up its tributary, White Tail Creek, at what is now the east end of Lake McConaughy. This is supported by a 1931 letter from rancher John Bratt to Nebraska State Historical Society director Addison Sheldon in which Bratt relates that the Cheyenne made camp a few miles west of his Big Baldy cattle camp. Luther North, rancher and officer of the Pawnee Scouts, relates in his recollections, *Man of the Plains*, that horses were stolen from his ranch, said to be 15 miles east of the Cheyenne camp, and he writes that Bratt's nearby ranch had been attacked. Sandhills human geographer C. Barron McIntosh explores these accounts and locates this temporary Cheyenne camp on two of his maps in *The Nebraska Sand Hills: The Human Landscape*. He writes that Cheyenne Lake in Arthur County gets its name from being the location of the camp.

While Mari Sandoz curiously does not write of this temporary camp between the headwaters of the Middle Loup and Dismal Rivers, the many maps she annotated or drew during her research for *Cheyenne Autumn*, her novelized account of the exodus, show the necessary eastward bulge of the Cheyenne's route just where it was located. And out of the hundreds of Sandhill lakes, Sandoz also includes on her maps a small dot labeled Krumpf Lake, approximately midway between the Cheyenne temporary camp and the main winter camp, which further illuminates their route.

In 1937 the mixed-blood Lakota interpreter from Pine Ridge who Sandoz had worked with while on her research trip for her Crazy Horse book, gave her or

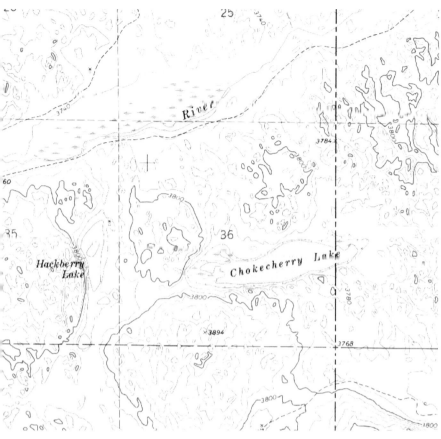

Topographical map showing the location of Little Cherry Valley in the Nebraska Sandhills. U.S. Geological Survey.

showed her a map made by a Lakota man who had visited his Cheyenne wife at that final hidden winter camp in the Sandhills. The Sandoz map collection includes a pencil sketch made from that map with the notation: "From John Colhoff, winter 1937. Original map made by Sioux named Hawk whose wife was a Cheyenne and who went to Little Cherry Valley [sic] while Little Wolf's people were there." The map shows the shape and orientation of the lake and keyed identifying features surrounding it. Also included in the collection are three photostat copies of it with all of the text typewritten. Because photostats, an early form of making photocopies, was a time-consuming and bulky process, this was clearly an important piece of evidence for Sandoz.

As much as possible, Sandoz insisted on familiarity for the places she wrote about. She retraced the entire

Cheyenne exodus route, surveyed on foot and in detail the Fort Robinson breakout, and according to neither "could she rest until she was able to identify the place where Little Wolf and his followers survived the harsh Nebraska winter undetected after they had earlier parted from Dull Knife's band and thus avoided the fate that group suffered. To accomplish her purpose, she enlisted the aid of several of her siblings. When they finally helped her locate the place after tedious and prolonged efforts, she identified it as Lost Chokecherry Lake. To her surprise, it was located in a remote region of the ranch of her brother Jules A. Sandoz, Jr.," as LaVerne Harrell Clark wrote in 2005 in an article for *Whispering Wind*. The site of the Cheyenne winter camp that kept Little Wolf and his people safely hidden and protected during the winter of 1878–79 was only a few miles from where she had grown up.

It was in 1949 that Sandoz identified the camp site at Chokecherry Lake, just south of the Snake River on the Cherry County–Sheridan County border. Her typed notes about the trip with her siblings read:

> Oct 11, 1949
>
> LITTLE CHOKECHERRY, valley in Sandhills
> Legal Des: T30 R41 SE½ SEC 36, T30 R40 W½ SEC 31
> App 140–160 acres in valley, about 40 acres in lake, usually.
>
> Protected from wind, water sweet. . . .
>
> Rushes, probably muskrats then, and timber along north slope full of deer. Timber includes a few evergreens, cedar, hackberry, cottonwood, plum, willows, buckbrush [coralberry], chokecherry, rosebrush.
>
> Suggested by Jules. Flora driving, Caroline along. Walked across where no road led to valley. Located it then went around on trail made by mowers. No road into valley. Got in ok, with car. Ate lunch under hackberries on slope of west end.

Mari Sandoz was the first white historian to identify and locate the elusive winter camp of Little Wolf's fleeing

Cheyenne where they managed, apparently without tipis, to live off of deer, elk, and the escaped cattle that wandered the hills. The map from Hawk matched the lake and its environs on her brother's land; as Sandoz wrote, "Lost Chokecherry turned out exactly as both the Sioux and Cheyenne described it to me." Cheyenne sources later told Sandoz that they, as well as the Lakota, knew this lake as in the past they would make their final night's camp there when they traveled to Frederick LaBoue's trading posts a few miles away along the Snake River. They explained, "Because there were always enemies in the region, Poncas and Pawnee come to trade too . . . because it offered all that a camp needed, including escape gaps in each direction and brush enough to hide out."

Lieut. G.K. Warren's words proved true: the Lost Chokecherry camp was so close to the Kearney–Black Hills trail, used by miners and the military, that the road could be seen from the Lone Tree on a nearby hill (F on the sketch map). Despite traffic on the trail, army camps on the Snake and Niobrara Rivers, and patrolling reconnaissances for the Cheyenne from these camps, the Cheyenne remained safely hidden. When troops tried to search for the Indians, they were driven back by the bitter cold and snow. Eventually, they concluded that Little Wolf's band had slipped away again, headed north, they believed, to Sitting Bull in Canada Toward spring, however, the troops would stumble on the large trail made by the Indians when they eventually left the valley in late February. Only then, backtracking the trail, did they discover the Chokecherry Lake camp, so near yet never found over the course of almost four months.

Little Wolf guided his people east when they first left the lake, thus avoiding the Niobrara crossing of the Kearney–Black Hills trail and all the soldiers camped in the area. Eventually they turned northwest and continued along the east side of the Black Hills, finally making it to their homeland where 114 people—33 men, 43 women, and 38 children—surrendered peacefully to their old friend Lieut. Philo Clark, who they called White Hat, on March 25, 1879, near Fort Keogh in southeast Montana. The Cheyenne Sweet Medicine Chief had led his people home.

Emily Levine is an independent scholar of the Great Plains focusing on Indigenous history and culture.

Little Wolf. Photograph taken by Alexander Gardner during the 1868 treaty negotiations at Fort Laramie. Signal Corps Photo, National Archives and Records Service.

Settlers
Ranchers, Homesteaders, Immigrants

Andrew S. Pollock

Sandhills settlers posed with their animals and garden outside sod houses and barn. The photo was taken about 1910 by John Nelson, a commercial photographer based in Ericson, Nebraska. RG3542 Nelson, John, 1864–1942 RG3542.PH000132-000009, History Nebraska.

Our earliest records describe the Nebraska Sandhills as "a great desert of shifting sand" unfit for settlement. The great desert sands do not shift. They are stabilized by grasses. On the question of fitness for settlement, however, were they correct? Europeans settled the Sandhills over the last three decades of the 1800s. Populations peaked in the 1920s. Since then, depopulation has been precipitous. Questions of sustainability remain.

On May 9, 1869, the last spike was driven on the first transcontinental railroad, opening access to markets on both coasts of the United States. Records from the same year show the Lonergan brothers raising a small herd of cattle they had driven from Texas to the lower Sandhills in upper Keith County. To the surprise of many, the cattle flourished. Over the next decade, massive herds of Texas cattle were driven to Nebraska, arriving gaunt from the long trail. More ranchers settled in the Sandhills, fanning out east and west from where Kingsley Dam now blocks the North Platte River. They fattened beef over the winter, then trailed south to a new Union Pacific Railroad line. From the new terminus of the Texas Trail at Ogallala, the rail line followed the Platte Valley east to Omaha and transected west across the lower Panhandle, through Kimball County, toward developing western markets.

Often teachers in one-room schoolhouses were not much older than their pupils. A famous story tells of the bravery and heroism of a school-teacher who saved her pupils during a vicious blizzard in 1888. This image, ca. 1910, was taken in Wheeler County. RG3542 Nelson, John, 1864–1942 RG3542.PH000092-000003-1, History Nebraska.

Some of these early Sandhills cowboys had given up the trail after driving from Texas. They pushed cattle farther north into Arthur and McPherson Counties. By 1873, the year barbed wire was invented, ranchers were also filling up the South Loup valley upstream of Kearney into Custer County, while others began moving into the Sandhills from the north into Brown County. Before long, Nebraska was producing its own beef for the rest of the country. Ranchers settled in the valleys scattered among the Sandhills. Herds roamed unfenced open range, land in the public domain. Branding was critical During blizzards masses of cattle drifted southeasterly across the open range into homestead land along the rivers. Ranches consolidated and grew. Opportunities for ranching were promoted in advertising and books, including Gen. James Bisbin's 1881 bestseller, *Beef Bonanza, or How to Get Rich on the Plains*. New railroad lines expanded access to market. By 1882 the Fremont, Elkhorn & Missouri Railroad, curving across northeast Nebraska, had reached Valentine. Before the end of the decade, the Burlington and Missouri River Railroad had sliced its way through the center of the Sandhills from Grand Island to Alliance.

The cold, snowy winter of 1880–81 was a harbinger of a tumultuous decade. Relentless blizzards drove off many cattle ranchers, especially the smaller operations, during much of the decade. Weather was not the ranchers' only adversary. While larger ranches prospered, the economic and cultural landscape changed. In 1882 a lower Sandhills rancher saw the "trickle of homesteaders into the big North Platte Valley" as a portent of things to come as Nellie Snyder Yost wrote in *The Call of the Range*. Like all cattlemen, he "feared the plowman." Before the middle of the decade, grangers were "flocking in by the hundreds . . . plowing up little patches of land for corn, picketing out their milk cows, sending complaints against the cattlemen to Washington."

Throughout the early settlement of the Sandhills, cattlemen and farmers fought over loss of livestock and crops, the battle lines haphazardly drawn in fence laws at the local, state, and federal levels. Separating livestock and crops was a challenge in the Nebraska plains. The stone walls of New England were not possible. There were few rails to be split; fence laws had little value without fence. Many a farmer found satisfaction in eating a good beef cow that had strayed through his crops. On occasion a granger corralled a few head and trailed the collection to town for sale. The story of Print Olive hanging cattle rustlers who killed his brother resounds through the Sandhills today.

In his 1931 *Great Plains*, Walter Prescott Webb wrote: "Barbed wire made the hundred-and-sixty-acre homestead both possible and profitable on the Prairie Plains; it made the homestead possible in the dry plains, but it did not make it profitable. The farmers took the homesteads there, but they did not and could not always hold them. Conditions were still too hard."

Good fences did not guarantee good crops, nor did they necessarily mean good neighbors. Fights continued between granger and cattleman. Wire cutters were deployed by both sides. Ranchers became notorious for fencing the public domain to build cattle empires. The war for the Sandhills took on epic scale when a former rancher named Teddy Roosevelt used the power of the U.S. presidency to lock up Bartlett Richards of the Spade Ranch on charges related to illegal fencing. In 1911, before his one-year sentence was served, Richards died; he was the last of the cattle kings.

Richards outlived the other cattle kings because he fought the longest. Most of the range was "stitched up with fences" before the 1880s were over. The last round-up in Cherry County was in 1885. The finale, conducted with great fanfare in Cheyenne County, followed three

Congregation of the first African American church established in Brownlee, Nebraska, one of three Nebraska communities created by African Americans who took advantage of the Kinkaid Act. The 1910 census recorded eighty-two Black residents in Cherry County. The number of occupied African American homesteads peaked in 1914, although some settlers had already canceled or sold their claims and moved away. Note the sod construction. RG2301 Photographer unknown (ca. 1910) RG2301.PH000001-000003, History Nebraska.

years later. As Yost wrote, "By the end of 1888 the cattle kingdoms were virtually gone. . . . In time, the ranches would be big again, never as big as in the fabulous '80's, but good-sized outfits; and they'd be managed after a new fashion, under fence, with winter feeding."

Over the three decades from the 1880s through the 1910s, grangers and ranchers fought over the edges of the Sandhills, until the matter was mostly settled. The 1904 Kinkaid Act, by granting up to 640 acres, allowed the homesteader one last fighting chance at making a go of farming in the Sandhills. This act brought one of the few ethnic settlements into the Sandhills. Two dozen African American families claimed about fourteen thousand acres in Cherry County and established a town they named after one of the business owners, DeWitty. Like nearly all homesteads in the Sandhills, the DeWitty settlement failed. Yet, it is not the homesteader who was unfit for the Sandhills; rather, it was the Sandhills that were unfit for the homestead.

A prominent windmill was a key part of being able to set up a viable homestead. This family's sod house featured windows. Solomon Butcher, known for his photographs of pioneers, took this photo in 1887. RG2608 Butcher, Solomon D. (Solomon Devore), 1856–1927 RG2608.PHO-001199, History Nebraska.

Beyond grangers pushing the limits of the Sandhills, other industries critical to the business of livestock have defined the Sandhills with different edges. The establishment of the Union Stockyards in 1883 linked Omaha to the Sandhills. The stockyards brought immigrants flooding into South Omaha from Europe. Omaha, of course, is 250 miles east of the Sandhills. As the days of the Omaha stockyards waned, meatpacking plants were established along the edges of the Sandhills. As the stockyards of Omaha once did, the meatpacking plants

of Schuyler and Lexington draw immigrants. Yet immigrants have not moved into the Sandhills. They remain on the edges.

Nearly all academic literature on immigration in Nebraska is devoid of information about the Sandhills. Rare anecdotes—such as DeWitty and a small group of Japanese laborers who slept in holes dug in the ground while helping build the potash factories near Antioch—only emphasize the lack of ethnic and racial diversity in the Sandhills. The statistic that perhaps best paints the picture is that 2.8 percent of the populations of Sandhills counties is Hispanic, compared to 33.3 percent in Dawson County, where a meatpacking plant has operated since the 1980s.

A year after the Union Stockyards were built in Omaha, T.B. Hord shipped 235 cattle from range in Wyoming to a farm north of Central City, where he put them on feed, and a separate industry was spawned on the edges of the Sandhills. Today, stockyards and feeders remain largely on the edges of the Sandhills.

Over the decades, the granger invasion abated. By 1920 populations in most Sandhills counties had peaked. The Depression chased the hardiest homesteaders from their claims, and farmland retreated to better soils. Today, tilling the Sandhills has taken on its own ethos, although eight-dollar corn squeezed the edges in the early years of the twenty-first century.

Current estimates indicate the average population loss since the peak in all Sandhills counties is 59.3 percent. Over the past hundred years, the Sandhills have experienced economic stagnation, ranch consolidation, and population loss. Certainly, there are exceptions. Entrepreneurs, who understand the need for diversification in both attraction and audience, are creating authentic local experience in breweries, premium beef, canoeing wild rivers through backcountry more remote than the Rockies, bird-watching tours, star-gazing parties, and world-class golf.

Barbed wire, the windmill, the revolver, and the railroad were essential to the early settlement of the Sandhills. Continued infrastructure development has been important to the long-term settlement of the Sandhills. Rural electrification made life more bearable for the isolated rancher. Paved highways, blacktopped roads, and telephone lines allowed ranchers more connection with the rest of America. Modern broadband infrastructure offers affordable access to markets around the globe. All such infrastructure is critical to diversification of life in the Sandhills.

Although the foregoing instruments give shape to the human settlement of the Sandhills, they do not altogether define the Sandhills. Humans themselves are, of course, part of the Sandhills—part of the grit felt by outsiders—but humans are more defined by the Sandhills than they are a defining agent. The Sandhills are not Broadway; they are not subway graffiti.

Who, by definition, is a Sandhiller? A sampling tells of one made independent, tough, stubborn, self-reliant, innovative, and perhaps wealthy by the nature of their place of life and business. We might roughly define humans and their assorted constructions and agree they are all part of the Sandhills, but, still, what then are the Sandhills?

To answer that, return to the question the first correspondents reporting from history asked and answered. Are the Sandhills fit for habitation? Is settlement in the Sandhills sustainable? Perhaps, rather, the inquiry should now be, what is this that we want to sustain? Or, is it even for us to ask, what do we want the Sandhills to be?

The Sandhills are remnants of antiquity, treeless deserts, vast grasslands, pristine landscapes, largely undisturbed by people. Our attempt to tame them with the plow backfired. These lands were meant to be wild, wilderness, backcountry, the range of bison and cattle.

Andrew S. Pollock is a partner with Rembolt Ludtke law firm. He grew up in Keith County, Nebraska.

The Black Homesteaders of DeWitty

Richard K. Edwards

African Americans filtered into the Great Plains after Southern whites defeated their hopes for owning land in the South. They came to Cherry County to homestead from a variety of places, including Custer County, Omaha, even Canada, to seek land in the Sandhills made available through the Kinkaid Act.

Leroy Gields and his sister Matilda Robinson entered the first claims, in 1902 and 1904. Charles and Hester Meehan, an Irish man and Black woman arrived in 1907 to live in open and undisturbed defiance of Nebraska's anti-miscegenation law. In all, fifty-eight Black people successfully proved up their claims and gained owner- ship of nearly thirty thousand acres in the homesteader community of DeWitty.

DeWitty settlers believed strongly in education. They es- tablished three school districts in 1908–9, and for at least one year, Black and white schoolchildren sat side by side in class. In 1912 Miles DeWitty set up a combined post office and tiny general store; only a few other structures stood nearby. It was more a rural neighborhood of con- centrated homesteading than a town. Despite their large farms, families were connected by kinship ties and by church, schools, and community social events. Residents converted an old sod building into the St. James African Methodist Episcopal (AME) Church.

The community initially prospered, reaching its maximum population of 150 in 1915. DeWitty residents and white ranching families seemed to interact harmoniously at a time when anti-Black prejudice in the nation turned increasingly violent. In 1919 white people in Omaha lynched Will Brown, a Black man, and in 1929, a mob in

Hester Freeman Meehan photographed by her son, William Meehan, between 1915 and 1918 in front of the family's sod house in DeWitty. Used with permission, Catherine E. Blount.

North Platte drove all Blacks, about two hundred people, out of town. But in the Sandhills, Black and white resi- dents respected each other, and no incidents of hostility or violence against DeWitty residents were recorded.

DeWitty declined in the 1920s as farmers struggled with the nationwide farm depression and drier times locally. Families moved to find more favorable farming conditions, children left to attend high school and college, and some residents moved to cities for work.

Today all that remains of DeWitty is a building foundation, a historical marker, and the memories of those whose ancestors dreamed big and homesteaded in the Sandhills.

Richard K. Edwards is director emeritus of the Center for Great Plains Studies at the University of Nebraska–Lincoln. He is co-editor of *Homesteading the Plains: Toward a New History* (2017).

This man was a member of the North Loup Sluggers, a baseball team composed of players from DeWitty. The Sluggers were one of two teams, the other being the Yellow Jackets, managed by George Riley who barnstormed exhibition games. Photograph from the William Meehan collection (1918–1923). Used with permission, Catherine E. Blount.

William Meehan photographed this woman and her horse between 1918 and 1923 in DeWitty. Used with permission, Catherine E. Blount.

Town Life—A Photo Essay

Mark Harris

Candling of a chicken egg to check the chick's stage of development holds the attention of Yael Estrada, Carter Jones, and Eli Brogden. All Loup County students attend the county's sole school in Taylor. Most ride school buses, some making a 70-mile round trip each day. Megan Helberg, an English teacher, said that with each class averaging six students, a sense of community and helpfulness is evident. "Older kids just stop and help. It may be tying a shoe in the hallway, or a senior might show up to class late because they saw the need to help a class of fifth graders get going. Everyone is seen here. No one slips through the cracks."

Anna Rudloff of Verdigre competes in shot put in the Niobrara Valley Conference Invitational track meet at West Holt High School in Atkinson. Anna, a seventeen-year-old junior, competes for the consolidated Niobrara-Verdigre Cougars track team. Many Nebraska towns have consolidated their schools as student populations dwindle. It's a touchy subject; often mergers involve long-standing historical rivals and parents and grandparents lament the loss of town identities and school pride. Usually all participants vote on new names, mascots, and colors. When the Niobrara Lions and the Verdigre Hawks merged in 2010, they became the Niobrara-Verdigre Cougars. Over the last several decades, hundreds of small-town Nebraska schools joined through other forms of unifications, mainly financial and academic fusions, which allow schools to continue operating unchanged from the students' perspectives.

About once a week Isabelle Wenger, twelve, and her two siblings travel from nearby Springview to take music lessons from Emily Shook, a violinist and economic development director in Bassett, at the Old Feed Store Art Center, a creative hub for the region that opened in 2018. Grant-and-donor funded, its 3,200 square feet includes a permanent exhibition area, a gallery for local artists, and workshop and classroom spaces. Volunteers renovated the space in about six months. Sustained now by the Rock County Community Foundation, the center has proven to be a model creative operation.

Off-road vehicle engines roar through eastern regions of the Nebraska National Forest just south of Halsey. After breaching the top of the popular Hill Climb area, a father and son spin aggressively in the fine sand before diving back down the steep incline to repeat. The U.S. Forest Service maintains around 36 miles of narrow, winding trails for motorized four-wheeled vehicles such as ATVs. This hill takes speed to summit—timid attempts result in grinding stops and embarrassing retreats. Motorbikers take note: two wheels can't handle this much sand.

Ava Koenigsberg (*left*) and Brooklynn Gideon, both of Burwell, ride the Sizzler at the annual carnival produced by D.C. Lynch Shows of Chapman. Mike Lynch is a third-generation owner of the family's business, created by his grandfather in 1957. Lynch's two sons add a fourth generation as they travel with the carnival each season. Employing forty seasonal staff, the carnival travels May through September to thirty small towns, some of which employ them for county fairs. In several locations, like Burwell, the carnival is an annual fundraiser as Lynch passes a percentage of revenues back to the local chambers of commerce.

Allyson Starr, ten, and her friend Everley Jones, one, play on a warm evening in Taylor. Allyson's parents own and operate the 1960s-era Starr's Wildlife Inn, a six-room motel popular with folks who hunt, fish, or boat on the nearby Calamus Reservoir. Allyson and her friends often bike the quiet streets of Taylor, population 140.

When a hailstorm struck the Congregational Church in Ashby, insurance funded the installation of a new roof and repairs to just a couple of broken stained-glass windows. But the congregation funded restoration of all the other stained-glass windows and replaced the aging front doors and floors. Jason Kruse of Kruse Stained Glass in Hartington, Nebraska, sets the project's final trim nail into place before packing up for the 320-mile drive home—the farthest distance west his company has ever traveled. Founded in 1925, the church shares its pastor with a sister church in nearby Hyannis; the combined forty-person congregation swaps Sunday worship locations monthly.

Dillon Barta welds windmill sections together at Daniels Manufacturing Co. in Ainsworth. This family-owned business supplies feedlots with livestock-handling equipment such as cattle pens, gates, and "squeeze chutes," which hold individual animals for veterinary or other care. Operating since 1958, the company's products are used in twenty-two countries and every U.S. state. Most of their windmills stay in the Sandhills, pumping water from sandy depths normally between 60 and 150 feet, although some windmills' pipes probe as deep as 400 feet.

Cattle are the economic engines of the Sandhills, with most destined either for large-scale slaughterhouses or local butchers, such as Husker Meats in Ainsworth. A federally inspected business, all their products are locally raised. Jim Pinney, along with his wife, Lisa, own a butchering operation that also helps educate the next generation of Sandhills ag leaders. The Pinneys assist the Sandhills Cattle Association's Steers for Students program. Ranchers donate young steers that are penned in feed yards that track development data until the Carcass Contest, the end of the line for the steers but the beginning of the students' hands-on learning. Students and beef producers learn about carcass evaluation and packing-plant operations, such as inspection, butchering, meat processing, and marketing.

The calm of an opening prayer belies the chaos yet to come at the Arthur rodeo. An approaching storm will strike but not stall bronc riding—riding wet with thunder crashing: this is how you live in cattle country. Eyes will grow wild in both man and beast when the gate swings open, kicking off an evening of competitive events deeply entwined in Sandhills culture.

Local boys cheer as a playful water truck operator sprays water at their feet while dampening a dusty rodeo arena in Clearwater. Since 1967 this northeastern Nebraska village (population 320) has hosted one of Nebraska's most outstanding rodeos. Saddle bronc riding starts the event, followed by roping, barrel racing, and steer wrestling. The night's highlight comes at the end as sinewy young men climb aboard violent bucking bulls, illuminated by bug-assailed stadium lights.

Using a vaguely bovine-looking, PVC-constructed "dummy steer" mock-up is one way to practice team roping. A difficult maneuver with live animals, roping is more than a rodeo stunt; it's a way to capture cattle. Ranch kids pick it up early in life as did (*left to right*) Brady Brown, Tyler Barta, Gage Pollard, and Russel Beard. "I would guess that 85 to 90 percent of all people in this area would know how to sling a rope," said Tyler, who adds that he and his friends practice weekly. Lawn chairs and coolers of beer just outside of this photo give away the other reason they gather.

Pilot and aerial applicator Ryan Stuhlmiller of Alliance oversees his crew preparing his 940-horsepower crop duster to fertilize a potato field. Although there's not much need for spraying grasslands, north and west of Alliance lie corn, sugar beets, beans, sunflowers, alfalfa, and wheat. With fungicide, insecticide, or fertilizer payloads of up to 5,500 pounds and roundtrips as far as 170 miles, Stuhlmiller maintains remote sites at airports in Gordon, Oshkosh, and Scottsbluff. It's a dangerous profession to perform GPS-assisted racetrack spraying patterns just 9 feet above the ground at 140 mph with steep P-shaped turns at field's edge. A pilot since age seventeen, Ryan, or "Rhino," as friends call him, started Flying Rhino Aviation in 2018. Close calls while flying? Only early in his career, when an older plane's radial engine blew a piston in flight. "I was able to limp back to the airport," he said. "Twice."

A $500 prize goes to the last man standing after a bull is released into the arena at the Bassett Rough Stock Challenge's Cowboy Pinball contest. After being folded into a pitiful pile, bruised all over by a furious, 1,700-pound snot-flinging bull, Riley Christensen, of Rose, Nebraska, recounted, "My plan to duck clear didn't work so well." Earlier that week and unknown to Christensen, a friend signed them up. "My buddy bailed out right after watching the first guy go down," he snickered. "When the bull squared up on me, I thought, there ain't no gettin' out of this one. But when it threw me up, I thought, 'Oh, this ain't so bad.' Landing wasn't a problem either, but when it started smashing me into the ground with its head and hooves I just thought, 'Oh crap.' As dumb as it looked, we had a lot of laughs later."

A brass spittoon holds tips at Cactus Jack's food trailer at the Sandhills Ranch Expo in Bassett. An expansive ranching trade show and widely anticipated annual event, the expo draws regional sales representatives and mom-and-pop shops to sell their products in massive tents and open-air spaces. Cactus Jack's, based in St. Libory, Nebraska, has been owned and operated by the Leo family since 2009 and travels to dozens of locations across the state.

Anticipation grows at Alliance's Laing Park Lake as fourteen-year-old Graydon Zahn hooks something unseen and enormous. Fighting the line for several minutes, eventually the channel catfish is dragged to shore by Graydon's friends David Standage and Jonathan Gibson. After a quick weigh-in (6.3 pounds) and some close-in examination, Graydon releases the fish safely back into the water. Nebraska Game and Parks occasionally stocks this groundwater-fed lake with catfish, bluegill, large-mouthed bass, yellow perch, black crappies, and rainbow trout, raised at Rock Creek State Fish Hatchery in the far corner of southwest Nebraska. Said Graydon, "We figured we might catch a few bluegills. I didn't expect to catch a fish that big in the little town of Alliance."

Terrified and speechless, first-timers Mutton Bustin' nervously await their turns at riding a sheep out of a rodeo chute. Veterans like this girl at the Alliance Cattle Capital Rodeo might ride backward purely for style. Like many ranch kids, she likely rode horses before learning to ride a bike. Sheep sprint frantically to escape their life's most bizarre episode as riders desperately grip their wool. Kids strive to hang onto the farthest distance but ultimately all end up in the dust. Tears or smiles may follow, though most exit the arena utterly dazed.

Sharing stories of the good ol' days on dance night in a local Gordon bar, couples and old friends enjoy the evening while drinking cold beer. Located in the far northwestern reaches of the Sandhills, just 13 miles from the state's border, Gordon's events draw regulars from South Dakota and many miles in all other directions.

Visions of big money drive lemonade tycoons Henry (*middle*) and Theodore Freshour of Alliance; sister Amelia just likes eating the cookies. Stationed along one of the town's busier streets, waving at passers-by is part of their successful marketing strategy. In 2021 their grand opening brought in $150 in just one hour. Many "customers" handed over money without awaiting a product, simply to show their appreciation for the phenomenal adorability of the setup. Though business slowed after their initial novelty wore off, Henry is saving up. "He wants to buy a Mount Rushmore Lego set," said their mother, Rose. "The boys just love seeing money go into the jar. It absolutely amazes them."

Vibrating machinery rumbles as Roel Rodriguez of Alliance dumps pinto bean hulls and stems into gigantic shipping bags. New Alliance Bean and Grain Co. of Alliance sells bean by-product to nearby feed mills that use them as a binder in livestock mineral blocks, soon to be licked by cattle's rough tongues in pastures. Half of the regionally grown beans processed at the company ship across the United States, and the rest are exported to other countries. Western Nebraska is a world leader in the production of great northern beans, the bulk of New Alliance's business.

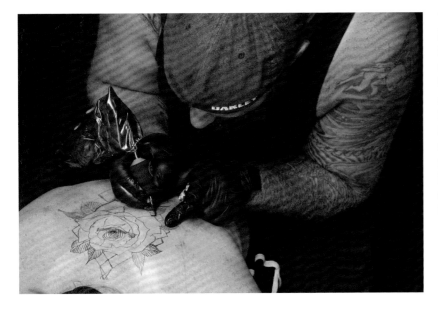

Tattoo artist Sam Mullins of Alliance operates the only tattoo business for 55 miles. Many of his clients want versions of their ranch's cattle brands, those distinctive emblems that often date back several generations. "It's about pride in their family and their ranches," says Mullins, shown here tattooing over a stencil on the back of his wife, Breanna Smith-Cole. Designs are a collaboration between artist and client, and Mullins tries to guide them. The eighteen-to-thirty-five crowd are more likely to walk into Sam's Pins & Needles Tattoo shop with wild designs in their heads, while the older crowd often leans toward memorial themes. Humor helps calm fear and, according to Mullins, "Only one person ever told me that it hurt more than they thought it would."

Working on other weekly community publications when not working on their own, Matt Esterly of the *Ainsworth Star Journal* runs the press's controls while printing the *Springview Herald* for the village 27 miles to the north. Lovingly dubbed Mabel, the press is 50 years old. "The Ainsworth paper has existed for over 125 years," said publisher Rod Worrell. Printed newspapers have been weakened by the internet in towns, cities, and metropolises across the United States and though the Sandhills region felt that effect as well, Worrell feels it has stabilized. "People here rely on us as their source for weekly local news," he said. "I think our future looks good."

Mark Harris is a former associate director of the University of Nebraska State Museum and a freelance photographer and author of *Rodeo Nebraska* (2015). All photographs by Mark Harris. Used with permission.

Nebraska's Human-Made National Forest

Carson Vaughan

The Platte River was running high in the blistering summer of 1901, and the mules were prone to startle. So the plucky young scholars improvised. Using picket ropes, they tethered their saddle horns to the wagon tongue, remounted their horses, and slowly—one step at a time—began to ford the braided river, nearly two hundred yards across.

"The old cow ponies knew more about pulling from the saddle horns than the riders [did]," teamster Charles A. Scott later admitted, but they soon reached the opposite shore, supplies dry and wagon upright, and continued merrily on their way: collecting plant specimens, felling trees, counting rings, taking notes, singing songs, writing letters. In the coming decades,

The Becoming an Outdoors-Woman event at the Nebraska State 4-H camp at the Nebraska National Forest near Halsey features canoe and kayak classes.

Hoarfrost-covered landscape near the Bessey Ranger District of the Nebraska National Forest near Halsey.

the seven men who comprised the Nebraska Sand Hill Reconnaissance Survey—recent college graduates, all of them—would usher the science and practice of forestry into the twentieth century. They would chair the deanships of budding forestry programs across the country. They would write books and bulletins and shape federal forestry legislation. But in the summer of 1901, a summer so hot it soldered their cookware, they were united with a single mission: to determine once

and for all if the Nebraska Sandhills—long considered a desert wasteland—could nurture a forest after all.

No one was more hellbent on the idea than botanist Charles Bessey, who had been publicly flirting with a radical "solution" to Nebraska's timber shortage ever since accepting the first deanship of Nebraska's College of Agriculture in 1884. Noting the "moist stratum" beneath the sand and the numerous rivers that gurgled to life in the grass-covered dunes, he quickly rejected

Nebraska National Forest near Halsey on a hazy fall day.

Rain falls on the Nebraska National Forest, Bessey Ranger District, near Halsey in Thomas County.

the Sandhills' prevailing reputation. In fact, to the contrary, Bessey eventually concluded that a great forest had once covered this mysterious terrain—a forest later razed by wildfire and trampled by grazing bison. He'd located isolated pockets of cedar and pine throughout the region, and the same dense cover of ponderosa that swaddled the Black Hills and Rocky Mountains, he noted, also swaddled portions of the Nebraska panhandle. All told, Bessey wrote, "We are forced to assume that the forest areas must have formerly been more extended, sufficiently so to connect these isolated canyon forests with one another."

And extended again they could be.

"That it would be desirable to do so needs no argument," he wrote in his annual report for the Nebraska State Board of Agriculture in 1894. "The beneficial influence upon the state would be almost incalculable."

Well before Bessey began his investigation of the Sandhills, those who reaped the rewards of America's westward migration championed tree planting as a means of "ameliorating" the climate. But it wasn't just land agents and railroad boosters. It was writers and government officials and scientists too—even professional foresters. Similar to the once-popular myth that "rain follows the plow," many also believed that rain follows the trees.

But as theories of increased rainfall gradually died out toward the end of the nineteenth century, Bessey and others refocused on the more tangible benefits of tree planting: the conservation of moisture, protection against the plains' unrelenting winds, a source of shade in a land sorely without, even a touch of beauty to "break up that monotonous skyline."

In January 1891, at Bessey's urging, the Nebraska Division of Forestry agreed to finance an experimental plantation in Holt County, Nebraska, on the eastern fringe of the Sandhills. Though hardly a runaway success, "It seems already to have proved what was intended,"

wrote Division Chief Bernhard Fernow just two years after planting, "namely that in the sand-hill region of Nebraska coniferous growth, especially of pines planted closely, is the proper material and method." Unable to stretch their shoestring budget any further, the division soon refocused on other priorities, and the so-called Holt County Plantation gradually fell off the radar.

Fernow, meanwhile, resigned to accept the forestry deanship at Cornell. But his successor, a politically astute Yale graduate named Gifford Pinchot, quickly reignited the gospel of plains forestry. After first hiring Bessey to continue studying "the causes which produce treeless

Dove hunters at windmill overflow tanks in the Nebraska National Forest, Bessey Ranger District.

Storm clouds and lightning over the Nebraska National Forest near Halsey.

prairies," he then authorized the Nebraska Sand Hill Reconnaissance Survey. Over the next three months, the eager party cut a wide swath through the Sandhills, compiling an exhaustive record of woody plants along the way. In the panhandle they discovered ponderosa pine and red cedar thriving on barren slopes where nothing else could grow, some with nearly three hundred rings. The Sandhills proper showed far fewer signs of established tree growth, but the soil and climate were essentially the same, and the Holt County Plantation—now towering 20 feet above the plains—offered additional proof of concept. If precautions were taken to avoid fire and overgrazing, the team concluded in its final report, similar forest conditions could be achieved.

Despite pushback from cattlemen and railroad executives, President Theodore Roosevelt finally approved Bessey's wild vision in April 1902, withdrawing more than 200,000 treeless acres from homestead entry and establishing the Dismal River and Niobrara Forest Reserves in the heart of the Sandhills. In 1906 Roosevelt added the 347,000-acre North Platte Reserve, and in 1908, all three were combined to create the Nebraska National Forest.

"This was the first project of its kind ever attempted in the United States," wrote Scott, who was subsequently hired to survey the boundaries for the Dismal River Reserve near Halsey and establish a supplementary eighty-acre nursery. "No one in the Bureau of Forestry could advise us, and the commercial nurserymen of the country had no experience with this type of work and we were told we would have to use our own judgement and do the best we could."

But after years of trial and error, Scott and his team slowly reaped their reward. Eventually the forest would blanket nearly twenty thousand acres of central Nebraska, making it the largest hand-planted forest in the world.

A federal afforestation program in China's Tibetan Plateau would later surpass it, but the Bessey Ranger District today remains the largest in the Western Hemisphere.

"It isn't an amazing forest like the Sequoias—it's shaggy and small," says District Ranger Julie Bain. "It is, however, a feat of human endeavor, and for that reason it is interesting."

Were it not for the ultimate success of the Bessey Nursery, however, the Nebraska National Forest would likely have followed so many other plains forestry reserves into oblivion—and the nursery itself was once on the chopping block.

"If we wouldn't have put up greenhouses, they would have closed us—guaranteed," says Manager Richard Gilbert. "The oldest federal tree nursery in the U.S. would have been closed, and it would have been a shame."

Now 120 years old, the Bessey Nursery provides seedlings for every national forest within the USFS Rocky Mountain Region and to a slew of other public entities throughout the Great Plains. And as wildfires and pest infestations continue to devastate public and private lands throughout the American West, demand for seedlings from the Bessey Nursery only continues to grow.

But perhaps more than anything else, the forest today is a living monument to the ethos behind Nebraska's former nickname.

"We, of Nebraska, have taken to ourselves the distinguished name of 'Tree Planters,'" Charles Bessey wrote in 1894. "Let us show to the world an example of tree planting and forest production worthy of the energy of our people."

Carson Vaughan is a freelance journalist and author of *Zoo Nebraska: The Dismantling of an American Dream* (2019).

Women package bare root trees for shipment from Bessey Nursery at Halsey as part of the federal Clarke-McNary reforestation program, ca. 1950. Photographs, Agricultural Communications Records, RG 08-16-06. Used with permission, Archives & Special Collections, University of Nebraska–Lincoln Libraries.

A woman packages a tree for shipment from Bessey Nursery at Halsey as part of the federal Clarke-McNary reforestation program, ca. 1946. Photographs, Agricultural Communications Records, RG 08-16-06. Used with permission, Archives & Special Collections, University of Nebraska–Lincoln Libraries.

Gate entrance to the "forest" in 1930. C. Barron McIntosh lantern slide collection, RG 12-11-11. Used with permission, Archives & Special Collections, University of Nebraska–Lincoln Libraries.

A man notes tree growth in Clarke-McNary trees in 1947 at Halsey. Photographs, Agricultural Communications Records, RG 08-16-06. Used with permission, Archives & Special Collections, University of Nebraska–Lincoln Libraries.

Trees planted beneath protective wooden structures at Bessey Nursey at Halsey, ca. 1918. Note the treeless grassland in the background beyond the Loup River. Raymond J. Pool, Botany Papers, RG 12-07-12. Used with permission, Archives & Special Collections, University of Nebraska–Lincoln Libraries.

Roads, blowouts, and erosion are evident in areas adjacent to the established trees, whose roots stabilize the soil. C. Barron McIntosh lantern slide collection, RG 12-11-11. Used with permission, Archives & Special Collections, University of Nebraska–Lincoln Libraries.

Bessey Nursery near the Loup River as viewed from a ridgetop, ca. 1918. C. Barron McIntosh lantern slide collection, RG 12-11-11. Used with permission, Archives & Special Collections, University of Nebraska–Lincoln Libraries.

Is the Experiment Over?

Kim Hachiya

Separate fires in 2022 burned portions of the Nebraska National Forest and Grasslands near Halsey. In May, the 201 East Fire burned 4,192 acres, the majority in the hand-planted forest. The Bovee Fire that started October 2 burned 18,930 acres, of which 5,130 acres were within the footprint of the hand-planted forest. It also burned sixteen of seventeen buildings at the State 4-H Camp and the historic Scott Lookout Tower. The Bessey Nursery, offices, and fire hall were saved, as was the town of Halsey, which was evacuated. A volunteer firefighter died fighting the Bovee Fire.

Since 1965, 89 percent of the fires in the nation's largest hand-planted forest were caused by lightning strikes, said Julie Bain, district ranger with the U.S. Forest Service. A vehicle accidentally started the Bovee Fire.

Bain said it would be a year or longer before decisions are made on restoration. She said a salvage sale to remove as much of the dead timber as possible would be a first step. The fire consumed invasive eastern redcedar, ponderosa pine, jack pine, and some deciduous trees.

"Where does the experimental forest go next?" she mused. "It was started as an experiment. Is the experiment over? Do we want it to continue with different kinds of trees? We want to not create unintended consequences." When the forest was planted in the early twentieth century, the destructive invasiveness of eastern redcedar wasn't known. Now efforts to remove it are ongoing.

"Is forest the best use of this land? That's a good question," she said.

The forest, she noted, is well loved by the public. "It's become iconic. Yet it's not ecologically correct. Can we do something without the unintended consequences? I don't know. We're humans. The Great Plains is a fire-adapted ecosystem. Fires are inevitable."

Public input will help inform Forest Service decisions about restoration, she said.

The Bessey Ranger district oversees the 90,170 acre Nebraska National Forest at Halsey (Blaine and Thomas Counties) and the 116,060 acre Samuel R. McKelvie National Forest in Cherry County.

Kim Hachiya is a retired communications specialist for the University of Nebraska–Lincoln and author of *Dear Old Nebraska U* (Nebraska, 2019).

Separate fires in 2022 burned more than 22,000 acres of the Nebraska National Forest and Grasslands near Halsey. The Bovee Fire burned 16 of 17 buildings at the historic Scott Lookout Tower and State 4-H Camp; a firefighter died during the blaze.
Photograph by Carson Vaughan. Used with permission.

LAND

Dawn breaks northwest of Burwell, Loup County.
Photograph by Mark Harris. Used with permission.

Physical Setting of the Sandhills in Maps

R. Matthew Joeckel, Clayton L. Reinier, Paul R. Hanson,
Jesse T. Korus, Troy Gilmore, and Aaron R. Young

A. USGS Physiographic Divisions of the Conterminous United States

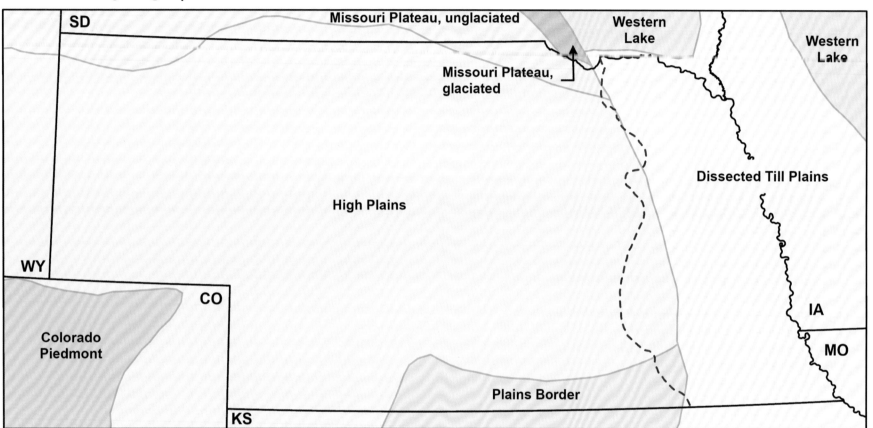

The Nebraska Sandhills in the context of regional landscapes. (A) Physiographic divisions of Nebraska as recognized by the U.S. Geological Survey. The Sandhills lie in the High Plains section of the Great Plains province. The Great Plains in the context of this map includes the High Plains, Plains Border, the unglaciated Missouri Plateau, and the Colorado Piedmont. The Dissected Till Plains in eastern Nebraska is technically not part of the Great Plains because it was glaciated during the Pleistocene epoch. Despite the subdivision of landscapes in this map, many regional geologists map the westernmost limit of Pleistocene glaciation slightly farther to the west (blue dashed line), because of buried glacial sediments encountered by drilling. Nebraska's major land resource areas (MLRAs) is a classification system that incorporates soil types, landforms, geology, surface water, groundwater, and land use. The Sandhills are a discrete MLRA, as are the adjacent Central Nebraska Loess Hills, which have some of the thickest loess (windblown dust) deposits in North America and even the world. Loess was deposited during the Quaternary period in large part due to actively migrating dunes in the Sandhills. Thus, sand and dust, dunes and loess hills are intimately related landscape-forming processes in recent geologic times. The legacy of those processes is apparent in land-use patterns and other aspects of human geography.

B. USDA Major Land Resource Areas

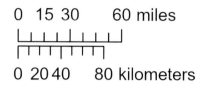

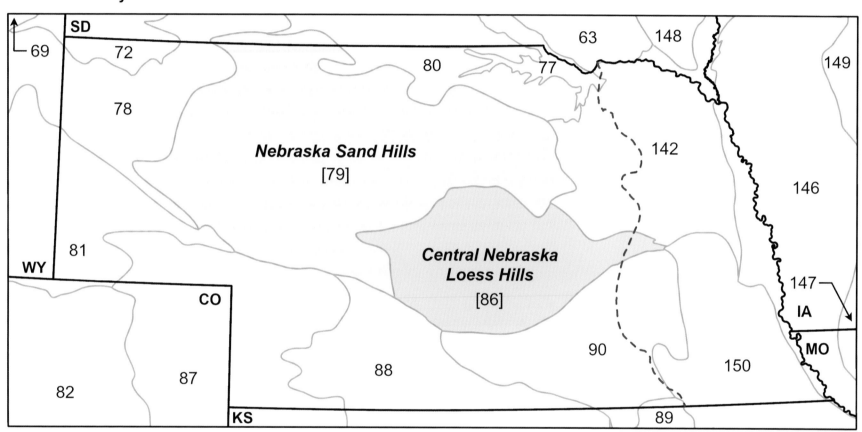

- - - Glacial extent

63 Southern Rocky Mountain Foothills	87 Central High Tableland
69 Northern Rolling High Plains, Southern Part	88 Rolling Plains and Breaks
72 Pierre Shale Plains	89 Central Kansas Sandstone Hills
77 Southern Rolling Pierre Shale Plains	90 Central Loess Plains
78 Mixed Sandy and Silty Tableland and Badlands	142 Loess Uplands
79 Nebraska Sandhills	146 Iowa and Missouri Deep Loess Hills
80 Dakota-Nebraska Eroded Tableland	147 Illinois and Iowa Deep Loess and Drift
81 Central High Plains, Northern Part	148 Till Plains
82 Central High Plains, Southern Part	149 Central Iowa and Minnesota Till Prairies
86 Central Nebraska Loess Hills	150 Nebraska and Kansas Loess-Drift Hills

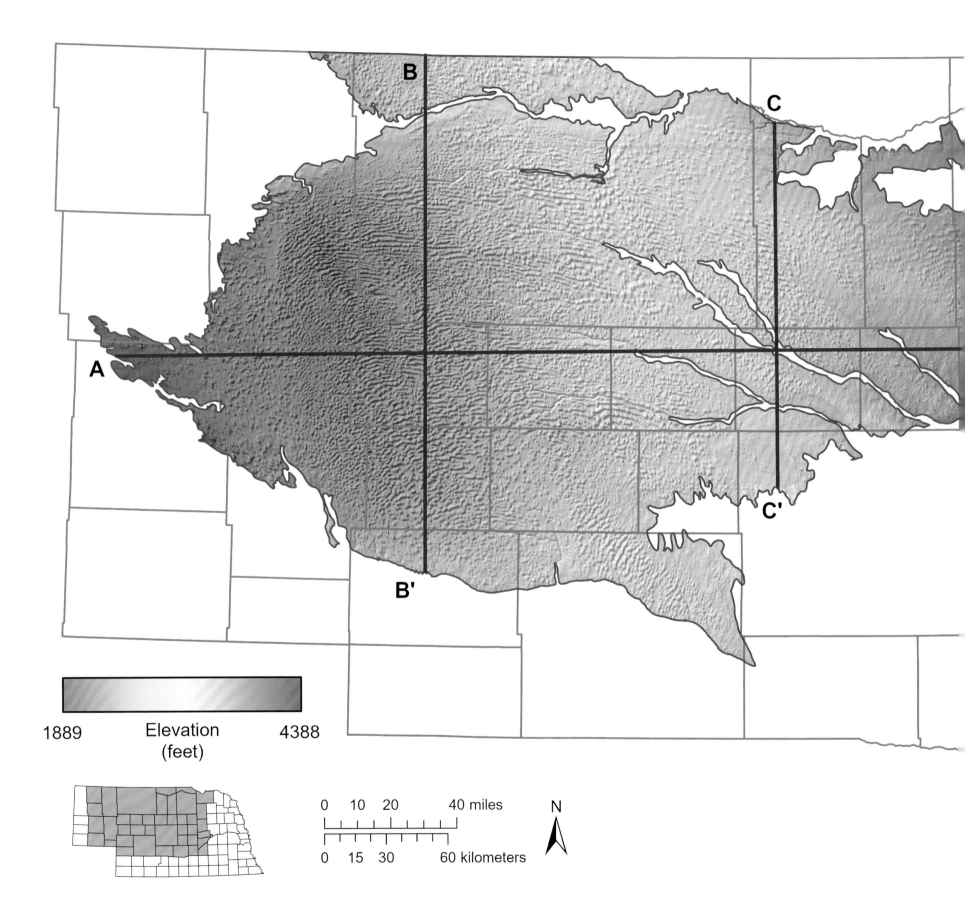

B

C

A

B'

C'

1889   Elevation   4388
              (feet)

0   10   20   40 miles   N

0   15   30   60 kilometers

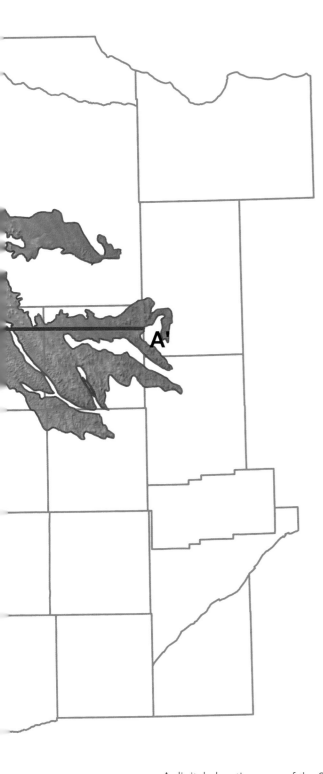

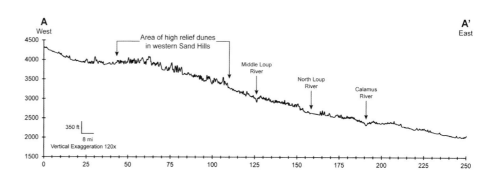

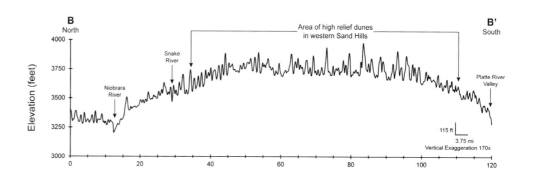

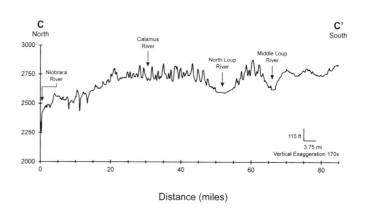

A digital elevation map of the Sandhills showing the topography created by the dunes and interdunal valleys. The red lines delimit the locations of the three topographic profiles shown to the right. Elevation is the altitude of a feature above sea level, whereas relief is the difference in elevation from low points to high points in a local area. The small-scale "sawtooth" aspect of the profiles is chiefly due to (1) the relief of large sand dunes, which appear as individual peaks, and (2) the valleys of small streams. Profile A–A' (top) extends across the Sandhills at their widest point. Elevation declines markedly eastward, as does dune relief. In profile B–B' the high-relief dunes of the western Sandhills are more prominent than in the graph above, because of the greater vertical exaggeration. Both elevation and relief reach a maximum toward the middle of the profile. In profile C–C' (bottom), there is a general increase in elevation from south to north, in contrast to the pattern evident in B–B'. Note that scale and vertical exaggeration in B–B' and C–C' are the same but are different from A–A'.

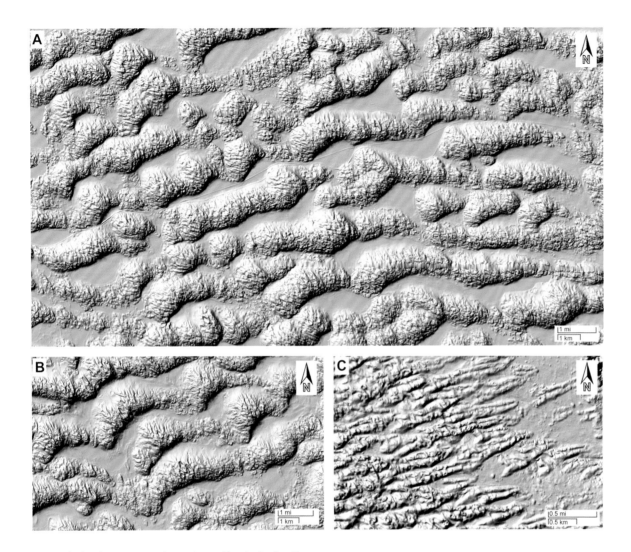

LiDAR (light detection and ranging; effectively the "laser scanning" of Earth's surface) images that show common dune types in the Sandhills. *(A)* Barchan and barchanoid ridge dunes. Individual crescent-shaped barchan dunes have locally coalesced into elongate barchanoid ridges. These dunes rise between 270 and 380 feet above adjacent interdune areas. The steeper slopes on the southeast sides of these dunes indicate that the primary formative winds blew from the northwest. These large dunes formed during the Pleistocene epoch, but they were reshaped when sand moved again during Holocene droughts. Thus, much smaller dunes, including elongated linear dunes, moved over the large dunes and now appear superimposed on them. The interdune areas now contain lakes and wetlands. *(B)* Crescent-shaped barchan dunes. These dunes range from 296 to 330 feet in height, and their steep southeastern slopes indicate they, too, were formed by northwesterly winds. Elongated oval pits, oriented northwest to southeast along the crests of many dunes, are blowouts, erosional hollows that are produced by wind. *(C)* Linear dunes. The tallest dunes, in the western half of the image, rise 54 feet above interdune areas, whereas the lower-relief dunes toward the east are only 18 feet in height.

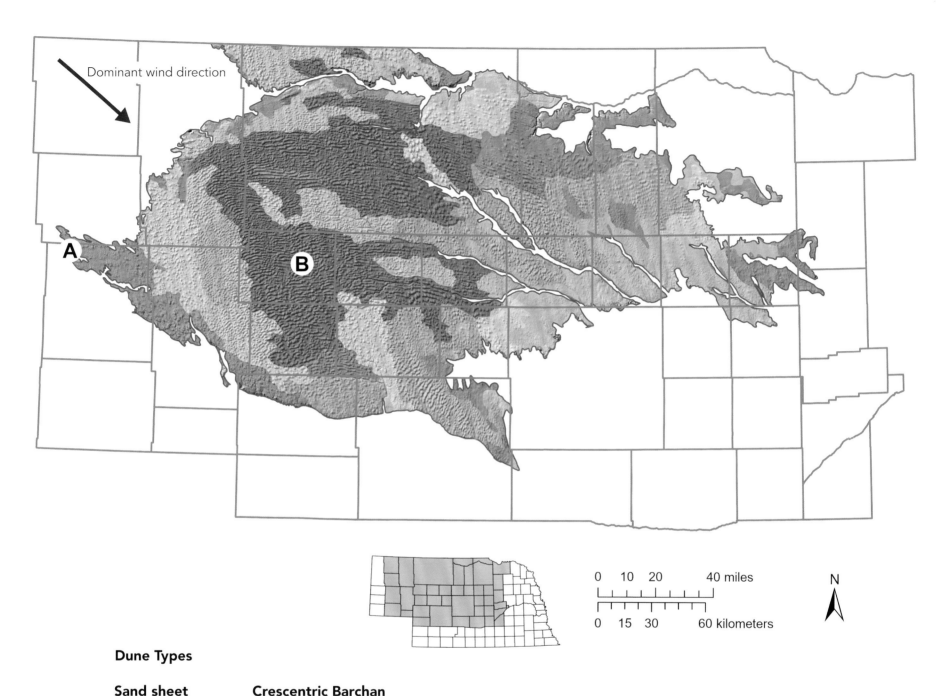

Dominant wind direction

A

B

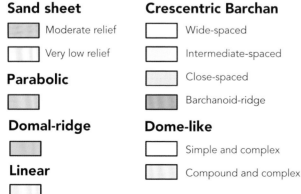

Dune Types

Sand sheet

Moderate relief

Very low relief

Parabolic

Domal-ridge

Linear

Crescentric Barchan

Wide-spaced

Intermediate-spaced

Close-spaced

Barchanoid-ridge

Dome-like

Simple and complex

Compound and complex

0   10   20   40 miles

0   15   30   60 kilometers

N

Shaded-relief map of the Nebraska Sandhills showing the classification of dune types. The highest elevation in the Sandhills, 4,388
feet above sea level (A), is a dune of comparatively modest size and
relief along the southwestern margin of the Sandhills in northern
Morrill County. This dune is highest in elevation, because the entire
region slopes upward to the west. The location of the greatest local
relief—approximately 400 feet—is in Grant County (B), within an
area of high-relief dunes. Here, the difference in elevation between a
depression in an interdune valley and the crest of a large compound
dune is essentially the same as the height of the Nebraska State
Capitol in Lincoln.

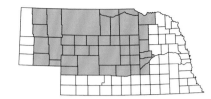

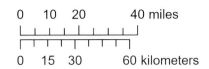

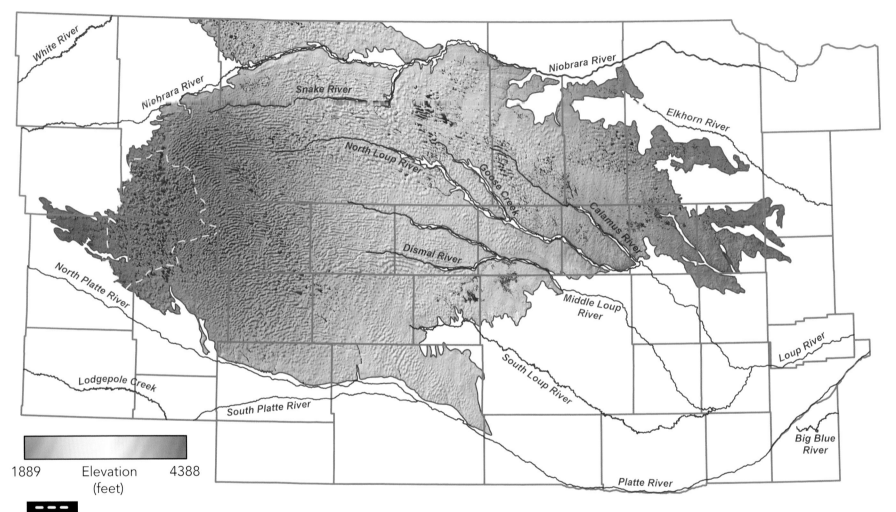

1889   Elevation   4388
(feet)

Alkali Lakes

Surface water (rivers and lakes) in the Nebraska Sandhills. Multiple rivers—the South, Middle, and North Loup Rivers; the Dismal, Calamus, and Snake Rivers—originate in the Sandhills, where they are fed by shallow discharging groundwater. The Elkhorn River originates at the eastern margin of the Sandhills, and the Niobrara River receives groundwater seepage from the High Plains Aquifer along its deeply incised canyon in Cherry County. Many springs are visible along and in the beds of these rivers and the tributaries that feed them.

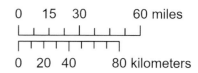

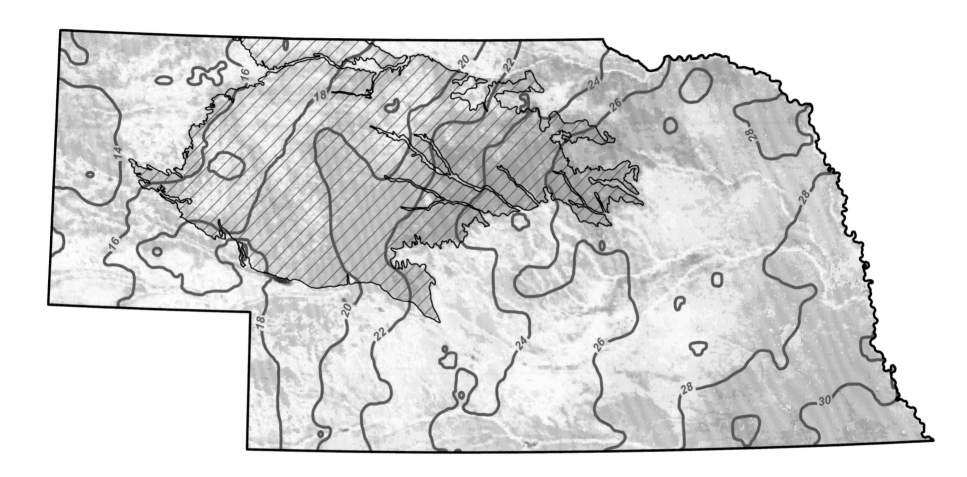

Average Annual Net Recharge (Inches)

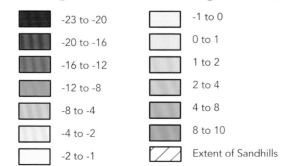

-23 to -20	-1 to 0
-20 to -16	0 to 1
-16 to -12	1 to 2
-12 to -8	2 to 4
-8 to -4	4 to 8
-4 to -2	8 to 10
-2 to -1	Extent of Sandhills

-20- Average annual precipitation (inches)

Estimated groundwater recharge—the movement of water from the land surface downward to the aquifer—with superimposed precipitation isohyets (lines of equal rainfall). The Sandhills have relatively high estimated groundwater recharge (shown in blue tones) despite modest annual rainfall, which declines more than 10 inches southeast to northwest. The thick permeable sands in Sandhills soils and the underlying strata readily transmit rainfall that infiltrates. Parts of Nebraska surrounding the Sandhills have markedly lower estimated recharge, shown in orange and yellow tones. Thus, the Sandhills are a critical aspect of the recharge of the underlying High Plains Aquifer.

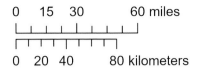

0 15 30   60 miles

0 20 40   80 kilometers

N

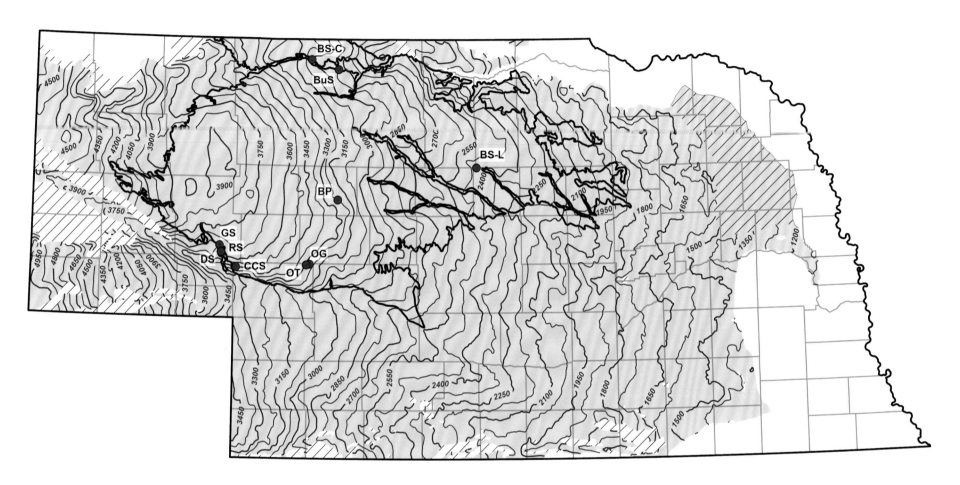

Elevation (feet)

	High Plains Aquifer
	High Plains Aquifer thin or absent
	Highly variable water levels
●	Majors springs
—	Extent of Sandhills

Contour interval 75 feet

Elevation of the water table in Nebraska and locations of some major springs (red dots) in the Sandhills. Just as the elevation of the land surface declines generally west to east across the state, so does the water table, which is estimated to drop more than 2,000 feet toward the east. Springs exist where the water table or the imaginary surface of groundwater hydrostatic pressure intersects or lies above the land surface. In Nebraska, springs tend to be at lower places on the landscape, such as the river valleys that cut across the Sandhills.

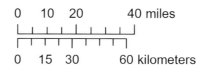

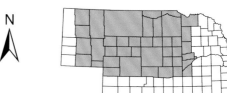

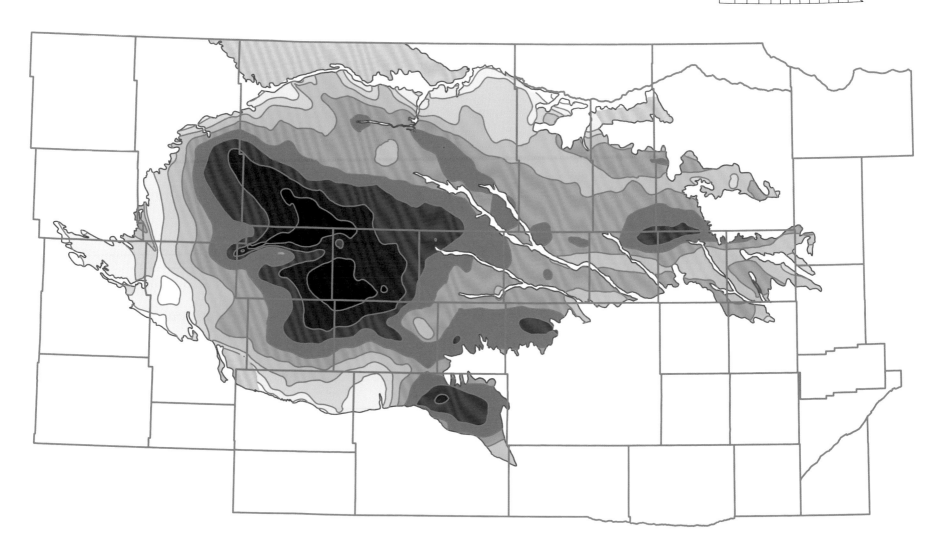

Saturated thickness (feet)

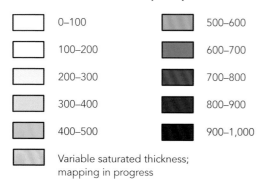

0–100	500–600
100–200	600–700
200–300	700–800
300–400	800–900
400–500	900–1,000

Variable saturated thickness; mapping in progress

Estimated *saturated thickness* (the vertical thickness of aquifer-hosting geologic materials in which pores are filled with groundwater) of the High Plains Aquifer under the Nebraska Sandhills. The greatest saturated thickness, and the largest amount of groundwater, is shown in dark blue. Saturated thickness decreases eastward, because the thickness of groundwater-bearing sediments and sedimentary rocks comprising the aquifer decreases in that direction. Likewise, aquifer-hosting strata also thin westward under the westernmost Sandhills and to the north and south, toward the Niobrara River and Platte River, respectively.

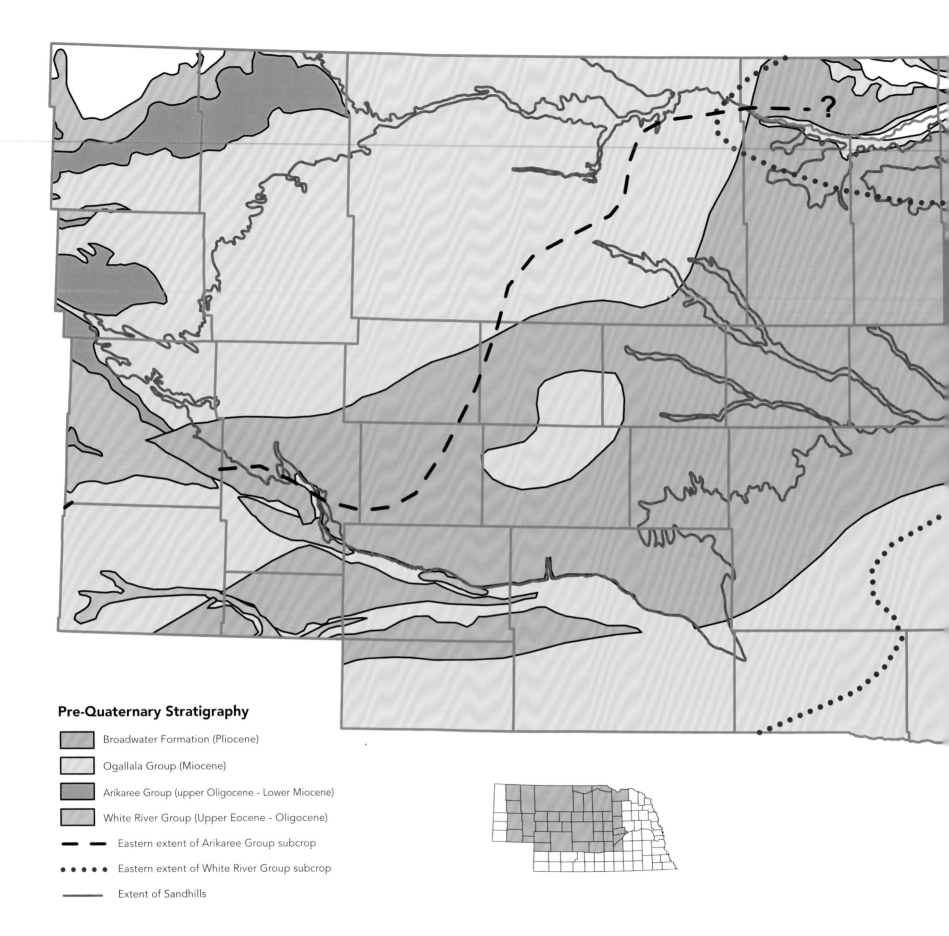

Pre-Quaternary Stratigraphy

■ Broadwater Formation (Pliocene)

□ Ogallala Group (Miocene)

■ Arikaree Group (upper Oligocene - Lower Miocene)

■ White River Group (Upper Eocene - Oligocene)

– – – Eastern extent of Arikaree Group subcrop

• • • • • Eastern extent of White River Group subcrop

——— Extent of Sandhills

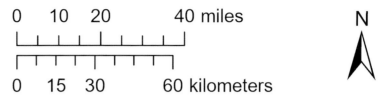

Pre-Quaternary geology underlying the Nebraska Sandhills, depicting the identity of sediments and sedimentary rocks that would be visible if the dune sands and related deposits were removed. The Broadwater Formation contains coarse sands and gravels deposited during the Pliocene epoch (5.33 to 2.58 million years ago) by a major river system draining the Rocky Mountains that flowed east to northeastward across present-day Nebraska. The Ogallala Group, consisting chiefly of the Valentine Formation and overlying Ash Hollow Formation, is a thick accumulation of Miocene deposits laid down by ancient rivers between 17 and 5 million years ago. It underlies the entire region, and—because it is thick, porous, and permeable—comprises the major part of the High Plains Aquifer. Recent geochemical research suggests that erosion of the Ogallala Group provided much of the sand in the present Sandhills. The Arikaree Group underlies the Ogallala Group in the western Sandhills and consists of ancient stream sediments and eolian sands. The White River Group, consisting chiefly of the Chadron Formation and overlying Brule Formation, crops out west of the Sandhills in the North Platte River valley and on the north flank of the Pine Ridge. It underlies the Arikaree Group and Ogallala Group under most of the Sandhills.

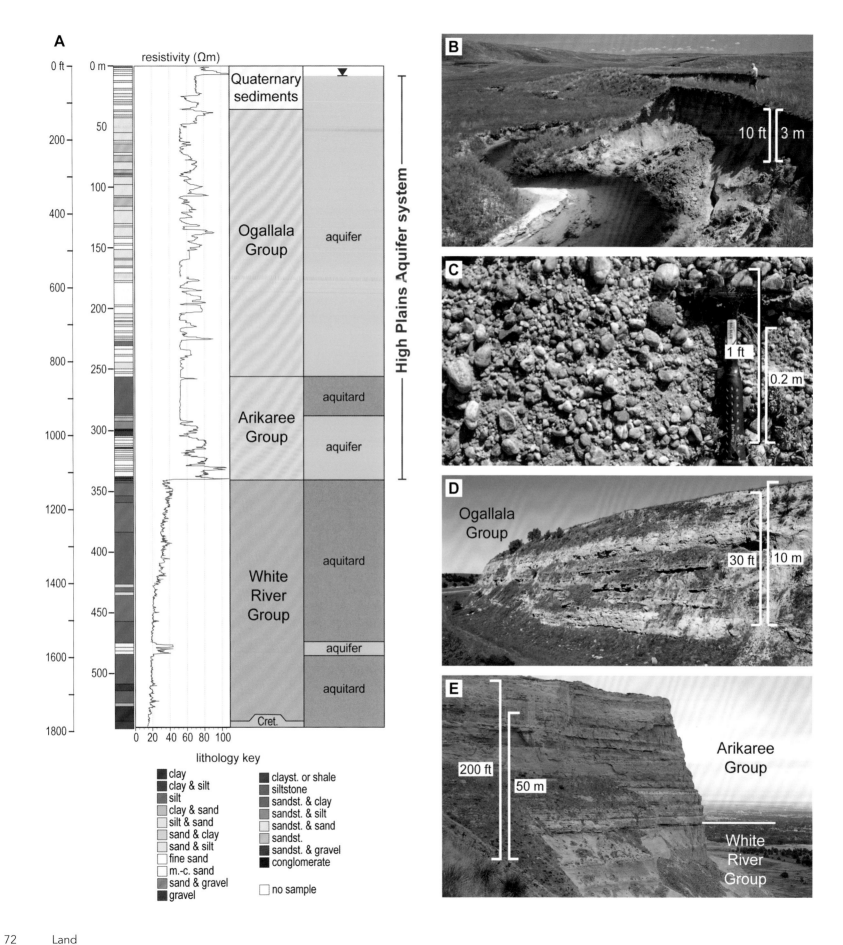

Sediments and sedimentary rock strata underlying the Nebraska Sandhills and their relationships with the High Plains Aquifer.

(A) A borehole log drilled in northern Grant County in 1989 to investigate groundwater. Formal geologic units that overlay the Pierre Shale of the Cretaceous System (Cret.) are named, and geologic layers serving as aquifers (layers that hold, readily transmit, and yield economically significant quantities of groundwater) and aquitards (geologic layers that are not aquifers and transmit groundwater only slowly) are identified according to the accompanying resistivity log (vertical, jagged blue line). The resistivity log depicts the resistance of geological materials to the flow of electrical current from a geophysical tool that is lowered down a borehole on a cable. The local thickness of the High Plains Aquifer is marked on the right side of the borehole log. The thickest and most complete succession of geologic strata in the High Plains Aquifer underlies the western Sandhills.

(B) Exposures of Quaternary sediments, including sandy alluvium and dune sand, at Gudmundsen Sandhills Laboratory, Cherry County. Sediments like these are identified at the top of the borehole log.

(C) Gravels of the Pliocene Broadwater Formation exposed near Broadwater, Nebraska. These strata are absent in the borehole because they were either never deposited in the immediate area or were eroded.

(D) An outcrop of Ash Hollow Formation of the Ogallala Group at the spillway of Kingsley Dam, Nebraska. Thick strata of the Ogallala Group are present in the borehole log.

(E) Outcrops of the upper Oligocene–Lower Miocene Arikaree Group and the Brule Formation of the Upper Eocene–Oligocene White River Group at Scottsbluff National Monument. The Arikaree and White River Groups are present in the borehole. The High Plains Aquifer in the borehole consists of the Arikaree and Ogallala Groups, as well as overlying Quaternary sands and gravels. Sandstone layers within the White River Group are, for the most part, physically isolated from the High Plains Aquifer, and, therefore, they are not considered a part of that aquifer system.

R. Matthew Joeckel is senior associate director of the School of Natural Resources, director of Conservation and Survey Division at the University of Nebraska–Lincoln, and Nebraska State Geologist.

Clayton L. Reinier is a GIS research specialist for the School of Natural Resources at the University of Nebraska–Lincoln.

Paul R. Hanson is a professor in the School of Natural Resources at the University of Nebraska–Lincoln.

Jesse T. Korus is an associate professor in the School of Natural Resources at the University of Nebraska–Lincoln.

Troy Gilmore is an associate professor in the School of Natural Resources at the University of Nebraska–Lincoln.

Aaron R. Young is a geologist in the School of Natural Resources at the University of Nebraska–Lincoln.

All maps were produced by the Conservation and Survey Division, School of Natural Resources. University of Nebraska. Used with permission.

The Sandhills through Time

David Loope, James Swinehart, and Joe Mason

Eolian sand exposed on the lower slopes of a barchan dune at a site in Hooker County called Vinton Blowout. Optically stimulated luminescence ages of 15,700 to 16,800 years on the lower dune sand indicate that the dune was migrating in that time interval, which was the terminal part of the Pleistocene ice age. This outcrop contains some of the oldest dune sand exposed anywhere in the Sandhills. Photograph by Joe Mason. Used with permission.

One long-standing question about the Sandhills is "How old are they?" Digging deeper, more specific questions emerge. If the question is "How old is the sand, and where did it come from?" the answer is easy, because many of the sand grains are radioactive. In the dunes, 99 percent of the sand grains are abraded crystals of two minerals—quartz and feldspar. Feldspar crystals (like bananas, potatoes, and our bodies) contain radioactive potassium. Age dating based on radioactive elements in feldspars from Rocky Mountain Front Range granites indicates that the crystals are between one and two billion years old, and so are the rounded feldspar crystals in the Sandhills.

Another question is "How old are individual dunes?" The answer is made possible by a new dating technique called optically stimulated luminescence (OSL) that also makes use of radioactivity. Instead of dating the sand itself, OSL answers the question "How long has this sand grain been buried in the dark?" While buried in the dark, silt- and sand-size quartz grains steadily accumulate energy from their radioactive (potassium-rich) components. When these grains are exposed to the sun, or to light of a certain wavelength in the lab, they release that energy. The longer they have been in the dark, the more energy is released (and measured). Moving like tanks, dunes recycle their sand as the sand grains continue to migrate downwind. Sand eroded from the upwind side is moved over the crest and deposited on the downwind side, only to be eroded, perhaps a hundred years later, from the upwind side. Today, in a big, stabilized dune where would we find the "oldest" (longest-buried-in-the-dark) sand? The answer is, at the base of the trailing (upwind) edge. So far, the oldest sand we have found (in a core retrieved from the southern Sandhills) was dated at about twenty-four thousand years, which is about ten thousand years before the last of the Ice Age glaciers left the vicinity of Des Moines, Iowa.

Split sediment core over 17 feet long from Jumbo Valley Fen. The brown to black layers are peat, which was deposited when the wetland was moist, whereas the gray layers are sand that was blown into the wetland during dry intervals. The peat at the base of the core is estimated to be about 11,000 years old. Photograph by James Swinehart. Used with permission.

Swan Lake in the southwestern Sandhills surrounded by 80- to 140-foot-tall compound parabolic dunes. The lake was the focus of early geological research on the age of Sandhills dunes and lakes. View is to the northwest. Photograph by James Swinehart. Used with permission.

A third question—not answerable by direct evidence—is "How long has there been a large dune field on the central plains?" This question is difficult to answer because the way dunes move limits the use of OSL. It is likely that there were big dunes in Nebraska long before twenty-four thousand years ago, but their sand grains saw daylight and lost their stored energy because they were completely recycled as the dunes migrated.

We think the Sandhills dune field may be as old as two million years. During a large portion of Nebraska's (and North America's) geologic history, the surface was the floor of shallow inland seaways, less than a thousand feet deep. The last of these seaways retreated to the Gulf of Mexico and to the Arctic Ocean about sixty million years ago, and the global climate started to cool. Twenty-five-million-year-old wind-deposited rocks comprise some western Nebraska cliffs and can be seen up close at Agate Fossil Beds and Scotts Bluff National Monuments. These sandstones (as well as the loose sand of the Nebraska Sandhills) record time periods when portions of North America's core became deserts. During the Ice Ages, much of the central United States was buried by thick glaciers. These glaciers did not reach the Sandhills, but they got close. The oldest glacial deposits in northeastern Nebraska and western Iowa are more than two million years old, the youngest are about fourteen thousand years old.

The most reasonable hypothesis for the age of the Sandhills dune field brings us back to plants. The cold climate that allowed continental glaciers to move so far south would have greatly reduced the length of the growing season. This severe cooling (starting about two million years ago) led to dramatic thinning of plant cover on the silt- and sand-rich land surface and ushered in a wind-swept desert landscape in north-central Nebraska. Sand grains in the unprotected river deposits started jumping and crashing, and silt grains took their long flights. Thus, dune fields and loess deposits soon started to take shape.

A final question involves the future of the Sandhills: "When and why were the Sandhills most recently desta- bilized?" This is, by far, the most important question for future humans and for future pocket gophers and other prairie creatures. In 1983, Jim Swinehart, together with Tom Ahlbrandt and Dave Maroney, published the first strong evidence that Sandhills dunes were actively mi- grating much more recently than the departure of nearby Ice Age glaciers. This claim is sobering, because if dune formation simply coincided with glaciation, there would be little need to worry about the return of desert condi- tions unless glaciers returned. Early attempts to answer this question (pre-OSL) had to rely on carbon-14 (C-14) dating, but there is not much carbon preserved in a sand dune. Bob Seger's song "Night Moves" is relevant here: "Working on mysteries without any clues."

After a tip from soil scientist Chuck Markley, we found a place (not within a dune, but in front of one) with a lot of carbon. Some of the wet meadows between the large dunes of the central and western Sandhills are actively accumulating peat—a deposit almost entirely composed of carbon-based molecules. Coring at Jumbo and Cutcomb Valleys in the late 1990s revealed (5 feet below the squishy muck on the surface) a persistent thin layer of sand sandwiched between older and younger peat. Radiocarbon dates from the peat above and below the sand at the two locations (21 miles apart) indicated that the sand accumulated seven hundred to a thousand years ago. The interpretation is that frequent severe regional droughts led to a lowering of the water table and drying of the meadows. The nearby dunes lost their grass cover, and winds drove the now-unprotected sand out onto the surface of the (no-longer-wet) meadows. When the period of frequent droughts ended, the water table rose and rewetted the meadows. Peat again accu-

Closely spaced linear dunes superimposed on large 250-foot-tall barchanoid ridge dunes at Gudmundsen Sandhills Laboratory, Hooker County. View is looking south. Photograph by James Swinehart. Used with permission.

mulated, ultimately leaving the sand buried under five feet of peat. More recent dating of the sand with OSL has confirmed the earlier results with C-14.

OSL dating of sand from Sandhills dunes and of silt deposits from loess exposures south of the Sandhills has also shown that, during the last ten thousand years, there have been at least four episodes of active dune migration, interspersed with times when—like the last seven hundred years—dunes were stable. Apparently, even after the glaciers were long gone, droughts caused the plant cover to lose its "grip," allowing the dunes to start migrating again. Another thing that OSL has

revealed is that episodes of dune activity coincide with episodes of loess accumulation. This makes sense if dust storms really are triggered by bouncing sand grains.

Happily, the Sandhills were not mobilized during the dust bowl of the 1930s. The droughts of seven hundred to a thousand years ago, indicated by C-14 and OSL dating, probably persisted for at least several decades, maybe several centuries; their cause is unknown. There are hints that changes in atmospheric circulation shifted over the Atlantic and Pacific Oceans, with long-distance effects on the flow of moist southerly air from the Gulf of Mexico that brings rain and snow to the central Great Plains. Historical records indicate that the Sandhills may be greener now than they were a hundred years ago, so those sand grains won't start bouncing . . . not in the near future, anyway. But they are certain to do so at some point in the future.

David Loope is a professor emeritus of Earth and Atmospheric Sciences at the University of Nebraska–Lincoln.

James Swinehart is an emeritus research geologist in the Conservation and Survey Division of the University of Nebraska–Lincoln.

Joe Mason is a professor of geography at the University of Wisconsin-Madison.

What It Takes to Form a Giant Dune Field

David Loope, James Swinehart, and Joe Mason

Aerial photo looking northwest at Hackberry Lake, Valentine National Wildlife Refuge, Cherry County. The lake is surrounded by 90- to 165-foot-high barchan and barchanoid ridge dunes with abundant healed blowouts.

Seen from Highway 2, the grassy landscape of the Sandhills is gently sloping, very extensive, and quite pleasant. Seen from a satellite (using Google Earth or Google Maps), the intricate repeating patterns made by giant stabilized sand dunes, shallow lakes, and green meadows are mind-boggling. The three of us have done geologic work in the Sandhills for a total of 117 years. Jim was the first of us to become obsessed with sand-sized particles (~1978), I fell for the crunchy stuff in 1981, and Joe joined us in 1990 (but, full disclosure, he has continued to flirt with silt). We've learned that the Sandhills are comparable in size, shape, and composition to the biggest deserts in the world today (which are also mind-boggling on Google Earth). The dunes rest on sand and gravel deposited by rivers, such as the Platte, that moved eastward from the Rockies across the Great Plains to the Gulf of Mexico. The trillions of sand grains in the dunes came from Colorado and Wyoming, but their journey toward New Orleans was paused when winds (blowing alternately from north and south) swept them out of dried-up riverbeds. The geologic history of the Sandhills spans just a couple million years—not exactly deep time, but our studies (and those of colleagues and grad students) have revealed a remarkable story involving repeated climatic and biologic shifts.

Modern-day sand dunes are restricted to deserts (as in North Africa and Arabia) and to coasts with broad beaches (think North Carolina's eastern edge or Michigan's west coast). Dunes form in deserts and along beaches not because they are so windy but because all other continental environments (not covered by ice) have plants that protect land surfaces from wind erosion. Most of today's deserts lie far from the ocean, in continental interiors. Today no portion of Nebraska is a desert, but the stabilized dunes in the Sandhills are clear evidence that it was a desert when the dunes were built.

Without land plants, strong winds at the bare desert floor can erode dry sandy sediment and drive the sand along the land surface. These grains don't billow up into clouds; most travel less than a foot above the surface. As they bounce, they form half-inch-high wind ripples. Silt grains are often too small to be raised directly by the wind, but each crash of a bouncing sand grain ejects several silt grains up and into the turbulent wind. Gravity quickly brings sand grains back to the desert floor, but silt grains can't fall through the air nearly as fast. Gusting winds carry them high in the sky, forming dust clouds hundreds of feet high. Like on today's Great Plains, the direction and strength of the ancient winds that built the Sandhills varied with the seasons. Reversals of wind direction allowed dunes to reach great heights—they built upward instead of spreading laterally. Silt that fell back to the desert floor (after the wind died down) was raised by the next windstorm that got sand bouncing again. Eventually, when silt grains fell on a grassy surface (beyond the edge of the sandy desert), they stayed there: the grass acted as a baffle that slowed the wind, so there were no crashing sand grains to eject the silt. This explains why the Sandhills are just sand, and why broad areas south and east of the dunes are underlain by sand-free silt (aka loess). It accumulated via fallout from many thousands of dust storms. Besides wind reversals, another factor limiting the size of dune fields is that, although bouncing sand grains can cross dried-up riverbeds, they cannot cross rivers that frequently flood. For example, at Sutherland, Nebraska, the landscape north of Interstate 80 and the Platte River is composed of sand; south of I-80 it's all silt, clear evidence of a river barrier at the south edge of the dune field.

How do we really know that these hills are wind-blown sand dunes and were not deposited by glaciers or rivers? First, they are very similar in size and shape to modern

Blowout on the backside of a barchanoid ridge dune overlooking Pullman Valley Fen, Cherry County. The fen has a maximum peat thickness of almost 24 feet and originated about 14,000 years ago. Ditches have been cut into the peat to facilitate drainage for cutting hay. The dune in the background is about 110 feet tall.

sand dunes. Second, they are entirely made of fine to medium sand—rivers and glaciers can carry (and deposit) clay, silt, sand, gravel, and boulders, but the wind carries only sand (that builds dunes) and silt (that is deposited as loess). Third, our coring and observations of the walls of excavations and blowouts revealed that the interior of the hills are made up of broad thin layers that are not flat, but instead slope 15 to 30 degrees. These "crossbeds" slope because they were deposited on the down-wind-sloping surface of migrating dunes. On some days, these soft, smooth surfaces were trampled by bison. Those sloping layers—distinctively deformed by cloven hooves—were buried during the next windstorm.

The biggest dunes are in the central and western parts of the Sandhills, near Hyannis and Bingham. Up to 400 feet high and several miles long, their southern slopes are steeper than their northern slopes. These are called transverse dunes; their unequal slopes show they were deposited by winds from the north. Crossbeds in the smaller dunes on the Sandhills' eastern edge (Burwell, Calamus Reservoir) were deposited by seasonal winds of nearly equal strength—the deposits of one season were not destroyed by winds of the next season. These are linear dunes.

Because, on this planet, water falls from the sky pretty often, streams have shaped most ice-free land surfaces, forming rills, gullies, canyons, and valleys as they charge downhill. Regardless of the climate—hot, cold, wet, dry—there is geologic evidence that streams (by the thousands) have been draining eastward across the Great Plains for more than 30 million years. River-laid sands and gravels of the famous Ogallala Formation (which lies directly under most of the central and southern plains) represent about a third of that time span. The Sandhills rest directly on river-deposited sand and gravel. The

scale of the dunes is impressive, but compared to the tonnage of sand that has been carried across the plains by the Platte, the amount of sand that comprises the Sandhills is—we hate to say it—trivial.

In the national parks of southern Utah and northern Arizona, there are big cliffs that display wind-deposited sandstones that range in age from about 300 million to about 150 million years. In Zion National Park, the Jurassic Navajo Sandstone forms cliffs up to 2,000 feet high. That formation stretches from southeastern California to central Wyoming. Will the deposits of the Nebraska Sandhills ever be cemented into rock and reach thicknesses like that? No. Plate tectonics explains not only the lateral movement of Earth's crust and upper mantle but also their vertical movement. During the Jurassic, the western United States—near the edge of the North American Plate—was slowly sinking while wind-blown sand was being slowly deposited. Cementation of the sand took place while it was water-saturated and deeply buried; uplift and canyon cutting started about 10 million years ago. Near the center of a continent and far from a plate margin, the Great Plains region is not subsiding, so great thicknesses of dune sand can't accumulate, and, sad to say, removal of the loose dune sand by rivers is more likely than their cementation into rock.

David Loope is a professor emeritus of Earth and Atmospheric Sciences at the University of Nebraska–Lincoln.

James Swinehart is an emeritus research geologist in the Conservation and Survey Division of the University of Nebraska–Lincoln.

Joe Mason is a professor of geography at the University of Wisconsin–Madison.

Sandhills Soils
Interactions among Topography, Water, Sand, Vegetation, and Grazers

Martha Mamo

The Nebraska Sandhills contain massive dunes and upland prairies that make up approximately 90 percent of the landscape. Wide valleys between the dunes contain lakes and meadows/interdunes making up about 10 percent of the landscape. This undulating landscape with its slopes, seasonally wet low-lying areas, wetlands, and stream terraces creates variable regions of microclimate, hydrology, geology, and vegetation type, which in turn produce variability in the regional soils.

Dunes in the uplands may reach 400 feet in height and be 2 to 20 miles long. Topography affects how the forces of wind and water dislodge soil particles and transport and deposit them on the land surface, in turn influencing soil formation and development. Slopes in the Sandhills range from nearly level, or less than 2 percent slope, to steep, or more than 30 percent slope. Other features of the topography and landforms, such as elevation and aspect, can also have a significant impact on microclimates and vegetation and therefore on soils. For example, south-facing slopes receive higher solar radiation than north-facing slopes, which can affect dryness and wetness of the land. On the other hand, interdunal areas—called swales—tend to have high soil moisture and therefore can be more productive than the tops of the dune or the slopes.

Parent materials are the geologic materials from which soils are developed, and the nature of a soil is greatly affected by the characteristics of its parent materials. Most upland soils in the Sandhills are formed from parent materials of eolian sand (wind-blown deposits), and some are from stream-deposited materials in low-lying areas and stream terraces. Eolian sands undergo limited soil development due to the semiarid climate and the resistance of sand to breakdown or weathering. Weathering describes how parent materials are changed by physical, biological, and chemical processes into other soil components. Upland soils in the Sandhills are considered to be "young" or less mature in terms of soil development because they have not changed very much from their original condition at the time they were deposited.

The upland soils of the Sandhills are classified as Entisols, which means "recent." An upland soil profile generally contains a thin, dark-color surface layer, called the A horizon, followed by unstructured subsoils that are mainly sand. Soil color tells part of the developmental story, as the different soil "shades" (i.e., red, yellow, gray, white, dark/brown) indicate the presence of certain minerals, biological activities, or the presence or absence of excess water. The dark color in the surface layer of the upland soil profile is characteristic of soil organic matter. Living soil organisms (flora and fauna) and other soil dwellers facilitate the decay of plant and animal residues and produce soil organic matter and release nutrients. One widespread Entisol soil type in the Sandhills is the Valentine series. Valentine soils have a surface layer of mineral material and organic matter that is one to five

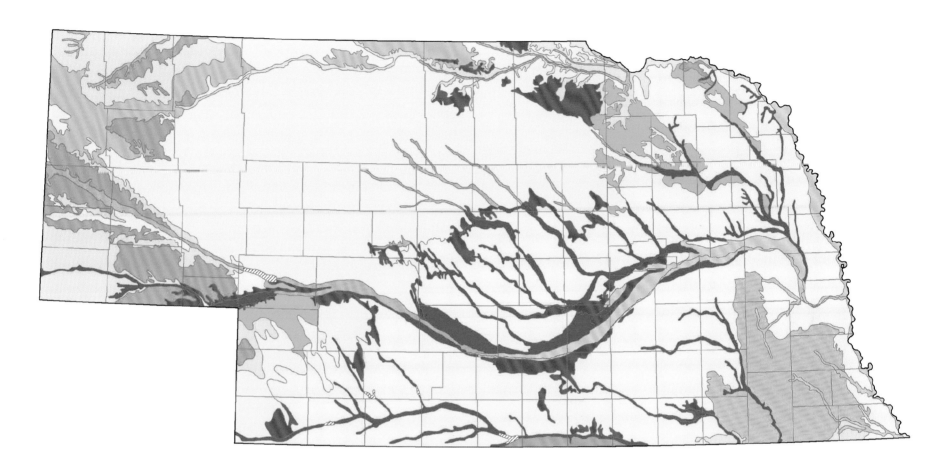

Soil Textures and Parent Materials

Sandy soils formed in eolian sand and sandy alluvium on uplands

Sandy and loamy soils formed in eolian sand and sandstone, siltstone, and shale on uplands

Silty soils formed in loess on uplands and terraces

Silty, loamy, and clayey soils formed in loess, and sandstone, siltstone, and shale on uplands

Loamy and sandy soils formed in loamy and sandy materials on uplands

Silty soils formed in alluvium and loess on stream terraces and bottomlands

Silty and clayey soils formed in loess and till on uplands

Silty and clayey soils formed in silty and clayey alluvium on bottomlands

Sandy and loamy soils formed in sandy and loamy alluvium on bottomlands

Loamy and clayey soils formed in sandstones, siltstone, limestone, and shale on uplands

Sandy and loamy soils formed in sandy and loamy materials underlain by coarse sand and gravel on uplands and terraces

Surface water

Nebraska Soil Parent Materials. Map of the major geological source materials that give rise to Nebraska soils. Throughout the Sandhills, eolian sands are the major source, with alluvium in the river valleys. From Conservation and Survey Division, University of Nebraska. Used with permission.

inches in depth, and these soils occur on slopes of up to 60 percent. They contain 78 to 98 percent sand, are well drained with low runoff, have high rates of water infiltration, and have low water holding capacity. Valentine series soils occur both in interdunes and on dunes and may be integrated with other soil types. These soils are neutral to slightly acidic, poor in nutrient holding capacity, and often contain less than 1 percent soil organic matter.

Loams are soils that are mixtures of sand, silt, and sometimes clay. The soils of meadows or of wide valleys with slopes of less than 3 percent range from loamy sand to sandy loam, with a sand content of 60–90 percent in the surface layer. Although sandy, these soils tend to be poorly drained and seasonally wet or frequently flooded because of their topographical position, the changing elevation of water table, or the presence of perennial creeks. Water tables in the wide valleys between the dunes can be within 2 and 4 feet of the soil surface throughout the growing season. These are referred to as sub-irrigated meadows, and they have greater overall plant productivity because water is available to support plant growth. Soils in the meadows are classified as either Mollisols (soft and dark from accumulation of calcium-rich prairie grasses) or Entisols. Unlike Entisols, Mollisols have a thicker surface horizon rich in soil organic matter, derived from the long-term addition and decay of grass roots and plant litter. Mollisols are rich

Valentine series soil on the crest of a dune at Gudmundsen Sandhills Laboratory. Photograph by Phil Schoenberger. Used with permission.

in calcium and more fertile than Entisols and thus are extensively used for agricultural plant production. Excess moisture from water-table rise in these low-lying areas contributes to the accumulation of organic matter in the surface soil, which varies in concentration because of variability in the rate of decay and/or productivity and the degree of wetness. Organic matter can range from less than 1 percent to as high as 10 percent in frequently ponded meadow areas.

Soil is the largest storehouse of carbon, and worldwide, soils store double the quantity of carbon found in vegetation and the atmosphere. Grassland soils store significant soil carbon—commonly 50 percent more than the carbon stores in forests. Soil organic matter is important because Sandhills grasslands depend on nutrients from decaying organic matter to sustain productivity and ecosystem functions. Soil organic matter increases soil fertility, serving as the storehouse for the energy and nutrients used by plants and other organisms. It also exchanges chemical compounds much more readily than soil clay, which allows it to retain and release essential nutrients, such as calcium, magnesium, and potassium. Organic matter also helps to retain water and acts as a glue in binding soil particles. Increasing and maintaining soil organic matter is especially critical for sandy soils because their fertility and available water capacity are low.

Grazing animals' excreta, such as dung and urine from grazing cattle, dead plant litter and trampled vegetation, decaying roots, and soil microorganisms serve as nutrient sources to grassland soils. The balance between these inputs and their decomposition determines soil carbon storage and release, as decomposition results in the biological transformation of the original organic materials and release of gaseous carbon dioxide and plant essential nutrients, such as nitrogen and phosphorus. Carbon inputs and their subsequent fate within Sandhills soils are controlled by a combination of factors, including weather (moisture and temperature), soil texture, grazing management practices, and topography. For instance, precipitation amount and duration can influence soil temperature and water content, which in turn affect microbial activity. Soil microorganisms (bacteria and fungi) are the main decomposers of soil organic matter, simultaneously impacting both soil carbon storage and the release of carbon to the atmosphere as gaseous carbon dioxide.

Improved grassland management can lead to soil carbon storage. Some Sandhill ranchers use high-intensity short-duration rotational grazing to increase soil organic matter by increasing trampling of standing vegetation. In the wide valleys, for example, grazing research has demonstrated annual litter accumulation of nearly two thousand pounds per acre—equivalent to about eight hundred pounds of plant carbon per acre. Synthesis of existing research also estimates that globally, grasslands have the potential to increase soil carbon sequestration by 0.25 ton (500 pounds) to more than 2.47 ton (4,940 pounds) per acre per year.

Yet in the Sandhills, overall knowledge of how grazing affects soil carbon stocks is quite limited. There is a need to evaluate Sandhills soils to better understand the fate and the patterns of nutrient return in pastures in relation to grazing strategies, climate, and topography. This research is essential in helping Sandhills ranchers manage their production and soil ecosystem functions using optimal grazing management strategies. Such strategies can help to mitigate the impacts of changes in precipitation and temperature and to stabilize landscapes by managing soil carbon for generations to come.

Martha Mamo is John E. Weaver Professor and Chair of Agronomy and Horticulture at the University of Nebraska–Lincoln.

The Last Five Million Years of Grasslands and Grazers

Chris Widga

In the summer of 1857, the conflict between the Sioux and the U.S. Army was heating up, and Lieut. G.K. Warren was commissioned to lead a mapping expedition deep into Nebraska Territory. The geographic and scientific goals of this expedition included the exploration of the natural history of the region. A young geologist, F.V. Hayden, accompanied Warren on this expedition. Hayden's eye for geology and fossils served them well once the expedition reached the Sandhills. As a prolific collector and a member of the Megatherium Club (boosters of a young Smithsonian Institution), Hayden made sure that some of the most prominent eastern paleontologists were able to analyze and report on important fossils that the expedition found in the Loup and Niobrara River valleys.

At one stop along the North Fork of the Loup River, near what is now Seneca, Hayden found teeth and bones. He had probably seen similar fossils during his work with James Hall, the first state geologist of New York. The small collection, as later described by Joseph Leidy of the Philadelphia Academy of Natural Sciences, included teeth of a jaguar, mastodon, and horse. A second location in the Niobrara valley of southern Sheridan County yielded a large mammoth tooth. Leidy, rarely cautious when it came to naming new species, used this specimen to describe a new species of large primitive mammoth, the imperial mammoth.

Leidy's concept of the imperial mammoth would soon fall into disuse, a casualty of better collections and,

eventually, analyses of ancient DNA from fossils. However, large mammoths remain emblematic of Nebraska paleontology. The 1922 discovery of a very large mammoth on a Lincoln County farm became the centerpiece of the newly christened Elephant Hall in the University of Nebraska State Museum. Nicknamed "Archie" and reconstructed in bronze, it now stands in front of the museum to the delight of Husker fans and fourth graders who walk under its massive, upturned tusks.

Since the mid-nineteenth century, the Nebraska Sandhills have hosted dozens of paleontological expeditions. Fossils from these expeditions reside in many eastern natural history museums, from the American Museum of Natural History to Harvard and Yale. Yet the largest collections continue to be held by the University of Nebraska State Museum, whose paleontologists led (and continue to lead) expeditions to key localities in Sheridan, Morrill, Garden, Brown, and Cherry Counties. A modern landscape of stabilized dunes, alluvial gravels, silts, and marls preserves the deep history of Sandhills plant and animal communities.

The Sandhills were not always dunes, nor were they always grasslands. The presence of herbivores with high-crowned teeth (useful for eating abrasive grasses) in regional paleontological assemblages have been key to understanding the timing and development of grassland ecosystems in North America. From modest Miocene beginnings, warm season grasses gradually

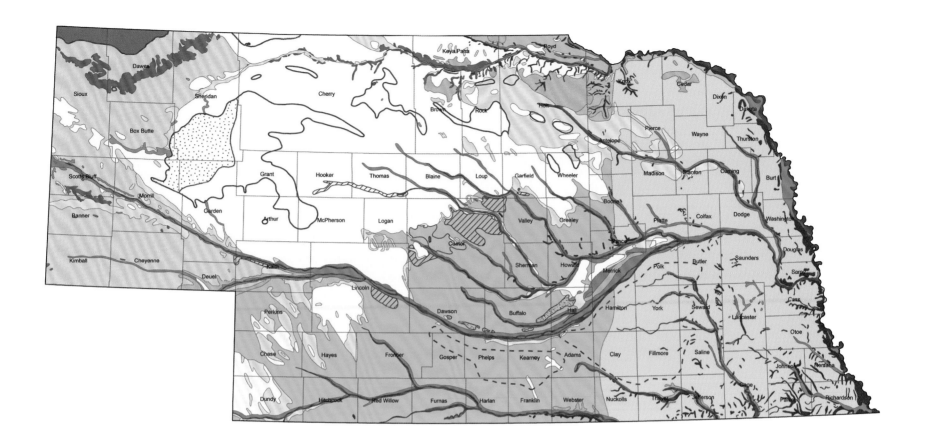

Native Vegetation of Nebraska Before 1880

Forests and Savannas

Ponderosa Pine Forests and Savannas

Red Cedar Forest and Savanna

Riparian Deciduous Forests

Upland Deciduous Forests

Aquatic Vegetation

Lakes, Ponds, Marshes and Fens

Rainwater Basins

Scattered Salt Marshes and Flats

Salt Marsh and Flats

Grasslands

Upland Tallgrass Prairie

Lowland Tallgrass Prairie

Loess Mixed-grass Prairie

Sandhills Mixed-grass Prairie

Sandsage Mixed-grass Prairie

Sandhills Borders Mixed-grass Prairie

Gravelly Mixed-grass Prairie

Shale Mixed-grass Prairie

Mosaic of Mixed-grass/Shortgrass Prairie

ROBERT KAUL / STEVEN ROLFSMEIER

Native vegetation in Nebraska before 1880. Map by Robert Kaul and Steven Rolfsmeier. Used with permission.

became larger components of the landscape during the Pliocene, reaching modern levels approximately 3 million years ago.

Some of the earliest Pleistocene sites in the Sandhills preserve animals of this earlier time and represent a transition from the warm mid-Pliocene to cooler glacial conditions. Giant camels, diminutive antelopes, llamas, stegomastodons, and borophagine dogs from the Lisco and Broadwater localities along the North Platte River are holdovers from these Miocene forests, when rhinos and oversize tortoises roamed the region. The Lisco quarry is famous for its giant camels and is estimated to be 4.5 million years old. Hundreds of extinct horses and a relatively complete skeleton of a stegomastodon were found at the slightly younger Broadwater quarry (3.5 million years old). Both sites represent a world that could come again. Over the next few decades, atmospheric CO_2 levels and temperatures will increase, reaching levels that were last experienced during this mid-Pliocene transition.

The first time glaciers from Canada made it to the mid-latitudes marked a one-way shift in the animal and plant communities of the Great Plains. Browsers occupying the open forests of the Pliocene moved elsewhere or went extinct, to be replaced by cold-tolerant taxa of the Ice Age. These communities included mammoths, musk oxen, horses, and camels, and a broad range of cold-adapted small mammals such as jackrabbits, voles, and muskrats. It is these smaller species that help us tell time during the Ice Age, as the teeth of younger taxa quickly adapted to diets in colder, drier landscapes. Sites near Mullen on the North Fork of the Loup River document this change from Pliocene survivors to early Ice Age faunas. Some of the earliest harbingers of a 2.5-million-year cooling period were not mammoths and musk oxen, rather they were jackrabbits and muskrats!

The Ice Age was not always cold. During this time the climate swung between warm and cold, dragging the ranges of animals and plants to the south during cool periods and back to the north as it warmed up. Collecting sites in the ancestral Niobrara River valley near Hay Springs, Rushville, and Gordon—made famous by Leidy's imperial mammoth—provide a picture of the Sandhills landscape as a cool, lush, relatively open forest. Ranchers of today would have recognized many of the animals that occupied the Sandhills at this time, as they were the ancestors of many modern forms. In addition to mammoths, stilt-legged horses and flat-headed peccaries occurred in these sites, as did the iconic saber-toothed cat, *Smilodon fatalis*.

In recent years new techniques, such as the recovery of DNA from fossil teeth and bones, have rewritten our understanding of some of these species. These studies suggest that mammoths were surprisingly similar throughout their range and that the genetic differences between woolly and Columbian mammoths were minor, despite measurable morphological differences. On the other hand, mastodon populations had evolved separately for much longer, and dire wolves are more closely related to earlier forms like Armbruster's wolf (found in the Sheridan County sites) than to modern gray wolves.

The end of the Ice Age happened quickly. Continent-wide glaciers covered Canada at the peak of the last glacial episode (~20,000 years ago) but had melted north of the U.S. border within a few millennia. By twelve thousand years ago many of the largest animals were extinct, leaving a landscape occupied by a single remaining species of megafauna, bison. This period of warming also corresponds to some of the earliest evidence of humans in the Great Plains.

Chris Widga is a vertebrate paleontologist, head curator, and adjunct faculty member in geosciences at East Tennessee State University.

Bison grazing in the Sandhills. Photograph by Chris Helzer. Used with permission.

Where the Buffalo Roam
. . . or Not

Chris Widga

Bison have been present in the Great Plains for at least a hundred thousand years. Their constant presence and the presumed gradual changes in the shape and size of their horns made them an ideal chronometer for some paleontologists to estimate the age of certain fossil assemblages. Although ubiquitous during the Late Pleistocene, they typically made up only a small portion of an entire faunal assemblage. This all changed about twelve thousand years ago, when the other Great Plains megafauna went extinct. With the loss of large herbivores, such as mammoths, horses, and camels, bison populations boomed. Sites at this time included dozens, sometimes hundreds, of animals and were often associated with evidence indicating a long-term, sophisticated use of bison by Indigenous communities.

Much of this drama also played out in the Sandhills, where bison bones are commonly found in archaeological sites. At one rare locality near Burwell, tracks are preserved in a buried lakebed. Despite long-held assumptions suggesting bison migrated often and for long distances, historic records of bison movements have been ambiguous. Some early chroniclers observed the year-round presence of small bison herds, whereas others provide convincing accounts of seasonal, long-distance movements. Both scenarios could be correct, but the chemical record of bison behavior in teeth and bones from paleontological and archaeological sites has provided a more nuanced picture of bison movement at some localities.

Over the last few decades, scientists have begun to explore the potential of certain isotopes for tracking the impact of animals within ecosystems. Isotopes of some elements in teeth and bones correspond with animal behavior. For instance, the ratio of ^{12}C to ^{13}C (notated as δ^{13}C) reflects the amount of warm season grasses (C4 plants) relative to cool season grasses, herbs, shrubs, and trees (C3 plants) in an animal's diet. This relationship has been very important in understanding the timing of the spread of grassland ecosystems during the Miocene and Pliocene. The ratio of ^{87}Sr to ^{86}Sr (notated as ^{87}Sr/^{86}Sr), on the other hand, reflects the underlying geology of an area that is grazed by an animal. Through careful sampling of rapidly growing teeth, scientists can reconstruct the movement of an animal across different geological substrates. This has led to surprising results when applied to bison from the Great Plains, suggesting that bison were local herbivores with a flexible diet throughout much of the late Pleistocene and Holocene. Long-distance, seasonal migration seems to be a behavior that only existed during the narrow window of time when early writers documented it. That is not to say that bison never moved. A ten-thousand-year-old herd in the southern Sandhills seasonally shifted its range between the Platte River valley and neighboring uplands over the course of a multiyear record. Over many years, the home range of a herd might drift a significant distance, or young male bison might disperse from a natal herd to a new range. These studies paint a picture of bison as highly flexible and able to adapt to rapidly changing environments, characteristics that would have served them well when other megafauna went extinct.

Changes in the evolution of animals and their associated plant communities in Nebraska over the past 16 million years. Used with permission, the University of Nebraska State Museum.

During the Barstovian Age (16 to 12.5 million years ago), temperatures were mild, and most large- and medium-sized mammals were leaf-eating browsers. These included *Cranioceras*, which had a third horn jutting from the back of its head, and *Merycodus*, a small, extinct cousin of today's pronghorns. The ancient horse *Merychippus* was among the earliest mixed feeders, which both browsed and grazed. Early cats, bears, and a four-tusked elephant called a gomphothere migrated from Asia during this period.

During the Clarendonian Age (12.5 to 9 million years ago), temperatures cooled and the resulting shifts in vegetation favored the evolution of grazing animals, such as the horse *Neohipparion*, which lived together with browsers, including the camel *Aepycamelus*, which had a long giraffe-like neck. The fauna also included predators, such as bone-crushing dogs and the saber-toothed cat *Nimravides*.

During the Hemphillian Age (9 to 4.9 million years ago), Nebraska grew steadily cooler and drier. Large rhinoceroses, such as *Aphelops* (a browser) and *Teleoceras* (a grazer), roamed the region. New arrivals from Asia included the large bear *Indarctos* and the large saber-toothed cat *Machairodus*.

During the Blancan Age (4.9 to 1.8 million years ago), the drying and cooling trend continued. Long-legged grazing animals, adapted for running across the grassland, dominated the landscape. The expansion of savanna-like grasslands coincided with changes in the dominant grasses, from C3 types to tougher C4, which were harder to chew and digest. This favored mammals, such as the giant camels and the elephant-like *Stegomastodon*.

Sandhills Grassland, Large Grazers, and Conservative Use

Al Steuter

Charolais cattle grazing along the Middle Loup River near Halsey.

Free-ranging bison disappeared from the Sandhills during the late 1800s. They were briefly replaced by free-range cattle, escapees of the Texas to Montana cattle drives that gave rise to the beginnings of open-range cattle ranches. Then the early 1900s saw a growing number of privately owned and fenced ranches. The cattle industry grew during the next five decades, even during the difficult years of drought in the 1930s and 1950s. By the 1960s, Sandhills ranches had become well-known as a source of high-quality feeder cattle for the expanding feed lots of Iowa and eastern Nebraska.

Early in the 1900s, bison were nearly extinct, with only about a thousand animals remaining. Three federal reserves were established to ensure that the bison would not become extinct: the National Bison Range near Moiese, Montana; the Fort Niobrara National Wildlife Refuge in the northern Sandhills near Valentine, Nebraska; and the Wichita Mountains National Wildlife Refuge near Lawton, Oklahoma. Bison numbers on the initial federal refuges and parks and selected state parks had increased to more than a hundred thousand by 1960. Surplus bison began to be made available to private ranches. The Peterson Ranch in the Sandhills south of Newport, Nebraska, was probably the first serious bison ranch in the Sandhills. Bison numbers on private ranches and conservation lands grew steadily through the 1970s and '80s,

then rapidly in the 1990s, only to have the market crash in 1998–2000. Since the early twenty-first century, the private bison industry has consolidated into fewer and larger operations.

In 2022 there were approximately 530,000 beef cattle and 25,000 bison on private ranches in the Sandhills. Within comparable grasslands, cattle tend to consume more forbs in their annual diet than do bison, who consume more grass. A gross calculation using Sandhills cattle and bison herd numbers, range site productivity, and total Sandhills rangeland area suggests that the current management of cattle and bison is sustainable at the large scale. However, there are a few species of specialized plants and fish in need of focused conservation action.

Cattle drive at Bowring Ranch State Historical Park, Cherry County.

Managing the Sandhills with adapted large grazers like cattle and bison provides an opportunity for a low-cost, high-value product that also provides important environmental and recreational values. Bison have resisted many attempts at domestication, whereas cattle have been domesticated worldwide for thousands of years. The Fort Niobrara National Wildlife Refuge plays a unique role in conserving bison as a species. The Fort Niobrara herd continues to be managed as a natural sex and age ratio herd at a population scale. In contrast, most private ranch and conservation herds of bison in the Sandhills are managed with an adult bull

Bison grazing at The Nature Conservancy's Niobrara Valley Preserve, Brown County. Photograph by Michael Forsberg. Used with permission.

Herding Hereford cattle north of Oshkosh in the Sandhills.

to cow ratio of 1:10 or a bit higher. Similar stocking rate calculations can be made, but the difference in social behaviors between cattle and bison also may influence factors, such as seasonal forage selection and soil disturbance. Cattle tend to drift with the wind during snowstorms, whereas bison stand facing into the wind. On hot summer days, cattle tend to form tight bunches in up-wind pasture corners, especially when flies are feeding on them, a behavior not seen in bison.

Whether raising cattle or bison, Sandhills ranchers focus on sustainably using the native rangeland for as much of their forage needs as possible. Bison adaptations provide them with advantages for using Sandhill forages year-round. An extra heavy winter coat covers a bison's head, shoulders, and chest, and limited blood circulation to extremities reduces body heat loss. Another

winter adaptation is a lowering of the overall metabolic rate, which reduces their need for forage. The downside of this adaptation is reduced winter growth potential and delayed sexual maturity, even if high-quality winter forage is available. Bison heifers typically breed as two-year-olds and have their first calves as three-year-olds. This results in lower herd productivity relative to a typical cattle operation. However, it is common for bison ranches to have more than 90 percent of three-year-old bison cows with live calves in the fall roundup.

Bison ranches that maintain their herds year-round on native Sandhills rangeland without supplemental feed have a defined calving season of late April into July, although their bulls are in the herd and fertile year-round. This is a result of the improved body condition of adult cows grazing the high-quality spring and early summer forage following calving. Another trade-off between cattle and bison operations is the extra feed and labor required by cattle at calving time. Bison calve on pasture without assistance by virtue of natural selection for smaller calf size. This is another example of lower cost with lower productivity.

When ranchers move cattle with calves to new pastures, the best practice is to take plenty of time to reduce stress on the cows, calves, and people involved. The move usually ends at the closest water source in the new pasture. This helps to congregate cows and calves for a drink and grazing of the new grass around the water source, holding most cows for a while. It typically takes an hour or more to ensure all the calves have paired up with their mothers in the new pasture before they head out to explore. If a cow and calf don't find each other, they are likely to return to where they came from, even if it requires going through fences. With moving bison, the calves are seemingly still glued to their mother's side when they reach their destination.

Over the last four decades, ranchers have seen that raising bison and cattle can range from highly profitable to less profitable. By combining multigenerational ranch experience with the management techniques proven by university research and extension scientists, the Sandhills will continue to provide high-quality grazing land requiring few inputs, other than those needed to maintain the diverse and resilient native plant communities.

Al Steuter is a landowner and rancher in Johnstown, Nebraska.

Pipe from a windmill stock tank delivers water from the aquifer below at Gudmundsen Sandhills Laboratory, Cherry County. Photograph by Michael Forsberg. Used with permission.

Cloud towers reflect in a Sandhills wetland, Grant County.
Photograph by Michael Forsberg. Used with permission.

WATER

Groundwater
How the High Plains Aquifer Shapes the Sandhills

Erin Haacker

Groundwater shapes the Sandhills in many ways, both visible and invisible. Not far below the surface—and at the surface in lakes and wet meadows between the dunes—the spaces between sand grains are filled with water instead of air. If you dig in these places, the hole will fill with water. This is called an aquifer: an underground unit of rock, gravel, or sand that stores water and allows it to flow beneath the land surface.

The Sandhills are part of the High Plains Aquifer, a large system of several interconnected layers of sediment that store and transmit water and that stretches from southern North Dakota to south of the Texas Panhandle. About two-thirds of the water in the High Plains Aquifer is in the Sandhills. The largest geologic unit of the High Plains Aquifer is the Ogallala Group, and the aquifer is often referred to as the Ogallala Aquifer. The Ogallala Group is made up of sediments that eroded from the Rocky Mountains and were carried by streams from present-day Colorado and Wyoming. As the mountains rose, gravel and sand were washed down the slopes to create an extensive blanket of sediment.

In most places, a large proportion of water from rain and snowmelt "runs off" (flows across the land surface to a stream channel) or evaporates from puddles. The rest of the water soaks into the ground and, as it trickles through the soil, is taken up by plant roots and

transpired through leaves. Usually, only a tiny percentage of the water in soils makes it past the root zone and into the deeper unsaturated zone, where it eventually reaches the water table and becomes what is known as groundwater recharge. In the Sandhills, this precipitation partitioning is very different than most regions. The Sandhills is like a giant sponge. When rain falls, almost all the water quickly sinks into the sandy soil rather than running off into surface depressions or streams. Although other parts of the High Plains commonly have more rain and snow than the Sandhills, the Sandhills receive by far the greatest proportion of precipitation flowing to the aquifer, because water moves through the coarse sandy sediments so quickly. This abundant infiltration keeps the water table shallow, close to the surface of the landscape.

Groundwater flows down a slope, just as surface water flows downhill. When the water table intersects the land surface, a natural spring forms. In the Sandhills, this often takes the form of wet meadows in low spots between dunes. Wet meadows are a common, visible, and ecologically sensitive consequence of the water table's proximity to the land surface. Like wet meadows, many regional streams and rivers of central Nebraska also are fed by cool groundwater from the Sandhills. These streams act like giant drains, preventing groundwater from accumulating and turning the region into a

single vast wetland. Occasionally the sandy soils cannot absorb all the water from a rainstorm or blizzard, and large floods occur. When this happens, the Sandhills can stay flooded for months at a time as the water slowly evaporates or drains to streams.

In addition to having a high water table, the Sandhills sediment extends deep below the surface. Most aquifers have a base of less-permeable rock that serves as a barrier to deeper water infiltration, and the Sandhills is no exception. But while other areas of the High Plains Aquifer have an impermeable layer up to a few hundred feet below the land surface, the base of the Sandhills aquifer is generally more than 500 feet below the surface. In some places, the water-bearing sediments are more than a thousand feet thick. This is another reason that the Sandhills store so much water. Much of this

Groundwater occurs at the surface in the interdunal valleys, giving rise to Sandhills wetlands, such as this wetland on South Whitman Road, south of Whitman and east of Hyannis in Grant County. Photography by Mariah Lundgren, Platte Basin Timelapse. Used with Permission.

water is likely to be thousands of years old, but its age is hard to determine and varies with depth.

Sandhills groundwater flows in the same general direction as the rivers, from west to east, but much more slowly. According to measurements taken by the U.S. Geological Survey, the groundwater in the Sandhills may travel about 30 feet per day, much faster than groundwater in most places. This west to east flow is why declining groundwater levels to the south in Kansas and Texas have no effect on Sandhills water levels.

Groundwater withdrawals from the High Plains Aquifer are greater than groundwater withdrawals from any other aquifer in the United States. About 97 percent of the water in the High Plains Aquifer is used for agriculture, and the aquifer is known for its declining water levels due to irrigation of corn, soybeans, and cotton. Yet in contrast to other parts of the aquifer, the water level in the Sandhills has remained fairly stable since recordkeeping began. One likely reason is that the Sandhills is not a profitable place to grow crops because the sandy soil does not retain sufficient nutrients to support intensive agriculture.

The large quantity of water stored in the Sandhills has led to suggestions to pipe the water to other parts of the aquifer where water availability is declining because of excess withdrawals. Despite its huge water storage, the Sandhills is a fragile, groundwater-dependent ecosystem that would be damaged irreparably by significant withdrawals. For example, along the cliffs of the Niobrara River, there are many springs where groundwater meets the surface and flows into the stream channel. Other areas of the High Plains once had many of these springs that provided water for plants and animals, but most stopped flowing when the water table declined. If this happened in the Sandhills, rivers like the Loup, Dismal, Elkhorn, and even reaches of the Niobrara could stop flowing and become dry, and the wet meadows would disappear.

Maintaining Sandhills groundwater quality is a major environmental challenge. The close relationship between groundwater and surface water makes this area vulnerable to contamination. Fertilizers, such as nitrate, and pesticides, such as atrazine, move readily with water through the unsaturated zone. In other regions, it is estimated to take decades for a drop of water to travel from the land surface to the underlying aquifer. In the Sandhills, the surface water—and anything in the water—goes straight into the water table. When it reaches the aquifer, it may travel to a nearby stream in a matter of a few years. Once contaminated, groundwater is difficult to clean up. Despite this vulnerability, groundwater in the Sandhills remains cleaner than in other areas of the state with more intensive agricultural and urban development.

Next time you pass through the Sandhills, notice the wet meadows, the irrigation pivots, and the windmills, many of which have a small stock tank at their base. The windmills are used to transport water from the aquifer to the surface. This was the first technology used to pump water from the High Plains Aquifer, and these small wind-powered wells are still a common sight across the region. The windmills, pivots, and wet meadows are reminders of the ways in which groundwater has shaped this unique landscape over thousands of years and continues to do so today.

Erin Haacker is an assistant professor of Earth and Atmospheric Sciences at the University of Nebraska–Lincoln.

Sandhills Streams and Rivers as Influenced by Groundwater, Climate, and Humans

Jessica Corman and Troy Gilmore

Waterfall along the North Loup River, Cherry County, at twilight. Photograph by Michael Forsberg. Used with permission.

Meandering Dismal River, which is fed by regional groundwater, and the associated flat-topped stream terraces, which are the remnants of a time when the river flowed at a higher elevation. Photograph by Phil Schoenberger. Used with permission.

Within the valleys of the undulating Sandhills landscape lies a network of flowing waters. Flowing southeasterly across the Sandhills, the streams include the Calamus, Dismal, Middle Loup, North Loup, and Snake Rivers. Flowing easterly, the Niobrara and Elkhorn Rivers trace the Sandhills' edge in the north, and the North Platte River traces its edge in the south.

Streams and rivers derive their water from a variety of sources. In grassland regions, this generally includes water directly from overground sources, such as rain or melting snow, called overland flow, and belowground sources, like springs or groundwater seepage. The belowground sources derive from a vast body of sediment, saturated with groundwater, that lies beneath the Sandhills. Those saturated sediments start as much as a thousand feet below the surface, extending upward to the water table. The higher land and water table elevations in the west drive groundwater generally to the east, where it finds an exit at lower elevations. The lowest elevations on the landscape are usually streambeds. The varying streamflow quantity (and even the color of the water) throughout the year is largely an expression of that hidden groundwater.

To examine the characteristics of streamflow in the Sandhills more closely, consider the Loup River system. The Loup River is fed by headwater creeks and straightened drainage ditches that flow from wet meadows in the western valleys in the Sandhills. The creeks and ditches then flow into meandering streams before feeding into the Loup. In dry times, the streams are smooth and clear, although sometimes stained the color of tea from organic matter that is leached out of valley soils. During wet seasons, the valleys may flood, straining or overtopping culverts at ditch crossings and downstream road crossings. Where the channels are sinuous, the turbulent stream water almost appears to boil as it swirls at the channel bends. At these times, the stream has a light-brown color in part due to fine white sand that is suspended in the water, a reminder of the power of these waters to shift and reshape the stream channel over time. Along the edges of the stream, the waterlogged fine sands can produce pockets of quicksand, an unpleasant surprise for the unsuspecting newcomer.

Scientists studying the streams in the Loup River system have made some exciting discoveries. In particular, they have discovered that the river and its tributaries are receiving groundwater from different parts of the dune sands and from the aquifer below. In the headwaters of the Middle Loup River, measurements of the age of groundwater, just before it seeps into the stream, suggest that much of the groundwater discharging to the headwater creeks has been traveling through the aquifer for years to decades before discharging into the stream. Farther east, in the main channel of the Middle Loup River near Seneca, Nebraska, at least some of the groundwater feeding the river is likely thousands of years old! This vast reservoir of "ancient" groundwater is the reason that these streams have flowed so reliably over the years. For those who "tank" in the Middle Loup, that cool water at your feet was recently groundwater that may have traveled for a thousand years or more to greet you.

Smith Falls in Smith Falls State Park on the banks of the Niobrara River, Cherry County. A groundwater-fed stream plunges over the canyon walls to give rise to the tallest waterfall in the state of Nebraska (63 feet).

Riverine Flora and Fauna

The Sandhill streams and rivers provide habitat for a multitude of plants and animals. In contrast to the surrounding landscape full of grasses and other prairie species, the riparian areas stretching on either side of the flowing waters support a variety of sedges, rushes, bulrushes, reeds, and forbs. The larger rivers can support some forested communities along their banks, although the tree canopy does not extend across regions of flowing waters at the stream's center. Yet this lack of canopy cover does not mean that river and stream waters are always warm. Instead, the consistent groundwater inflows generally keep waters cool. Indeed, this groundwater influence tends to minimize temperature variation in Sandhills streams throughout the year. The cooler waters are necessary for a favorite fish of anglers, the trout, to live and reproduce. Brown trout (*Salmo trutta*), rainbow trout (*Oncorhynchus mykiss*), and brook trout (*Salvelinus fontinalis*) can all be found in Sandhill streams, although the rainbow trout are often stocked. Perhaps the most interesting fish of all is the plains topminnow (*Fundulus sciadicus*). This olive-green fish, no more than the length of a playing card, with an upturned mouth, prefers the heavily vegetated, slower moving backwaters of streams and rivers. Stream degradation, nutrient pollution, and other stressors have decreased its population size over much of its range in the central United States; hence, the Sandhill streams remain important in maintaining this fish population.

Human Impact on the Flow of Rivers and Streams

While the Sandhills region is considered less impacted by human activities than much of the Great Plains, the region still faces local and regional pressures. Indeed, area ranchers can recall streams that were once fordable by truck, foot, or hoof and are now so downcut or entrenched that they resemble small canyons and require some ingenuity to cross. Ditching and straightening of streams, done to aid agricultural endeavors, increases streamflow and, ultimately, rates of erosion. Often, this increased erosion has occurred on the streambed, resulting in a further lowering or downcutting of the stream channel. While many ranchers have maintained a sustainable balance in managing their land, many have not. Thus, in some places, unsustainably managed grazing has not only led to increased stream bank erosion but loss of riparian vegetation and compromised water quality as well.

The overall water balance in the region has also changed. Within some local areas, extraction of groundwater for irrigation has diverted water from streams and rivers, moving it to cropland systems. At a regional level, climate change has increased precipitation in the Sandhills over the last hundred years, mostly through an increase in heavy precipitation events, which can cause catastrophic flooding, as witnessed in the March 2019 flood. While it may be difficult to pinpoint whether specific rain or flood events are caused entirely by climate change, the overall trend toward more extreme weather events is consistent with the output of climate model experiments that investigate the impacts of increased greenhouse gases in the atmosphere.

Jessica Corman is an associate professor in the School of Natural Resources at the University of Nebraska–Lincoln.

Troy Gilmore is an associate professor in the School of Natural Resources at the University of Nebraska–Lincoln.

The Niobrara
A National Scenic River

Jessica Corman and Troy Gilmore

Niobrara River in Cherry County winds through its canyon in fall color. Photograph by Michael Forsberg. Used with permission.

In the northern Sandhills lies the Niobrara River, which begins as a narrow cold-water stream in the high plains of eastern Wyoming. As the waters move eastward, springs from the High Plains Aquifer continuously feed the river. And as it grows, the river flows through wide valleys and narrow, sinuous canyons, exposing rocks that are millions of years old in the canyons and bluffs. Parts of the river even flow directly over bedrock, an uncommon feature of the many sand-bottomed, sediment-laden rivers in the Sandhills. Along its narrow corridor, the Niobrara River valley hosts a rich diversity of vegetation, including species from western coniferous, eastern deciduous, and northern boreal forests, some of which likely survived as relicts of the last glacial period and its cooler, moister climate. These attributes, along with the lack of significant impoundments and relatively undeveloped shorelines, led Congress to designate a 76-mile corridor beginning just east of Valentine, Nebraska, as a National Scenic River. Each year, thousands of tourists flock to the Niobrara River, enjoying the waters as they float, explore waterfalls, hunt, fish, or camp.

Birdwood Creek, one of two streams that drain directly into the Platte River from the Sandhills. Photograph by Michael Forsberg. Used with permission.

March 2019 Floods

Jessica Corman and Troy Gilmore

In mid-March 2019, the most powerful bomb cyclone to hit the region in decades swept across the Great Plains. Nebraska was both particularly cold when it hit, with soil frost levels unusually deep, and hit hard by what would become two to three-plus inches of rain across the region. The water could not infiltrate the soil, and so the absorbent Sandhills soils did not absorb. Instead, water flowed overland to streams and rivers in the region. The overland flow quickly melted much of the snow on the ground, further increasing the amount of water draining the landscape. Because of the earlier cold weather through much of February and March, river ice was particularly thick and when the waters rose, that ice began to break up. The floodwaters carried these massive ice blocks—some as large as pickup trucks—until they inevitably got caught in bends in the rivers, under bridges, and at dams. The ice jams and resulting flooding led to more than $2.6 billion in damage. Throughout much of 2019, precipitation rates and water table levels remained elevated. In the spring, while researchers at the University of Nebraska–Lincoln worried about when water levels would decrease enough to safely continue ongoing investigations of these aquatic ecosystems, residents of the Sandhills wondered when roads, bridges, pastures, and, in some cases, homes would once again be usable. Highways in the Sandhills remained flooded for months. In June, Highway 83 was still under five inches of water, and the flooded highway in August was still flanked by stoplights, dictating one-way traffic on the stretch, and the soaked, overtopped sandbags along the edge of the road seemed like omens of our inability to manage climate-change-related crises without a substantial, coordinated effort.

Sandhills Lakes in Space and Time

Sherilyn C. Fritz

One might not imagine hundreds of lakes in a sea of sand and grass, but indeed, the Nebraska Sandhills contain more than fifteen hundred lakes scattered throughout its hills and valleys. Strange as this might seem, lakes in dry, sand-dominated regions also occur in other places across the globe, including the Badain Jaran Desert of Inner Mongolia and in some of the sand seas of the Sahara. These lakes exist because of the large aquifers beneath the fields of dunes, which provide a continuous source of water. In the Sandhills, it is the High Plains Aquifer that rises to the surface in areas of low topography and is the major source of water for many of the region's lakes and wetlands.

Ironically, most of the Sandhills lakes likely formed during past intervals of extreme drought. Some lake basins are relatively small depressions formed by deflation of the sand by wind in places with sparse vegetation cover. When the climate got wetter, and the rains returned, these wind-carved basins filled with rainwater. In other cases, river and stream drainages were blocked by blowing sand during major droughts, forming a dam. Subsequently, the water table rose behind the dam, flooding low-lying areas and giving rise to lakes and wetlands.

These deflation depressions and dune-dammed lakes likely formed during multiple so-called megadroughts over the millennia. The most recent of these megadroughts occurred about eight hundred years ago, but these processes have occurred for thousands of years, yielding lakes of varied ages across the landscape. Some lakes that exist today are only hundreds of years old, whereas others have been present for millennia. In addition, remnants of ancient lakes that existed in the past, but were filled with sediment over time, are found along the Niobrara River and in other Sandhill drainages. These "paleolakes" are evident as large exposures of layered lake sediment adjacent to modern rivers and streams. Radiocarbon dating of the outcropping sediment indicates that some of these lakes existed more than forty thousand years ago, during wetter intervals of the last glacial period.

Because of their differing origins, the lakes of the Sandhills range in size from small, isolated basins of less than a hectare to large linear lakes that extend for miles between the dunes. These interdunal areas are sometimes filled with shallow lakes and in other cases are occupied by wetlands, depending on the steepness of the valley walls and the amount of water inflow from groundwater and rainfall. All Sandhills lakes are relatively shallow, ranging in depth from tens of centimeters to a few meters. The shallow depth of the basins combined with strong winds, which stir up and mix muds from the lake sediments into the water column, cause many of the lakes to be extremely turbid (opaque). This high turbidity limits the penetration of sunlight through the water column, limiting photosynthesis and the growth of aquatic plants.

Mosaic of lakes in the Sandhills region showing the diversity in size, shape, and setting.

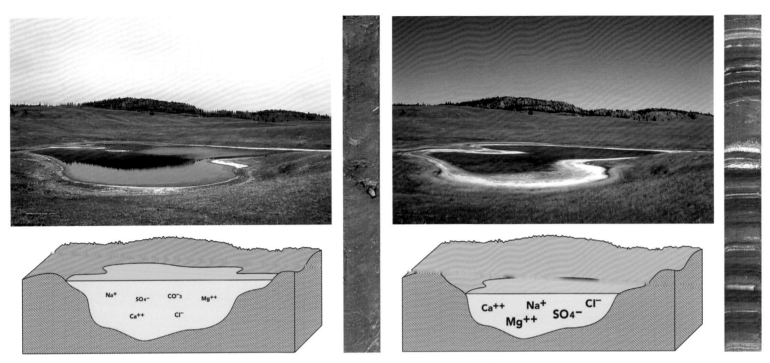

As lakes in the Sandhills region transition from wet (*left*) to dry (*right*) climate, the water level declines, dissolved ions become more concentrated by evaporation, and salts precipitate from solution, forming white layers in the sediments. Lake photographs by Brian Cumming. Used with permission. Sediment photographs by Sherilyn C. Fritz. Used with permission. Lake graphic modified from an image by Angie Fox, University of Nebraska State Museum.

The chemistry of Sandhills lakes is tremendously variable because of complex interactions between the mineral composition of deposits at the surface, the connectivity of basins to groundwater, the topography of the land surface, and climate (precipitation, evaporation). The lakes have pH values from mildly alkaline (~8) to highly alkaline (>10), and salinity ranges from freshwater to several times higher than seawater. In general, lakes at lower elevation are closer to the water table and have more groundwater inflow than those lakes higher in the regional flow system. Because most groundwater in the Sandhills region is relatively fresh (<2 g L^{-1}), the salinity of low-elevation lakes is lower than that of nearby lakes at higher elevation. Yet even in low-lying basins, salts are concentrated by evaporation, producing lake water that is saltier than the groundwater.

In regions of higher elevation, near the crests of dunes, many lake basins are fed mainly by precipitation and are cut off from groundwater inputs. In these areas, the in-

Aerial photograph showing dozens of lakes and wetlands amid the Sandhills landscape.

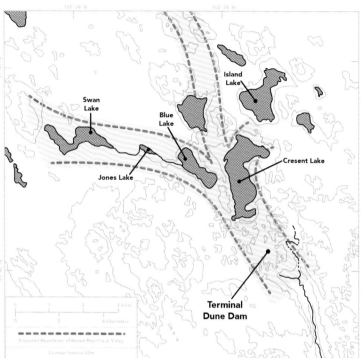

Aerial photo and map of Swan Lake, Crescent Lake, and Blue Lake in the western Sandhills, which are drained today by Blue Creek. The lakes were formed during different very dry periods during the last 14,000 years, when wind-blown sand accumulated in the valley (depicted by orange dotted line), forming dune dams. The most recent dune dam, which formed about 5,000 years ago, is located just below Crescent Lake and was identified by drilling into the dunes. Photograph by Jon Mason. Used with permission.

tense evaporation during the warm season concentrates salts over time, and these so-called perched lakes often have extremely high salinity and sometimes dry out. In contrast to the ocean, which is dominated by sodium chloride salts, lakes in the Sandhills may be dominated by carbonate, sulphate, or chloride brines dependent on the geology; carbonate salts are the most common. Among the more interesting of the Sandhill lakes are the alkaline lakes in Sheridan and Garden Counties, which are characterized by potassium salts and in some places were mined for potash for fertilizer.

The Sandhills lakes are an important water source for migrating waterfowl, other wildlife, and cattle. In addition, the lakes themselves harbor a rich diversity of microscopic plants and animals that vary in lakes of different depth and water chemistry. In comparison with other regions of Nebraska, the Sandhill lakes have not been affected by substantive human impact. Nonetheless,

the rich grassland soils and warm temperatures favor high algal productivity during the growing season, including blooms of cyanobacteria (blue-green algae that sometimes produce toxins) during summer months. Analysis of the history of Sandhill lakes via the record preserved in their sediments indicates these algal blooms existed prior to widespread regional settlement and the expansion of ranching.

Through the years and centuries and millennia, the size, depth, chemistry, and biology of Sandhills lakes have varied in response to changes in climate, particularly changes in precipitation and temperature-driven evaporation. As organisms died and sank to the lake bottom and layers of sediment accumulated over time, a record of each lake's history and the associated climate was preserved in the sediment layers, with the oldest layers deep in the mud and recent history at the sediment surface. Various mineral, chemical, and biological fossils contained in those layers of sediment can be used to reconstruct the climate and environment at the time of deposition and to put together a sequential history of the lake and its watershed.

Fossilized clues from lake sediments have been used in combination with other records of geological history, such as the records from the dunes themselves, to unravel the long-term history of the Sandhills region. Together these geologic records indicate that repeated droughts spanning decades and centuries—droughts that were more extreme and persistent than those of the last century or two—are a recurrent part of regional history. This long-term history preserved in Sandhills lakes and dunes shows the dynamic interaction of hydrology, vegetation, and wind over time in this sensitive grassland region, and the record suggests that drought is the rule rather than the exception for the Sandhills and its various long-term inhabitants.

Sandhill lakes are an enduring feature of the landscape that have provided resources and refuges for the region's people and wildlife throughout time. They exist because of the interplay between the region's geology and hydrology and are shaped by the interaction of sand, water, wind, and plants. Because of their sensitivity to changing climate and local environments, they serve as sentinels of the dynamic character of the Sandhills as they evolve and change in space and in time.

Sherilyn C. Fritz is George Holmes University Professor in Earth and Atmospheric Sciences and Biological Sciences at the University of Nebraska–Lincoln.

Deposits from an ancient paleolake above the Niobrara River that formed by dune blockage of the river about 50,000 years ago. Over thousands of years, the diatoms living in the lake died and fell to the lake floor, where they accumulated and formed tens of meters of diatom-rich sediment. Photograph by James Swinehart. Used with permission.

Sandhills Alkaline Lakes

David D. Dunigan

Between the Niobrara, Platte, and Loup Rivers and the east-facing buttes of Butte County, the Sandhills cradle the alkaline lakes of western Nebraska. The lakes flourish with wildlife and inspire wonder in all who visit and contemplate their subtle beauty. Surprisingly, the Sandhills alkaline lakes (SAL) are unique to the Western Hemisphere and are a true treasure—but they are also a well-kept secret, even to most Nebraskans. What makes this ecosystem so special? Potash.

Potash (potassium carbonate, K_2CO_3) was named for the ash formed from burning plants, but the term today is applied to several potassium-containing salts. Potash leaches slowly through soils and into closed water basins, where the salts accumulate as water evaporates. Many of the interdunal lakes in Garden and Sheridan Counties are highly alkaline (pH > 10), and it is common to see their shorelines encrusted white from evaporated brine. Are there alkaline lakes in other places? Yes, but what makes the alkaline lakes of the Sandhills unusual is the high carbonate (alkalinity) coupled with the high potassium content of the water. Most other known alkaline lakes on Earth are relatively high in sodium, rather than potassium; these are referred to as soda lakes. The other two regions of the world with lakes similar to those of the Sandhills are the northern playa of Lake Chad in Africa and Qaidam Basin in China.

These lakes are intriguing because a potassium-rich environment is anathema to most cellular life, and yet these lakes are teeming with life, microbial life. How do these organisms adapt to the otherwise toxic environment? The potassium-to-sodium ratios in the highly alkaline lakes are approximately ten times higher than ocean water or fluids of the human body. This means that the organisms living in these conditions are expending enormous energy just to maintain their standard physiological state, assuming they have physiologies similar to other known organisms. Or perhaps they have unknown physiological mechanisms. These questions are central to understanding how anything can live in such a harsh environment and also how these environments fostered their evolution. Our preliminary studies on the diversity of bacteria of the alkaline lakes indicate that many are from groups classified according to terms that refer to life in extreme conditions, including haloalkaliphilic (loving alkaline salty environments), chemolithoautotrophic (making energy from rocks), and salt-tolerant polyextremophiles (tolerant of more than one extreme condition). Given the unusual and harsh conditions of the Sandhills alkaline lakes, a team of scientists is working to describe the diversity of microbial life and to uncover just how they carry out life in such a strange and wondrous environment.

David D. Dunigan is a research professor in the Nebraska Center for Virology at the University of Nebraska–Lincoln.

Diverse Groundwater-Fed Sandhills Wetlands

Ted LaGrange

I am not a native Nebraskan. Growing up in our neighbor to the east, I had only a vague idea of what the Sandhills were and had never set foot in them. That changed in 1982 when my wife and I took a month-long honeymoon trip through the western U.S. and Canada. We departed Iowa headed west on Highway 20 and before long were passing through some of the most amazing country I had ever seen. Miles and miles of grass-covered dunes interspersed with innumerable wetlands and lakes. This unique landscape rivaled the Rockies and the Pacific coast that we would later pass through, and the Sandhills of Nebraska began working their way into my heart and soul.

Eleven years later, I was hired as the wetland program manager for the Nebraska Game and Parks Commission, and I set out to explore my new home state. One of my first trips was to head back to the Sandhills. I was soon in an airboat speeding across the Marsh Lakes at Valentine National Wildlife Refuge. I visited with other biologists and ranchers to learn more and eagerly read *An Atlas of the Sand Hills*.

To the casual observer, the Sandhills may appear to be a dry landscape, and there certainly are large expanses of upland prairie. However, in many places, especially in interdunal valleys, there are also numerous lakes and wetlands. The vast groundwater underneath the hills reaches near the land surface, and lakes and wetlands arise. Wetlands are defined as having soils and a plant community that developed under periodically wet

conditions, with the water either ponded on the surface or contained as groundwater near the surface. Some wetlands are associated with lakes, rivers, and streams, but many are isolated from other water bodies and immersed in the prairie landscape. Wetlands are dynamic and respond to changes in groundwater level, so their water levels can fluctuate dramatically over time.

The Sandhills is, by far, the region of Nebraska with the most wetlands. It is challenging to estimate their real extent, but the number of acres ranges from 369,606 to over 1.3 million. Individual wetlands range in size from less than an acre to over 2,300 acres, with greater than 80 percent estimated to be 10 acres or less.

Wetlands across the Sandhills are surprisingly diverse, and the main types include marshes, wet meadows, fens, lake and stream fringes, and alkaline wetlands. Many of these types intermingle across the landscape, so they can be a challenge to define. Marshes tend to have surface water from a few inches up to six feet deep. They are generally dominated by robust emergent plants, including cattails, bulrushes, sedges, rushes, arrowheads, even wild rice in some places, and in the deeper zones, floating-leaf and submergent plants occur. Wet meadows usually do not have standing water, but groundwater is within twelve inches of the surface. Meadows are mostly dominated by grasses, sedges, and rushes but also have a variety of wildflowers. The edges of nearly all Sandhills lakes, rivers, and streams have a wetland fringe, and the floodplains of rivers and streams can contain meander cutoffs (oxbows), which are a type of marsh. Fringe wetlands can be very narrow or wide depending on the lay of the land, are marsh-like in the deeper portions, and can grade into wet meadows if the landscape is relatively flat. Alkaline wetlands are mostly located in the western Sandhills, with the largest concentrations in Garden and Sheridan Counties. They generally do not have surface water outflow and receive much of their water input through groundwater discharge. Their alkalinity can become very high due to

Alkaline wetland in the western Sandhills. The white deposits are not snow but alkaline salts. Alkaline wetlands do not have surface water outflow, and therefore minerals in the water become concentrated over time due to evaporation. Photograph by Ethan Freese, Platte Basin Timelapse. Used with permission.

minerals that are concentrated through evaporation. This high alkalinity makes these wetlands home to a variety of unique plants and animals.

Wetlands of the Sandhills provide diverse benefits to people, especially considering that they cover only about 10 percent of the region. Not many people associate wetlands with clean water, though wetlands act as a filter, slowing water down and allowing sediment and many pollutants to settle out. As water slowly moves through the wetland, a series of chemical transformations take place that bind or alter some pollutants. The net result is that, generally, water leaving a wetland is of higher quality than water entering. This is important because the origin of much of the drinking water for many communities in Nebraska, including Omaha and Lincoln, ultimately is the Sandhills. Although the hydrology of Sandhills wetlands can be complicated, some wetlands help to recharge groundwater. Surface water held by wetlands can also reduce the impacts of flooding, because water would move downstream more rapidly if the wetlands were drained.

Two boiling springs in the Sandhills. The "boiling" is not caused by heat, but by groundwater that reaches the surface with enough power to suspend sand grains. In places where cold groundwater continues to reach the surface in dry years, fens can form. The cold groundwater also creates a microclimate that allows cold-adapted plants that lived in Nebraska during the last Ice Age to persist. Photograph by Dakota Altman, Platte Basin Timelapse. Used with permission.

Wetlands are among the most productive biological systems known. They produce more plant and animal life per acre than cropland, prairies, or forests. Wetlands provide migration, breeding, nesting, and feeding habitat for millions of waterfowl, shorebirds, songbirds, and other wildlife. They are home to thousands of different plant and animal species, including many that are threatened or endangered. The Nebraska Natural Legacy Project (State Wildlife Action Plan) identifies all or parts of eight biologically unique landscapes (BULs) within the Sandhills, and all contain wetlands. Within these BULs are seven tier-1 at-risk plant species and thirty tier-1 at-risk animal species. The Sandhills are the most important waterfowl production area in Nebraska and one of the best duck production areas outside of the Prairie Potholes region just to the north. The abundant fish and wildlife of wetlands support many recreational uses, including wildlife observation, boating, hunting, and fishing. The amazing productivity of wetlands is not lost on ranchers, who rely on the land to make a living. Wetlands provide water for livestock, and the lush vegetation in and adjacent to wetlands provides important livestock forage, with wet meadows being especially valuable for hay production.

Thanks to the good stewardship of ranchers, the Sandhills remains an intact landscape. However, these wetlands are not entirely unaltered. Fragmentation has impacted wetlands via conversion of areas to row crops and development of some types of infrastructure. Plant and animal communities, including in Sandhill wetlands, evolved with natural disturbances, such as fire and grazing by native ungulates. These natural disturbances have been eliminated in many parts of the Sandhills, which affects the wetlands. Some wetlands were drained, or partially drained, by the installation of drainage ditches to improve hay production. Some streams were straightened to move water more quickly. The combined effects of ditches and straightening have caused some Sandhill

Aerial view of the Calamus River and adjoining wetlands in its floodplain, Loup County.

streams to cut deeper (degrade), which lowers the water table and dries out adjacent wetlands.

A number of non-native invasive species are impacting wotlands, including the introduced variety of common reed (*Phragmites*), reed canary grass, redtop, garrison creeping foxtail, hybrid cattail, purple loosestrife, Eurasian water milfoil, and common carp. These invasives can crowd out native species and alter their habitat. But by far the greatest potential threat to Sandhills wetlands would be a decline in groundwater levels below normal cyclic variation. Wetlands are only present because groundwater reaches the surface, and their persistence depends on groundwater within at least twelve inches of the surface in most years. If groundwater levels were to drop even slightly, due to either human withdrawals or climate change, the wetlands would disappear, along with the benefits they provide.

Despite the losses and threats, there are still plenty of reasons for hope. When I came to Nebraska, I had the honor of joining the board of the Sandhills Task Force. Ever since, I have been inspired by the ability of ranchers and conservation agencies and organizations to work in partnership to implement projects that benefit wetlands, grasslands, wildlife, and people. I believe that if we continue to work together, the wonder of Sandhills wetlands can be sustained for future generations, including for my grandchildren. My hope is that long into the future, someone will still be able to head west from Iowa and fall in love with the land that we call the Sandhills.

Ted LaGrange is wetland program manager for Nebraska Game and Parks Commission.

Marsh marigold, a common plant in Sandhill fens, is a relic of the Ice Age.

Cattle grazing alongside a wetland in Cherry County. Most of the wetlands in the Sandhills are in private ownership, and thanks to the good stewardship of ranchers, these wetlands are in very good condition and are important sources of water and forage for livestock.

Fens

Ted LaGrange and Gerry Steinauer

One of the rarest and most unique wetland types in the Sandhills is the fen. Fens are characterized by slightly acidic (~pH6) water and peaty (undecomposed plant parts) organic-rich soils that form in areas fed with a nearly constant supply of groundwater, which continues even in the driest years. Because they are constantly saturated with cold groundwater, dead plant material decomposes very slowly, over thousands of years. These organic soils can be many feet thick; the deepest recorded in the Sandhills is 23 feet and dated to over twelve thousand years. In places the organic soils and associated mat of vegetation are suspended over a pool of groundwater, causing a slight mound that shakes when you walk across it. Most fens are one or two acres in size, but some are over five hundred acres. Fens are usually found in the upper portions of valleys or lakes where groundwater flows in, and they are often bordered by wet meadows and marshes. Fens harbor several plant species rare in Nebraska, including cotton grass, buckbean, and marsh marigold. The primary range of these plants is mostly in colder regions north of Nebraska. The populations in the Sandhills are likely Ice Age relics that have survived in fens since the retreat of the last glaciers.

Fens are especially susceptible to alterations due to ditching or declining water tables. If the organic soils dry out, they can rapidly decompose, and the fen will disappear. They also are impacted by non-native plants that also affect other wetlands in the Sandhills. Many conservation efforts for Sandhill wetlands, such as plugging ditches, addressing stream bed degradation, and controlling invasive species also help to sustain the fens of the Sandhills.

Ted LaGrange is wetland program manager for Nebraska Game and Parks Commission.

Gerry Steinauer is a botanist-ecologist for Nebraska Game and Parks Commission.

A River in Motion
Platte Basin Timelapse

Michael Farrell, Michael Forsberg, Kim Hachiya, and Mary Harner

At a stock tank in the Sandhills, cattle come and go. A windmill turns furiously. Fall arrives, and the tank goes dry. Snow and ice accumulate. Spring comes, and the grass greens. A rancher turns the cows and calves loose in the pasture. The cycle repeats. An oxbow in a Sandhills river continually cuts backward, the river's fragile banks eroding with the water's flow. Birds arrive, nest, fledge their young, and leave a Sandhills lake as the four seasons progress. Ranchers move cattle about on meadows to take advantage of new grass and to allow pastures to recover. These meadows, marshes, and wetlands are critical pieces of the Sandhills ecosystem responding to climate, weather, and people. Small daily changes, nearly imperceptible, mount up over seasons and years. What if you could see a decade of seasonal change in thirty seconds? Would it change how you interpret the Sandhills and its ecosystems?

Over a dozen time-lapse cameras dot the Nebraska Sandhills, documenting the daily events of the landscapes, animals, and waters. It may seem like a static, unchanging region of grass, water, and sky, but the cameras tell the story of a robust ecosystem as it adjusts to weather, animals, people, and the progression of time.

The cameras are part of Platte Basin Timelapse (PBT), a long-term project that seeks to uplift and describe the natural and human-influenced processes of a river system that traverses three states. PBT presents a vision of a watershed as a set of motion picture images, capturing the river and adjoining land as they unfold

Platte Basin Timelapse camera maintenance at a station in Schilling Wildlife Management Area at the confluence of the Platte and Missouri Rivers. Photograph by Michael Forsberg. Used with permission.

Inside view of a Platte Basin Timelapse camera system installed in the high country of the Rocky Mountains, Colorado. Photo by Mariah Lundgren, Platte Basin Timelapse. Used with permission.

Windmill at Gudmundsen Sandhills Laboratory, Cherry County. Photograph by Michael Forsberg. Used with permission.

over time from multiple viewpoints. The largest river system in the Sandhills, the Loup, is among the Platte's major tributaries, and much of its flow is from the aquifer system beneath.

Since 2011 PBT cameras have been collecting images from over sixty points throughout the Platte River Basin, from the high country of the river's sources in the Rocky Mountains of Colorado and Wyoming and eastward through Nebraska, where the river is fed by tributaries that traverse the Sandhills, to its confluence with the Missouri River south of Omaha. Cameras record an image once an hour each hour of daylight. Those images are collated into time-lapse motion pictures that show the river and its watershed unfolding in ways that compress and intensify the normal human perception of time.

When the many camera positions and viewsheds are assembled into collections of interrelated movies, questions arise, and stories emerge. The river as a process of nature wants to be one thing; through technology

and engineering, humans urge it to be something else. These conflicting tendencies are the essence of the stories PBT producers tell.

Platte Basin Timelapse co-founder Michael Farrell notes that people who see the river every day, or even infrequently, often are only vaguely aware of seasonal changes. But if those seasonal changes are captured and compressed into films, the reality of change becomes apparent. The rapid compilation of years of images into a short film causes the viewer's perceptions to both speed up and slow down as they observe the passage of the river and time.

"The hundreds of camera images can show you the cycle of the seasons over several years in a matter of minutes," Farrell said. "The subtleties of dry versus wet years are made manifest to those who take the time to look to see the differences."

Farrell and PBT co-founder Michael Forsberg conceived the project during conversations they had while working together on a film about the Great Plains, based on a book by Forsberg. Farrell, then a filmmaker at Nebraska Public Media, and Forsberg, a freelance conservation photographer and author, both had vast experience telling the stories of the river.

After securing funding, Platte Basin Timelapse was launched and based at Nebraska Public Media. Later PBT moved its administrative offices to the Center for Great Plains Studies at the University of Nebraska–Lincoln, and in 2019 PBT became an entity within the School of Natural Resources at UNL's Institute of Agriculture and Natural Resources.

View from a Platte Basin Timelapse camera at the Audubon's Rowe Sanctuary on the Platte River on July 2011 (*left*), June 2013 (*center*), and September 2013 (*right*). Flow at a single site varies greatly, season to season and year to year, dependent on snowmelt, climate over the basin, and irrigation withdrawals. Platte Basin Timelapse. Used with permission.

A stable of producers, photographers, filmmakers, scientists, graduate students, and undergraduate interns have produced web-based multimedia, films, and other creative works and have used images to support research and communication about a myriad of topics. Subjects include American dippers, sandhill cranes, trumpeter swans, fire suppression in the Wildcat Hills and Sandhills, bighorn sheep reintroduction, beavers and otters, prairies and their restoration, and the state's wetlands, including those in the Sandhills. The latter is part of a large grant-funded project undertaken with Nebraska Game and Parks Commission. Platte Basin Timelapse's images and stories inform a large educational outreach project for Game and Parks.

Much of science is the study of change and its impacts— looking at what changes over time, how events prompt changes, how organisms and ecosystems respond and react to stimuli. Before and after images can give a snapshot of one point in time. Time-lapse films, however, show change while it is occurring. These kinds of images are invaluable to scientists, such as PBT member Mary Harner, an associate professor of communication and biology at the University of Nebraska at Kearney. Harner, her students, and colleagues have used PBT cameras and techniques to study the Sandhills and the Platte River in Nebraska; she also has applied these techniques to investigate the Rio Grande and Gila Rivers in New Mexico.

"Time-lapse images and the story-telling approach of PBT help advance both scientific research and public communication about natural resources," explains Harner. "Images provide a way to connect people with the beauty of places—like wetlands in the Sandhills—and to portray complex processes and change unfolding across time. PBT also offers ways for students to use and learn from images, by placing cameras in places they seek to know more about and analyzing existing image libraries to catalog biodiversity and ecosystem change."

The research aspects of PBT stand alongside the value it offers to lay audiences, Farrell said. "It is not a huge leap of imagination when viewing the timelapses of the Platte River to begin to reflect on the evolution of this watershed," Farrell said. "How did this river come about to begin with? What forces were at work to lift the mountains and carve the canyons, deposit the sands and gravels? How has this work of nature evolved prior to any human awareness of its existence?"

For Forsberg, Platte Basin Timelapse has created community by connecting the river, the land, the wildlife, and the people. "Everyone on the planet lives in a watershed making all of us neighbors upstream and downstream of someone else," Forsberg said. "That recognition is important. The old adage 'Whiskey's for drinking and water's for fighting' has proved out over history, and life has suffered. But understanding that we are all stewards of this most precious resource and have responsibility to each other levels the playing field and brings us together in a shared community we all belong to. I firmly believe that the role of water in our future can build community rather than tear communities apart. But first we have to know it. Then we have to love it."

As some debate the reality of climate change, PBT cameras portray change in undeniable visual ways that human perception can easily miss, gloss over, or choose to ignore. Farrell views the project as a Trojan horse, in which viewers are drawn first to the images, which then unlock the doors of perception, to allow and entice viewers into a new way of perceiving the river.

"When we began the Platte Basin Timelapse, one goal was to help people understand the complexities behind the seemingly simple question, 'Where does your water come from?'" Farrell said. "As time has passed, the cameras have observed and recorded the ongoing impacts of climate change, urban growth, and agricultural expansion. As those continue and as we hear talk of aquifer pumping and learn of new pipeline plans, we might now begin to ask, 'Where *will* your water come from?'"

Michael Farrell is a photographer, filmmaker, and co-founder of Platte Basin Timelapse.

Michael Forsberg is a conservation photographer and research assistant professor in the School of Natural Resources at the University of Nebraska–Lincoln. He is a co-founder of Platte Basin Timelapse.

Kim Hachiya is a retired communications specialist for the University of Nebraska–Lincoln and author of *Dear Old Nebraska U* (2019).

Mary Harner is an associate professor of communication and biology at the University of Nebraska at Kearney.

A composite of monthly images from 2013 taken by a Platte Basin Timelapse camera at Mick's Slide along the Middle Loup River as it winds its way through the Sandhills. Photographs by Mariah Lundgren, Platte Basin Timelapse. Used with permission.

CLIMATE AND WEATHER

Bald eagles and swans on a Sandhills lake.
Photography by Michael Forsberg. Used with permission.

The Times They Are A-Changing
Seasonal, Inter-Annual, and Long-Term Variability in Sandhills Temperature, Wind, Rain, and Drought

Martha Durr

The climate crossroads. The place where east meets west and north meets south. Blizzards. Heavy downpours. Heat waves. Damaging hail and tornadic winds. From torrents of rain one year to devastating drought the next. In this unique crossroads of North America lies the Nebraska Sandhills. It is subject to rugged and extreme weather, which could also be said of its inhabitants.

Moisture is a defining climate feature of the region. This unique part of Nebraska is perfectly positioned at the meridian dividing the relatively wet eastern U.S. and the dry intermountain West. In fact, eastern Nebraska receives twice as much annual precipitation as the Panhandle in the West. In a given year, precipitation averages about twenty-three inches in the Sandhills. But does the average ever really mean much? What is often more descriptive is the range of precipitation scenarios. Systematic weather observations began in the late 1800s, and the last century of observations shows precipitation has been greater than thirty inches in some years (34.89 in 1915, 33.05 in 2019, and 31.06 in 2018) and less than fifteen inches in others (12.02 in 2012, 12.79 in 1989, 13.56 in 2002, 13.93 in 1934, 14.32 in 1936, 14.69 in 1974).

Distinct wet and dry seasons characterize the Sandhills. Precipitation is low during the colder months. Thus, from November through February, when snow is common, liquid equivalent precipitation averages about a half inch per month. Precipitation totals start to increase in March, and by May and June, the monthly average is more than three inches. Through the rest of summer and autumn,

monthly totals typically start to decline. The driving factor for warm season rain is something called mesoscale convective systems, which is just a fancy term for an organized group of thunderstorms. You might be asking yourself about the source of the water vapor that helps fuel these storms. Part of it is transported all the way from the Gulf of Mexico with the help of southerly winds called a low-level jet. Another part of it is "recycled" and is water from previous rain events that evaporates and adds moisture to the atmosphere.

Historically, snow has occurred in all months of the year, even if just a trace (enough to notice, but not enough to measure) in June through August. February and March are typically the months with the most snow. On average, the region gets about 35 inches per year. Some seasons in recent years have seen more than 50 inches, whereas a few years had 80 to 100 inches. The year 1915 stands out as the wettest year in the Nebraska Sandhills, going back to 1895, and snowfall helped contribute. The observing station at Ainsworth reported a whopping 102 inches that year. In 1984, the area received 83 inches. More recently, the 2018–19 winter had 53 inches, and this snowpack was one of the factors leading to the historic March 2019 flood. Thick river ice, frozen and wet soils, and the trigger of the big storm were the other key factors.

There is a notable trend of increasing precipitation for the Sandhills. Over the last century, this part of Nebraska is gaining about a quarter inch of precipitation

Canada geese and trumpeter swans amid a snowstorm, Cherry County.

per decade. The trend has been amplified in recent decades, and since 1991, precipitation has increased more than an inch per decade. This recent trend is superimposed upon the three driest years on record (2012, 2002, and 1989)—a reflection of increased climate variability. As climate extremes shift so rapidly, this can cause added stressors to management of the area's precious natural resources.

Drought is a normal part of any climate regime, and the Sandhills is no exception. Whereas drought in general represents a prolonged period of dryness, there are different types, or perspectives, of drought. These perspectives include meteorological, hydrological, agricultural,

socioeconomic, and ecological. The primary differences in these types are the impacts, such as low streamflow, crop losses, supply and demand inequities, and ecosystems stress. Many different indicators are used to determine the occurrence of drought. The 1930s was a well-known time of multiyear drought with the detrimental combination of low precipitation and high temperatures. Since then, drought has continued to punctuate the climate record, including the mid-1950s, 1974–76, 1989–90, 2002–3, and 2012. However, these dry years are occurring amid an overall trend toward wetter conditions. When it comes to impacts from drought, one thing to consider is the soil type. Rainfall infiltrates the sandy soils of this region relatively quickly. Therefore, timely rains are an important factor in grass productivity, as sand doesn't hold on to water very long. What isn't taken up by plants (or evaporated) percolates to the shallow water table, near or even above the surface. This aquifer recharge is incredibly important, because irrigation is so widespread and helps to bring previous years' rain to crops growing in this year's drought, so to speak. The beautiful native prairie grasses, and the people and animals dependent on them, are impacted most during drought. Thus, water level declines in the aquifer and in the low-lying wet meadows are significant impacts of drought.

Whereas precipitation is highly variable, wind is most definitely a constant. The direction and intensity may change, but it is usually always blowing. In this part of the Great Plains, some say that the only thing stopping Arctic air is a few barbed wire fences between here and Canada. The typical wind direction during the cold months (roughly November through February) is from a northerly direction, most commonly the northwest. In about March, winds start to shift during the seasonal transition, and southerly winds are just as common. From June through September, it is these warmer winds from the south that are predominant, until seasons change, and we shift back into winter and cold Arctic air.

The average wind speed in the Sandhills is around 10 miles per hour. High wind events can occur any time of year and are typically associated with various types of storms. During the colder time of year, intense winter storms gain strength and speed as they flow out of the Rocky Mountains. Sometimes these storms result in dangerous blizzard conditions, which are the combination of snow and wind causing reduced visibility. Winds higher than 60 miles per hour can occur and are brutal this time of year, due to the resulting low

Sunrise on the day of first frost in early October 2019 at Walgren Lake State Recreation Area, Sheridan County.

Mist at sunrise on the day of first frost in early October 2019 at Walgren Lake State Recreation Area, Sheridan County.

wind chill temperatures. This is especially impactful for Sandhills ranchers, and extra effort is required to keep cattle safe. In warm weather conditions, during what is sometimes called the convective season by meteorologists, the mesoscale convective systems mentioned previously often result in strong straight-line or rotational tornadic winds. These high winds typically impact a smaller area when compared to cold season high winds but are damaging nonetheless. Hail is another common summertime severe weather event, and hailstone can range in size from peas to softballs. The

large hail events can be life threatening and damaging to infrastructure and forage production.

As precipitation has a seasonal pattern, so does temperature. The warmest month of the year is July with highs approaching 90 degrees F and lows around 60 degrees F. January is typically the coldest month with highs right around freezing (32°F) and lows around 10 degrees F. For the annual average, temperatures are about 48 degrees F. The warmest year on record was 2012 (51.6°F), while the coldest year was 1951

(44°F). High temperatures can exceed 100 degrees F, although historically these days are fairly rare and occur only a few times in a given year or not at all. The record warm year of 2012 was a notable exception with about two weeks' worth of extremely hot days. Temperatures below zero are common during winter and occur about twelve days in a given year.

In addition to getting wetter over time, the Sandhills are also getting warmer. Temperatures show an increasing trend over a century-long timespan, warming by about 1.3 degrees F (0.1°F per decade). In recent decades, the warming trend has picked up speed and is 0.3 degree F per decade. Nighttime lows are warming twice as fast as daytime high temperatures, due in part to increasing humidity.

In short, one thing is certain about weather in the Sandhills—day to day, year to year—it's always changing.

Martha Durr is a professor in the School of Natural Resources at the University of Nebraska–Lincoln, state climatologist, and director of the Nebraska State Climate Office.

Cold front approaching McKelvie National Forest, Cherry County.

Hoarfrost covers a pasture fence and windmill, Arthur County. Photograph by Michael Forsberg. Used with permission.

How and Why Storms Form in the Sandhills

Location, Location, Location

Adam Houston

Dissipating supercell, small rainbow, and anticrepuscular rays on June 6, 2022, McPherson County. Photograph by Adam Houston. Used with permission.

The Sandhills are impacted by diverse phenomena broadly encompassed by the term "storm." While important distinctions exist between snowstorms, windstorms, and thunderstorms, in general, all storms are manifestations of the atmosphere's efforts to remove imbalances in principal atmospheric forces. Disequilibria are ubiquitous in the atmosphere and are ultimately a consequence of the unequal heating of the Earth by the sun. Each imbalance necessitates an atmospheric response to reestablish balance, which usually involves only small corrections to the atmospheric state. A shallow cumulus cloud, for example, is the visual manifestation of a small correction: within it, energy is redistributed vertically to correct an unbalanced vertical stratification of temperature. However, the complex interplay of land, water, and air combine to yield significant and sustained imbalances that cannot be removed via small corrections. It is only through highly energetic responses that these high-amplitude disequilibria can be eliminated. Storms are the vigorous atmospheric responses to very large imbalances.

The geography of the Sandhills makes them particularly favorable for storm formation. First, they are located in midlatitudes (~30° to ~60°) on a continent that extends from the tropics to poles. Given the primary role played by the unequal heating by the sun in driving imbalances, it stands to reason that storms should be more prevalent where lateral differences in temperature are largest. A net loss of energy from the poles and a net gain in energy in the tropics places the midlatitudes in the globally preferred location for the largest lateral gradient in temperature. However, differences in the thermal properties of land and water mean midlatitude continents and midlatitude oceans will not be characterized by the same latitudinal temperature gradients that support storm formation. Owing to the large heat capacity of water, oceans mute the impact of solar radiation on temperature.

Thus, all else equal, midlatitude continents tend to be a preferential breeding ground for storms.

The second geographic characteristic of the Sandhills that favors storm formation is its position east of a north-south mountain range. Large-scale (1000s of km in diameter) surface low pressure centers that enter the United States from the west exhibit a unique behavior as they traverse the Intermountain West: they seem to disappear. The atmospheric anomaly associated with a "disappearing" system still exists, however, and when the anomaly crosses the Front Range of the Rocky Mountains into the Great Plains, the surface low pressure center reappears. Conceptually, the process can be viewed as the vertical compression and spin-down of the system as it moves over the higher terrain of the western U.S. and an expansion and spin-up as it emerges into the Great Plains. The rapid reemergence of the low can result in an imbalance that necessitates violent equilibration. This is particularly true when polar-Arctic air, dammed up against the Rocky Mountains, sags south into the Great Plains, creating a large horizontal temperature gradient that provides energy for nascent storms.

In spring and summer, the north-south oriented Rocky Mountains serve another critical role in storm formation. Across the U.S. Great Plains, the land rises gradually from east to west toward the base of the Front Range. The slope is generally only one to two meters per kilometer but, under the influence of solar heating, even this gentle slope can create a significant pressure gradient that accelerates air westward, up slope. After a northward deflection from the Coriolis force, the heated sloping terrain ultimately yields a southeasterly wind near the ground over much of the Great Plains that transports tropical heat and moisture northward, providing energy for growing storms.

The final geographic distinction of the Sandhills that favors storms is its relative proximity to the Gulf of Mexico. Nebraskans who are longing to visit an ocean beach will surely consider the Sandhills to be anything but close to the Gulf of Mexico. However, tropical air originating over the gulf requires only about a day to reach the Sandhills, as it rides winds pulled north by rapidly amplifying surface low-pressure centers in the lee of the Rockies and accelerated by heated terrain.

Whether large (e.g., surface low-pressure centers thousands of kilometers in diameter) or small (e.g., thunderstorms tens of kilometers in diameter), each storm alters, even if just briefly, the personality of the Sandhills. Winter storms can transform the landscape for weeks, if not months, with snow that drifts in blizzards to depths that cover houses. This snow, with origins in water vapor wicked off the Gulf of Mexico, can incapacitate the Sandhills' residents. However, it can also quench the seemingly unquenchable thirst of the land and its flora and fauna, as winds, warmed through adiabatic compression, flow down from the Rockies into the plains and melt the blanket of ice. These Chinook winds also bring a respite from winter, if only briefly—a taste of spring that those farther east rarely enjoy.

The impacts from storms can be devastating. Rapidly amplifying low-pressure centers pull tropical air north across the Sandhills. Several kilometers above the surface, jet stream winds blow west to east, driven by strengthening north-south temperature gradients. With warm and moist tropical air in the low levels of the atmosphere (typically below 1–2 km in height) and seasonally cool air above this, an unbalanced (unstable) vertical stratification is created. Triggered to rise by a cold front or dryline (a frontal boundary between dry air to the west and moist air to the east), for example, this low-level air will accelerate upward as a thunderstorm, in a violent equilibration of the imbalance. If the change

Tornado on May 25, 2021, Dundy County. Photograph by Ethan Lang. Used with permission.

Wall cloud under a supercell thunderstorm on July 10, 2021, Morrill County. Photograph by Adam Houston. Used with permission.

Arcus cloud along the gust front of a supercell thunderstorm on June 16, 2014, Wheeler County. Photograph by Stephen Shield. Used with permission.

in wind speed and/or direction with height (known as vertical wind shear) is sufficiently strong, a storm can convert the kinetic energy of environmental winds into a storm-scale vortex (a mesocyclone) that spans the entire depth of the thunderstorm. This type of thunderstorm, called a supercell, is maintained through the complex interplay between the mesocyclone and environment within which it is embedded. This interplay promotes anomalously long storm lifetimes, creates anomalously strong upward motion, and produces the disproportionately severe impact of supercells on the people, places, and things they encounter because, on average, supercells produce the largest hail and the strongest tornadoes of any thunderstorm type.

Individual thunderstorms (tens of kilometers across), whether supercells or not, can aggregate into a self-organizing system several hundred kilometers across. Such mesoscale convective systems (MCSs) are multiple thunderstorms organized into a nearly continuous line or arc, pushed forward by rain-cooled air behind the line/arc, and sustained through constant regeneration of new thunderstorms where the cold air and warm/moist air ahead of the system meet. MCSs can produce all severe convective hazards: hail, tornadoes, severe straight-line winds. It is the latter hazard that is the most definitive aspect of MCSs. The term straight-line winds distinguishes these winds from those associated with tornadoes or other small-scale (<10 km) vortices. The practical differences are (1) on average, the damage area covered by straight-line winds (often in the thousands of square kilometers) is much larger than the damage area tied to vortices like tornadoes, and (2) the severity of damage at any one point within the damage swath of straight-line winds tends to be less than for vortices like tornadoes.

Due to both intrinsic and practical predictability, accurate storm forecasts are challenging. It unlikely that

Back side of a supercell thunderstorm near Rushville on June 6, 2022. Photograph by Kyle Pittman. Used with permission.

Intensifying storm and wall cloud near Gordon on June 6, 2022. Photograph by Kyle Pittman. Used with permission.

forecasts of small-scale phenomena (like tornadoes) will ever evade the intrinsic limits of predictability inherent in their size. However, it is possible to close the gap between intrinsic predictability and practical predictability; the latter can be addressed through improved understanding, improved numerical weather prediction models, and more precise observations. The remoteness of the Sandhills is arguably one its greatest appeals, but it also makes it difficult to improve the practical predictability of storms in this area because of the lack of observations. However, new methods of remotely sensed and targeted observing can contribute to improved predictions, even in the Sandhills where there are more dunes than people.

Adam Houston is a professor of Earth and Atmospheric Sciences at the University of Nebraska–Lincoln and director of the Severe Storms Research Group.

Developing supercell on June 6, 2022, Cherry County. Photograph by Adam Houston. Used with permission.

Storm Chasing

Adam Houston

I knew that the odds of catching the storms racing north-northeast along Highway 83 north of Thedford, Nebraska, were low. Storms had eluded me all day, and with the sun low in the sky, I assumed that this might be my last shot at salvaging something from the day. I had long since abandoned any hope of seeing a tornado.

I had never even heard of the Sandhills before this visit. I am a native Texan, and at the time, I was a PhD student at the University of Illinois at Urbana-Champaign, so maybe my ignorance was permissible. The Sandhills were stunning to me, but my hyper-focus on the line of cumulus congestus just to my west prevented me from giving them the reverence they deserved. I turned east off of Highway 83 onto a compacted sand road in southern Cherry County. Recent rain had made the roads as slick as, well, wet sand, and after sliding sideways through a sharp turn and dropping my right rear wheel into the bar ditch, I instinctively shifted my focus away from the fleeing storms and onto my driving.

The road rose slightly as it ambled northeast; I glanced to my left and saw a fan of crepuscular rays radiating away from the summits of the line of towering cumuli to my west. Near the top of the hill, a lone tree stood stalwart along the fence line paralleling the road. My photographer instincts took over, awakened by the majesty of this juxtaposition of light and shadow. I stopped the car, grabbed my camera, tripod, and bag and walked back down the road to the tree. A steady south wind pulled the scent of wet soil and grass from the surrounding fields. I reached the tree and watched, mesmerized, as lobes along the tops of each cumulus cloud cut shadows into the hazy light emanating from the sun hidden behind them. I took a handful of shots before the sun emerged from behind the last cumulus in the line. Illuminated by the late day sun, the texture of each dune was revealed through the contrast between warm western light and cool eastern shadow. I widened my gaze, and textures melted into simple shapes, hills of green and gold stretching to the horizon. The storms were gone, but I had discovered the majestic Nebraska Sandhills.

Thunderstorm with cloud-to-ground lightning north of Johnstown, Brown County.

When Too Much Rain Is the Problem
2019 and the Flooding of the Sandhills

Bethany Johnston

The Nebraska Sandhills. Waves upon waves of prairie grasses. "Unchanging," some say, when their shoes tread once again on the sandy soil, "forever unchanged." I consider myself lucky that I was born and raised and have lived my entire life (minus schooling) in the Sandhills of Nebraska. I never wanted to leave and find a better place—for I had already found it. I found security in the grand sameness where ancient winds placed the curls of the dunes, in the same plant friends (native long before I), and in the sense of comfort in the routines that follow the seasons.

In town, they referred to us as the "north hill people." Our predecessors carved out a living through grazing the upland hills and haying a few wet bottoms. These bottoms, which accumulate shin-deep water only in the wettest years, are small compared to the spacious subirrigated hay meadows north and east of here. Wet years meant more grass, not more standing water.

Mother Nature, of course, sets no easy schedules. I saw ranchers fight hot, dry droughts, when neither rain nor snow fed the grass, then ease into years of plentiful precipitation. Ranchers constantly evaluated, penciled out tough decisions, and forged on. The pendulum swings, ranchers adjust.

I didn't see the floods coming. My husband, young daughter, and I had just moved back to our family ranch in the eastern Sandhills. It was March 12, 2019, and the local news station reported a blizzard coming, with a term I had never heard of before: bomb cyclone. While we had never heard of a bomb cyclone, it seemed prudent to prepare for one.

That evening the winds howled, the snow blew, and the swirl on the radar indicated the snow would not let up. I remember waking up in the middle of the night to an eerie stillness, checked the radar again, and zoomed out. To my horror, I realized the swirling movement of the clouds resembled a hurricane, and we were in the eye of the storm. The calmness didn't last. Chaos set in.

Three inches of rain fell on frozen soil on March 13, according to the weatherman who now read through a growing list of flooded areas. In an instant, extreme flooding roared in and didn't leave. A second bomb cyclone hit in April, followed by rains that came with unusual force and frequency and didn't stop all year. I can only estimate that between seventy-five and a hundred inches fell that year; never less than two inches at a time, never more than three or four days between rains. The water rose frightfully with each rain, flooding the barn, outbuildings, corrals, calving lots, and pivots and wiping out the county roads. The first bomb cyclone flooded so near our house that we lost our septic system and sandbagged around our home. That summer, amid rising water, the kitchen faucet spit out amber water as the domestic well flooded. Nine months with no septic, two months with no drinking water.

Aerial view of water mounding in 2020 in upland areas of the Sandhills. The heavy rainfall in 2019 and early 2020 raised the groundwater table above the level of the land surface in areas that typically would be covered in grassland. Photograph by Bill Sitz. Used with permission.

We did what we had to do because we didn't have a choice. When headquarters flooded, my husband and dad slept in their pickups with the heavies during the bomb cyclones, picking up babies and putting them in a stock trailer full of hay. But the trailers, filled with warm hay and fresh calves, became islands as cold, slushy water rose in the night. We moved calving to our summer (hill) pastures, "swam" pairs to new pastures, attempted diverting water away with an irrigation pump (futile!), hayed the high ground (although most hay was soggy due to the unstoppable rains), doctored foot rot and pinkeye, lived in our Muck boots and fenced in chest waders, rotated sump pumps around, bleached mold off our saddles, and tried to get feed delivered in the short window of road repairs. The hay meadows and pivots sat underwater; gearboxes hidden. Everything took twice as long to do since getting anywhere involved weaving new routes through the flooded hills and getting stuck was a daily occurrence.

I read articles on the brilliance of the emergency response, but their splendor never reached this far. I don't

Flooded ranch in the Sandhills. Heavy rains and frozen ground starting in March 2019 resulted in massive flooding, which persisted through much of 2020. Photograph by Debra Sitz. Used with permission.

know how my husband or father managed in 2019, with water levels increasing into 2020. I don't know how other ranches, from Bartlett to Lakeside, managed either. You trudge on.

Land is a man's silent partner. Watching your partner succumb to natural disaster is painful for any rancher. For two years, we watched our land scream yet not utter a sound. In our "poorly drained" area of the Sandhills, a quarter to a third of our upland pastures were under deep lakes. The result: 25–30 percent of our grass drowned. Vegetation native to the hills could only tolerate two weeks of "wet feet." The first year, 2019, the lakes grew, large and clear, all vegetation dead underneath. Water levels continued to rise in 2020, when cattails and bulrushes appeared from seedbanks.

In the Sandhills, water always seeped away in the sand, so what caused this historic flooding? "Catastrophic water mounding" is the term Chuck Markley, a Natural Resources Conservation Service soil scientist, used to describe it. According to Markley, normally, about five feet of dry sand will hold three inches of rain. "Amounts over that normally percolate downward into the water table. But since water cannot be compressed, mounds of water within the dune rise and eventually flow outward, creating pockets of water," he said.

Beginning in 1990, our precipitation averages grew above normal, raising the Ogallala Aquifer water level unnoticed under our feet for decades. In 2019 even small rains significantly raised the water levels of our lakes, as water poured out of the hills and into the valleys. Water couldn't go down, so it went out, creating water mounds.

As a child, I remember praying for rain, as the dryness of the 1980s lasted for years. More rain was always welcome, as the thirsty sandy soils sucked it up. "How much rain did you get?" was a community question, and the winner was "living right." It felt sacrilegious, but I wanted to pray for the "d" word. Yes, a drought—to push the pendulum back the other way.

And late in 2020 it came, slowly evaporating water levels. The drought continued into 2021, and lakes faded away, leaving ugly bare ground. Annual weeds colonized these areas, but the native upland species have yet to return. Another year of 25–30 percent loss in pasture production due to dry lakebeds, plus losses from the drought. We thought about drilling native seed, but which seed do you choose: seed that tolerates wet conditions or seed that can survive a drought?

As a rancher drought is a "when," not an "if." But flooding? I wonder if my generation, and the next, will fight both drought and floods. The pendulum swings quickly now. Mother Nature changed the Sandhills.

Bethany Johnston is a University of Nebraska Extension educator at the Central Sandhills Extension Office in Burwell, Nebraska.

SEA
OF
GRASS

At sundown, it's obvious why the phrase "oceans of grass" describes the Sandhills prairie in Loup County.
Photograph by Michael Forsberg. Used with permission.

The Unique Diversity and Habitat Structure of Sandhills Grasslands

Chris Helzer

The resilience of an ecosystem relies heavily on the size of its habitats and the diversity of its species. There are few grasslands in the world that better exemplify those attributes than the Nebraska Sandhills. The dunes and valleys across the Sandhills provide a mixture of inter-connected habitats that support countless species of plants and animals. A dynamic climate and episodic grazing by cattle provide even more variety. The end result is a globally significant prairie landscape that supports both a thriving ranch culture and an incredible and resilient array of natural communities.

The immensity of the Sandhills prairie supports large and well-connected populations of both plants and animals. As a result, prairie species can withstand episodes of stress from weather, disease, or human management that might be catastrophic in more fragmented land-scapes. The Sandhills has plenty to brag about, but the overall magnitude and continuity of its prairie habitat may be its greatest strength.

Each prairie animal and plant species has its own habitat preferences. Some thrive in patches of tall, dense vegetation, others in short vegetation with abundant bare ground, and still others in various intermediate conditions. Because of those varied needs, the number of plant and animal species in a landscape is driven by the variety, or heterogeneity, of its habitats. Again, the Sandhills shine in this regard.

A broad range of topographic features across the Sandhills provides dry upland and moist lowland habitats, as well as warm sun-facing slopes and cool shaded slopes. Layered atop that topographic

Painted milk-vetch, a plant found in and around blowouts and other areas of open sand. Photograph by Chris Helzer, The Nature Conservancy. Used with permission.

Lesser earless lizards are associated with open sand habitats. Photograph by Chris Helzer, The Nature Conservancy. Used with permission.

variation is even more habitat heterogeneity driven by "disturbances," such as grazing, fire, and drought. Those three forces, and their interactions, are responsible for creating and maintaining prairies across central North America. Patterns of fire and grazing, separately or in combination, regulate the height and density of vegetation, which shapes competitive environments for plants and habitat structure for animals. Those patterns are, and have been for thousands of years, strongly influenced by people and their intentional management of the landscape.

The Sandhills environment has a remarkable ability to maintain productivity during extreme climatic events. The plant species that thrive during years of abundant moisture will fade into the background when drought hits. Those species remain present and ready to reassert themselves when rains return but temporarily cede territory to other plants more adapted to drier soil

conditions. As a result, the plant community transforms dramatically as drought enters the scene.

Importantly, that drought-adapted community still includes plants favored by large grazing animals, and the pollen, nectar, seeds, and other essential resources for other wildlife, large and small. The total amount of vegetation produced might decrease during a drought, but the prairie doesn't simply shut down and forfeit the game. Instead, it changes its lineup and sends a new set of players out onto the field. As a result, while animals might have to alter the specific kinds of plants, nectar, or seeds they eat, they can still find the food and cover they need to survive.

When rainfall picks up again and drought slips away, the plant community again transforms itself. Insect and wildlife communities follow suit. The ability to effectively adapt and respond to changing situations is driven by species diversity, especially by the plants and invertebrates that provide the foundational resources that support larger animals. The bigger the roster, the more options there are for providing an optimal lineup of players at any particular time. In addition to reacting to weather patterns, natural communities in the Sandhills also respond to variable habitat conditions caused by human activities, such as grazing, haying, and fire, each of which shapes habitats in different ways. Many animal species have specific habitat requirements and are found only in places where a certain height or density of vegetation exists. Others are more flexible or have varying habitat needs across seasons. In both cases, the diversity and abundance of animals depends upon a broad spectrum of ever-changing habitat conditions across the Sandhills.

Plants also have conditions in which they are best suited to compete successfully, but they can't pick up and move when the world changes around them. Instead, plants hunker down during less optimal times and wait for their opportunity to rise again when the time is right. Many plants struggle to compete with the more dominant grasses in the Sandhills prairie and assert themselves only when the canopy of those grasses has been temporarily diminished by something, such as fire or grazing.

When left to grow unimpeded by fire or grazing, prairie vegetation grows relatively tall and dense, dominated by perennial grasses and a selection of wildflowers (forbs) that can successfully compete with those grasses. As time goes on, thatch and litter from previous years' plant growth accumulates, increasing the density of the habitat even further. Small mammals, like voles, enthusiastically tunnel through that thatch, grouse hide their nests in the tall grasses, and deer and other animals use the thick cover as a place to rest in relative safety.

On the other end of the spectrum, recently burned, hayed, or grazed prairie provides equally valuable

Sand blowout with prickly poppy blooming along its edge. Photograph by Chris Helzer, The Nature Conservancy. Used with permission.

resources to a different set of species. Plants that need abundant light try to bloom and reproduce before the big grasses again overtake them. Birds, such as horned larks, upland sandpipers, and long-billed curlews nest in the short vegetation, and a very different wildlife community forms than is found in taller vegetation.

When a site is intensively grazed for several months or more and then allowed to rest, a particularly unique and valuable set of habitat conditions arises. An extended release from perennial grass dominance allows a flush of growth from opportunistic plant species, many of which produce copious amounts of nectar, pollen, and seeds. The structure of the vegetation, consisting of relatively short and sparse grasses and tall well-spaced forbs, provides a perfect place for grouse and their chicks to forage for the abundance of insects fostered by the same architecture. In the absence of grazing, the perennial grasses eventually reclaim their dominance, and the species that thrive in this transitional habitat move on or recede and wait for their next opportunity.

While abhorred by many ranchers, patches of open sand, called "blowouts," also provide a unique and valuable environment for many species. Plants, such as blowout grass, blowout penstemon, lemon scurf pea, and winged pigweed, thrive in the bare and shifting sands and help stabilize those areas for subsequent colonization by other plants. Distinctive Sandhills animals, like kangaroo rats, earless lizards, sand wasps, and others make their homes in or around these blowouts, and many others use them as places to hunt or bask in the sun.

Interspersed in the Sandhills prairie are patches of shrubs and trees, especially on north-facing dune slopes or along streams and wetlands. These woody plants, streams, and wetlands contain their own communities of plants and animals but also provide

Prescribed fire, an important management strategy for the Sandhills, helps control woody plant invasion, creates varied habitat conditions, and improves forage quality. Photograph by Chris Helzer, The Nature Conservancy. Used with permission.

Fourpoint evening primrose responds positively to disturbances, such as intensive grazing and drought, which create favorable habitat structure characterized by tall forbs above and short, sparse grass beneath. Photograph by Chris Helzer, The Nature Conservancy. Used with permission.

important resources for prairie wildlife. On the other hand, some native trees and shrubs, such as smooth sumac and eastern redcedar, are responding to climate change and fire suppression by spreading into prairies at an accelerated rate and threaten to decrease the diversity and resilience of grasslands.

The inherent size and heterogeneity of the Sandhills prairie makes it an incredibly valuable and unique place. Just as humans have helped shape the diversity and resilience of the Sandhills across many centuries, we will play a crucial role in the future. In addition to protecting the intactness of the prairie and water resources of the landscape, it is critically important to provide all the various habitat conditions that support the diversity of life in the Sandhills. As long as the species diversity and large contiguous nature of the prairie persists, its future is bright.

Chris Helzer is a prairie ecologist and The Nature Conservancy's director of science in Nebraska.

Dense thatch vegetation structure is important for some species of wildlife but is only one of many habitat condition types needed to support the full range of animal diversity in the Sandhills. Photograph by Chris Helzer, The Nature Conservancy. Used with permission.

Are the Sandhills Resilient or Fragile?

Chris Helzer

While the size and diversity of the Sandhills prairie makes it resilient in many ways, many ranchers are also careful to keep enough vegetation cover in their pastures to prevent wind-driven soil erosion. Those ranchers fear the creation of sand blowouts, which can grow progressively larger, leading to extensive areas of bare sand. As a result of ranchers' caution, Sandhills pastures are rarely grazed intensively, and cattle are often rotated out of a pasture when grass height is roughly half (or less) of what it was when they came in.

This conservative grazing approach, and the strong social pressure that perpetuates it, certainly reduces the likelihood of chronic overgrazing and the negative impacts it can cause. At the same time, habitat heterogeneity in the Sandhills may be restricted by a scarcity of intensively grazed and/or burned habitat patches. Areas of short, sparse vegetation, including patches of bare ground, provide important habitat for both plants and animals, as do transitional plant communities that accompany the recovery of grasses after fire or grazing events. Because of the value of habitat heterogeneity and the species diversity it fosters, a limited range of available habitat types could end up working against the overall resilience of the Sandhills.

Fortunately, recent research at the University of Nebraska–Lincoln has significantly changed the way we understand soil erosion in the Sandhills. Studies have shown that destabilization of Sandhills dunes is not influenced primarily by aboveground vegetative cover, but instead it's the belowground root structure of Sandhills prairie that holds the soil in place, regardless of what is aboveground. Even if all aboveground vegetation is repeatedly killed with herbicides, the network of fine roots will continue to hold the soil for several years before breaking down and allowing dunes to destabilize and blow.

Breaking through that root layer, the bulk of which is within the top twenty inches (50 cm) of the soil, can very quickly cause dramatic soil erosion—as seen in blowouts that form along trail roads and permanent cattle trails in pastures. However, simply exposing the soil for short periods of time, as occurs after a prescribed fire or a season of intensive grazing, doesn't trigger the same loss of dune integrity. Perhaps this knowledge will reassure ranchers who are considering fire or grazing treatments that expose bare ground for short periods of time. Rather than weakening the Sandhills, the increased heterogeneity of habitat caused by those treatments might actually make the prairie more resilient.

Sandhills Prairie

Gerry Steinauer

The Sandhills are the Great Plains' largest and most unspoiled grassland ecosystem. Spared from the settlers' plow by steep dunes, nutrient-poor soils, and a semiarid climate, this sea of grass stretches from horizon to horizon, the rolling dunes broken only occasionally by interdunal lakes, marshes, and meadows. One can drive for miles and see no signs of humanity except for barbed wire fences, windmills, grazing cattle, and a lonesome ranch house.

One might think this extensive Sandhills prairie is an ancient stable ecosystem, but the opposite is true. A mere fourteen thousand years ago, as the last Ice Age was releasing its frozen grip on the continent, the dunes were covered by northern grasslands and spruce and aspen woodlands and roamed by mammoths and other Ice Age animals. During the following millennia as the postglacial climate warmed, spruce and aspen retreated northward in the glacier's shadow, and the warm-season grasses and forbs characteristic of today's grasslands expanded to fill the void. Then, about ninety-five hundred years ago and for much of the next several thousand years, severe, long-duration droughts, called mega-droughts, frequently descended upon the plains, withering the dune's protective grass cover while winds set the sand to blowing. Sahara-like naked dunes slowly rolled across the land. Remarkably, some bison survived in the Sandhills during this interval of frequent droughts, likely by grazing in the still green, groundwater-fed valleys. Proof is found in the hoof prints they left in the blowing sand, which are visible today in cutbanks as pockmarks in the laminated sands.

Eventually rains returned, and grass stabilized the dunes, but mega-drought lurked in the shadows, again showing its face about

Prairie-covered Sandhills dunes reflect off the blue waters of an alkaline lake in Garden County. Photograph by Gerry Steinauer. Used with permission.

Today the Sandhills region is densely vegetated with prairie grasses, such as little bluestem and prairie sandreed, and a diversity of wildflowers. Photograph by Gerry Steinauer. Used with permission.

950 years ago, when several hundred years of frequent drought set the dune tops to blowing. In the late 1700s and early 1800s, the first Euro-American explorers traversed the region during an era of dryness, wildfires, and large bison herds. The dunes were stable, but grass cover was sparse, with much open sand between plants. The explorers struggled crossing the dunes on horseback and despised the Sandhills. J.H. Snowden of the 1857 Warren expedition lamented, "Much broken by and cut by winds, supporting a very scant vegetation . . . Our greatest wish is to be away from it [the Sandhills] as soon as possible and never return." They deemed the region not fit for man nor beast.

Cattlemen ignored that scathing report and in the 1870s began drifting into the Sandhills, finding the dune and meadow grasses splendid for fattening herds for eastern markets. The news spread, and more ranchers followed. Passage of the 1904 Kinkaid Act, which gave settlers 640 acres of free land, brought a minor rush of farmers to the region. The Kinkaiders scraped by, farming hardscrabble flats and dry valleys but lasted, at most, a few decades before vacating their claims. In all, they plowed perhaps 10 percent of the Sandhills prairie, which eventually reclaimed the abandoned fields.

Although the Sandhills remain rangeland, settlement brought ecological changes, primarily through wildfire

Prairie rose blooms near a lichen-covered bison skull in the bison pasture on The Nature Conservancy's Niobrara Valley Preserve in Brown County. The rose is a common Sandhills low shrub. Photograph by Gerry Steinauer. Used with permission.

control and replacement of roving bison with fenced cattle. These factors, along with a wetter climate in the early 1900s, led to denser grass cover on the dunes and less exposed sand. Thick grass benefited cattle but crowded out wildflowers. The once common blowout penstemon, which grows in open sand, now struggles to survive, with only a few thousand plants remaining. Compounding this issue in recent decades is a shift from season-long cattle grazing of large pastures to rotational grazing of smaller pastures, which has resulted in more uniform grazing and consistent grass cover. Grazing-sensitive wildflowers have declined, including the shrub, New Jersey tea, which is now mostly found in un-grazed road right-of-ways.

Today, abundant dune grasses include needle-and-thread, prairie sandreed, sand bluestem, little bluestem, and sand lovegrass. Less abundant are an array of wildflowers and other grasses, along with a few sedges and shrubs. The exact number of plants inhabiting Sandhills prairie is unknown, but a 2006 survey of the seventy-thousand-acre Valentine National Wildlife Refuge in Cherry County found 175 native and a few non-native species growing on the dunes, the latter arriving since settlement. Many of the native species, such as sand dropseed, lemon scurf pea, and bird's-egg milkvetch grow only in sand, while others, such as side oats grama and prairie rose, grow in other soil and prairie types.

In late March, sun sedge is the first dune plant to awaken from winter slumber. This short grasslike plant is sought out by grazers, a nutritious bite of green in the still winter-brown prairie. Spurred by spring rains and warming days, wildflowers soon follow into bloom. Among those splashing the hills with spring color are the pink to purple-red to blue pealike flowers of hoary vetchling, the bright blue blooms of spiderwort, the fluorescent yellowish-orange blossoms of hairy puccoon, and the spikes of purple locoweed. The latter's name reflects the fact that if eaten by livestock it can become addictive, and if consumed in abundance, causes animals, particularly horses, to become spooked and disoriented.

Among the Sandhills' spring bloomers are its only tall shrubs: American plum and chokecherry. Cloaked in white blossoms, they appear snowball-like among the greening dunes. Their flowers' sweet scent draws crowds of bees, butterflies, and other pollinators, while their summer-ripening fruit attracts wildlife and jelly-makers alike. The shrubs often form thickets on cool, north-facing slopes and moist pockets in high dunes, providing relieving summer shade for prairie grouse and deer.

Yucca adorns a sand dune in Cherry County. Native Americans ate the flowers, flower stalks, and young seedpods raw or cooked. Photograph by Gerry Steinauer. Used with permission.

Hairy puccoon, Brown County. The plant grows on dry, sandy soils nearly statewide but is most abundant on Sandhills dunes. Photograph by Gerry Steinauer. Used with permission.

With a rosette of bayonet-like leaves and a tall spike of spring-blooming white flowers, yucca is the quintessential dune shrub. Cattle relish its tender blooms and young seedpods, which rarely mature in spring- and early-summer-grazed pastures. Cattle and bison prefer to graze the evergreen leaves in winter, when it is the only green available.

When summer's heat settles on the dunes, a new flush of wildflowers come into bloom. Common perennial species include sand milkweed, prickly poppy, hairy golden aster, and silky purple-and-white prairie clover. Perhaps most abundant is fourpoint evening primrose, a biennial

that brightens roadsides and other disturbed sites with large spikes of yellow blooms. Midsummer is when most prairie grasses send forth their sun-harvesting leaves and flowers. The nourishing leaves fuel the region's beef industry, while the flowers mature into seeds that cater to birds and small mammals.

Late summer brings on the asters, goldenrods, and sunflowers. Annual sunflower, like fourpoint evening primrose, thrives under disturbance and, in years of plentiful rain, can turn hard-grazed pastures yellow with blooms. The flowers often linger into early fall, mixing with the now frost-hued vibrant purples, oranges, and tans of the prairie grass. The Sandhills' autumn colors rival those of eastern forests.

Change, whether throughout seasons, decades, or millennia, typifies the Sandhills prairie, and if the past foretells the future, human-induced climate change will also alter the prairie. Already, recent mild winters and longer and wetter springs appear to be favoring the spring-growing, non-native grasses, like smooth brome and Kentucky bluegrass. In some areas they are marching out of wet valleys onto lower dunes slopes, displacing native plants. Will this climate pattern continue and allow these grasses to creep farther up and over the dunes? Perhaps climate change will induce hotter and drier summers and set the dunes to blowing. A worst-case scenario would have slowly advancing, unstoppable dunes burying fences, highways, and other signs of settlement, in a sense, rewilding the land. At present, science can only guess what the future holds for the Sandhills.

What is known is that the Sandhills prairie is the pride of Great Plains grasslands—scenic, diverse grazing lands to be cherished and conserved for future generations.

Gerry Steinauer is a botanist-ecologist for Nebraska Game and Parks Commission.

Blowout Penstemon

Cheryl Dunn

Blowout penstemon *(Penstemon haydenii)* makes its home in blowouts of the Sandhills. It is the only federally endangered plant in Nebraska and is one of the rarest plants of the Great Plains. This penstemon was first collected in 1857 by its namesake, Ferdinand Hayden, and then later described in 1891 by a curator at Harvard University. It is an exceptional plant in that it is one of only a few penstemons in the world that are strongly scented. The scent, wafting from the predominately blue to purple flowers, has been likened to white chocolate. This rare plant can stand up to twenty inches tall, flowers between June and July, and is uniquely adapted to a blowout's harsh environment of blowing sand and lack of water. Its extensive belowground root structures and aboveground stems that have a waxy coating and become shorter and thicker, enable the plant to stand up to sandblasting. Blowout grass *(Redfieldia flexuosa)* and blowout penstemon have similar root properties that help hold sand together. Their stabilizing features allow the blowout to heal and for plants less adapted to harsh conditions to become established in blowouts. Once this occurs, the blowout penstemon can't compete and will disappear. The decline of blowout penstemon has been linked to sand stabilization due to changes in cattle grazing rotations and control of fires that have prevented the formation of blowouts. In 1940 the blowout penstemon was thought to be extinct until it was found again in 1968. Several state and federal agencies have worked to establish blowout penstemon in active blowouts, helping the population to increase over the past several decades. The blowout penstemon is federally protected, making it illegal to collect or have any portion of the plant in your possession without both a state and federal permit.

Cheryl Dunn is research manager and herbarium coordinator for the Department of Agronomy and Horticulture at the University of Nebraska–Lincoln.

Endangered blowout penstemon grows on the leeward side of a blowout, Cherry County. Photograph by Gerry Steinauer. Used with permission.

Grazing Management for Beef Production and Wildlife Habitat

Walt Schacht and Larkin Powell

Cattle grazing near the shores of a Sandhills lake. Photograph by Dakota Altman, Platte Basin Timelapse. Used with permission.

The Nebraska Sandhills is the largest contiguous grassland in North America, and 95 percent of its 19,300 square miles is privately owned and used for beef production. Cattle share their pastures with wildlife, and the regional biodiversity of wildlife is enhanced by unique habitat components within the sea of grass: alkaline and freshwater wetlands, aquifer-sourced streams, and linear woody vegetation in riparian zones or windbreaks. Yet it is the upland grasslands that provide extensive areas of forage for cattle and a refuge-like area of habitat for a suite of grassland wildlife species.

Forage Resources

Around 90 percent of the Sandhills is upland prairie characterized by rolling dunes composed of fine sands in the Valentine series. The dominant native perennial grasses in this semiarid environment are palatable to grazing cattle and productive, producing as much as fifteen hundred to twenty-two hundred pounds per acre annually. Warm-season grasses, such as sand bluestem, prairie sandreed, little bluestem, and switchgrass, account for 40 to 50 percent of total aboveground plant production. Cool-season grasses, such as needleand-thread, porcupine grass, prairie junegrass, Scribner rosettegrass, and sedges, account for 30 to 40 percent of production, with forbs (wildflowers) and shrubs accounting for the remaining 20 to 30 percent. As much as 80 percent of the perennial grass biomass is below ground in fibrous roots and rhizomes, which provide the water and nutrients required for the persistence of perennial grasses in this relatively harsh environment. The fibrous roots also are the major source of soil organic matter and are responsible for stabilizing the sand dunes.

Uplands are used almost entirely for grazing cattle, mostly during the growing season, although haying is a common practice on some ranches, particularly in high rainfall years. The other 10 percent of the Sandhills is wet meadow dominated by exotic cool-season grasses and some native warm-season grasses and sedges and rushes. Most wet meadows were ditched in the first half of the 1900s to drain surface water from these meadows and allow ranchers to use haying equipment by July. Wet meadows are productive, with annual average plant production of four thousand to six thousand pounds per acre. Because of high soil moisture availability, plants grow rapidly following the summer hay harvest and provide excellent forage for fall grazing.

Livestock Production

Sandhills ranches are a primary source of calves and yearlings for feedlots in Nebraska and are critical to the state's $12.1 billion beef cattle industry. As much as 95 percent of Sandhills rangeland is privately owned and used for cattle ranching, with cow-calf enterprises on more than 90 percent of the ranches and stocker-yearling operations on about 40 percent of them. Most cow-calf enterprises calve from March to May and wean in October and November. Sandhills vegetation is a good match for these cow-calf enterprises because of the abundant, diverse, and high-quality forage plants available during the summer grazing season (May–October); much the same can be said for forage availability for stockers-yearlings. The dominant warm- and cool-season grasses also are grazing tolerant, providing a long grazing season. Sandhills uplands are stocked near grazing capacity, and the native grasses remain dominant.

Ranchers generally depend on beef as their sole source of income from the ranch, making economic sustainability of ranches a challenge, especially considering the variability in beef cattle markets and weather from year to year. To diversify and increase economic sustainability of ranches, enterprises built on the value of ecosystem services found in the Sandhills are being developed, including fee hunting and ecotourism. A significant portion of Sandhills rangeland is owned by people who do not live on the property. These absentee owners commonly have land-use goals other than beef cattle production.

Grazing Practices

The principal grazing season on the upland range of Sandhills cattle ranches is from mid- or late May to October or November. Uplands are the only source of

Aerial view of cattle grazing on grass-covered dunes. Photograph by Craig Chandler. Used with permission.

forage for cattle during this five- to six-month grazing season. Sources of forage during winter and early spring are variable and include hay (mostly from the wet meadows), crop residue (mostly from neighboring cropland areas), and winter range in the Sandhills. Ranchers typically select rotational grazing systems in uplands during the summer season. Choices of duration, timing, and stocking rate create management alternatives that range from simple rotational grazing, where cattle rotate through two to seven pastures once during the grazing season, to management-intensive grazing with eight or more pastures and cattle rotating through the pastures multiple times (usually twice) during the grazing season.

Cow numbers in Sandhills counties have remained between 750,000 and 800,000 since the mid-1950s. Average liveweights of cows were a thousand pounds in the 1950s and 1960s but then increased to fourteen hundred pounds by the twenty-first century, primarily because of a transition to heavier breeds of cattle. Therefore, even though the number of cows on Sandhills grazing lands has not changed since the 1950s, liveweights increased by as much as 40 percent during the same period. Forage intake of individual animals increases with increasing liveweight, resulting in increased forage demand or stocking rate. This suggests that forage demand on grazing lands has increased considerably, with stocking rates increasing by as much as 40 percent. Some of this increase in forage demand has been met by using forage resources outside of the Sandhills, especially grazing cornstalks and other crop residues during winter in cropland areas near the Sandhills. However, much of this increase in forage demand has been met by increasing the efficiency of using available forage in the uplands. Distribution of grazing in large pastures with long distances between livestock water sites is commonly uneven, resulting in large areas that are not grazed or only lightly grazed along with areas that are heavily grazed. This unevenness, or patchiness, of grazing within pastures over a ranch property can be corrected by a number of different strategies.

The spatial distribution of cattle grazing, and associated plant defoliation, is more even for management-intensive grazing than with simple rotational grazing and continuous grazing. Over the last several decades, the USDA's Natural Resources Conservation Service and university extension programs have promoted rotational grazing and reducing pasture size, while increasing livestock water sites to reduce distance to water. Overall, these practices have increased the evenness of grazing over space and time, which has increased the percentage of available plant biomass that grazing livestock consume and increased carrying capacity.

Grassland Heterogeneity and Wildlife

The diversity of wildlife habitat types in grasslands is largely dependent on the patchy distribution of vegetation cover. Heterogeneity describes the patchiness of vegetation over time and space as measured by height, density, and composition of vegetation. Vegetation is naturally patchy at landscape scales because of changes in topography, soils, and past management. Upland plant communities in the Sandhills, however, are relatively homogeneous throughout because of the continuity of sandy soil, dominance of the gentle rolling dunes, and management strategies that favor even distribution of grazing. As cattle evenly graze pastures, the vegetation cover of the pastures become homogeneous, and patches of wildlife habitat become less distinct. Evaluating the tradeoffs of implementing different grazing strategies is part of the decision-making process of ranchers to achieve their management objectives.

The effect of increasing homogeneity of habitat on wildlife varies by species. Biologists have documented three hundred species of resident and migratory birds in the Sandhills, fifty-five species of mammals, and twenty-seven

Close-up view of cattle grazing on grass-covered dunes. Photograph by Craig Chandler. Used with permission.

Auction site at Fort Robinson State Park with bison and longhorn cattle.

species of amphibians and reptiles. Some species, such as western meadowlark, white-tailed and mule deer, and bullsnake are habitat generalists and can be found on a variety of habitats, including homogeneous grasslands. Others are habitat specialists and require unique patches of habitat. These species include northern prairie lizard (bare areas of blowouts), six-lined race runner (dense vegetation), meadow vole (wet meadows), and horned lark (bare ground). These specialists are the species affected the most by changes in habitat heterogeneity over time.

Managing for Habitat Heterogeneity

Ranchers use rotational grazing systems, fencing, and water distribution to spread livestock grazing evenly across pastures and to minimize creation of bare ground,

thus reducing the risk of overgrazing that can reduce beef production in subsequent years. Rotational grazing systems have been touted as beneficial to wildlife diversity in grasslands across North America. Yet field measurements in the Sandhills during the past two decades have shown that the level of heterogeneity in Sandhills grasslands created by rotational grazing may not provide the extremes in plant structure and composition—very dense, ungrazed vegetation and bare ground—needed to provide habitat for a diversity of grassland animals.

Walt Schacht is Emeritus Sunkist Fiesta Bowl Professor of agronomy and director emeritus of the Center for Grasslands Studies at the University of Nebraska–Lincoln.

Larkin Powell is a professor of wildlife ecology and director of the School of Natural Resources at the University of Nebraska–Lincoln.

Grazing, Landscapes, and Greater Prairie-Chickens

Walt Schacht and Larkin Powell

A large portion of the range of the greater prairie-chicken in Nebraska sits squarely on the Sandhills region because of the landscape of unfragmented grasslands. The Nebraska Game and Parks Commission has monitored prairie-chicken populations every year since 1955, and numbers fluctuate from year to year. Greater prairie-chicken numbers in Nebraska grew substantially during the 1980s. What factors are responsible for the population size of prairie-chickens each year? Although mortality from hunters has potential to affect the population, the number of grouse hunters in Nebraska has fallen substantially, and hunting mortality appears to be a non-issue. Other predators, such as raptors, coyotes, and bull snakes remove eggs, chicks, juveniles, and adults from the population. Severe winters, especially cold periods without the deeper snow that the birds use for thermal cover, most likely cause higher mortality of prairie-chickens. Cornfields are used as winter food by prairie-chickens on the edges of the Sandhills region, but the large-scale and long-term conversion of grasslands to croplands substantially reduces habitat. Whereas higher levels of rainfall and soil moisture provide for increased vegetation biomass and insect populations for feeding chicks, droughts reduce levels of cover needed to protect nests from predators and to provide habitat for insects.

Grazing is a complicated factor for prairie-chicken populations. Given what we know about the need for patchiness of habitat, some level of grazing is beneficial. Spring mating areas (lek sites or booming grounds) are typically found in closely grazed or trampled sites, such as those near water tanks. Recent research has found that population growth of prairie-chickens in Nebraska was lowest at moderate stocking rates. A positive response of prairie-chickens to higher stocking rates that have been used since the 1980s may be coincidental with implementation of rotational grazing systems that allow pastures periodic rest and regrowth of cover for prairie-chickens while cattle efficiently utilize an adjoining pasture. The relationship between grazing and prairie-chickens will continue to be a focus of research in the future, and this factor is representative of the complicated, interwoven nature of the landscape and environmental factors that constantly push and pull at prairie-chicken populations.

Once found widely throughout the U.S., greater prairie-chickens are now mostly limited to short-grass prairie due to extensive habitat loss. This male (*left*) is booming through orange air sacs, drawing the attention of the female. Photograph by Tom White. Used with permission.

Mule deer wading in a Cherry County lake in early spring.

WILDLIFE

Birds of the Sandhills

Larkin Powell

The North American Breeding Bird Survey has documented 171 species of birds breeding in the Nebraska Sandhills. Only 46 stay in Nebraska year-round. The late ornithologist Paul Johnsgard noted another 125 species that migrate through the Sandhills to northern breeding grounds. When we add 102 species that rarely wander into the region, our tally comes to 398 species.

The contiguous grasslands and distinctive wetlands offer a variety of habitat types that meet birds' diverse needs. Likewise, bird-watchers can visit expansive rangelands, wetland complexes, and small forest areas in the same morning in the Sandhills: the vastness of space and feelings of near-wilderness are impressive. Ranches are large and towns are small; the only signs of humanity seen from most dune tops and meadows are small roads, fences, local electric lines, and cattle that must belong to someone. Bird-watchers do not typically come to the Sandhills to see rare or threatened species, because any species of bird in the Sandhills can be seen somewhere else. The unique feature of a Sandhills birding trip is the backdrop, which is positively magnificent.

Birds' wings allow them to be choosy consumers of landscapes and pioneer new areas quickly. The relatively new geology of the Sandhills provides a chance to ponder the millennia over which birds have been making these decisions. Fossil remains from south-central Nebraska, dated to two million years ago, include species of birds that can be viewed today in the Sandhills: green-winged teal, northern harrier, pied-billed grebe, ferruginous hawk, and wild turkey. Those species were ready to move into the Sandhills as the dunes and wetlands formed.

Upland Grassland Birds

Grasslands dominate the Sandhills, and grassland birds are its most abundant breeding species. Four species—western meadowlark, red-winged blackbird, mourning dove, and grasshopper sparrow—are alone responsible for

Trumpeter swan stretches its wings near its nest in a Sandhills wetland in Box Butte County. Photograph by Michael Forsberg. Used with permission.

Trumpeter swan incubates eggs atop a nest in a Sandhills wetland in Box Butte County. Once nearly extirpated, this iconic species now breeds again in the Sandhills. Photograph by Michael Forsberg. Used with permission.

51 percent of the observations in the Sandhills on the annual Breeding Bird Survey. Three of these species are grassland birds, and red-winged blackbirds are associated with areas close to wetlands. If we use the survey as a guide, one in every four birds you see in the Sandhills is our state bird, the western meadowlark!

In fact, we can account for 90 percent of all observations on the Breeding Bird Survey in the Sandhills with only 30 of its 171 breeding species, and 20 of those 30 species are grassland birds. My research teams in the Sandhills found that two species—western meadowlark and grasshopper sparrow—accounted for half of our sightings. Grasslands are important systems, but they are relatively simple systems with one level of cover compared to forests.

Hunters and bird-watchers are attracted to the Sandhills with equal interest in two species of grouse: greater prairie-chicken and sharp-tailed grouse. Prairie-chickens moved into the region to escape the plow that removed grasslands in Illinois, Iowa, and eastern Nebraska. Sharp-tailed grouse in the Sandhills are at the southern tip of their range. The two species of grouse look and act in similar fashion. However, prairie-chickens tend to be found in landscapes with large valleys with their dancing grounds in mowed meadows or in areas made bare by livestock near windmills and water tanks, and sharp-tailed

Few birds are as striking as the yellow-headed blackbird. Its sounds are a mixture between techno and rock. For this summer resident, the Sandhills provide unique wetland habitat during the breeding and nesting seasons. Photograph by Dakota Altman, Platte Basin Timelapse. Used with permission.

grouse are the kings of rolling dunes with few valleys, and males dance on the sparsely vegetated tops of dunes. Prairie-chickens may move to near-field areas to find alfalfa or corn during the late fall and winter, while sharp-tailed grouse seem content to stay in their dunes.

Migratory Water Birds

Before and after winter, the wetlands of the Sandhills become especially busy with the sounds and activity of migratory birds. Management of migratory birds in North America is conducted in four flyways, and the Central Flyway through the Great Plains lacks a north-south geographic feature that the Atlantic, Pacific, and Mississippi Flyways have in the form of coasts and a large river. The wetlands of the Sandhills join with east-west rivers across the plains to serve as rungs on a ladder through which birds climb and descend during their annual migrations to and from their northern breeding grounds.

Avocet in the Lakeside Area, Sheridan County.

Ducks and geese make use of open water, and some stay to nest in the Sandhills. Our waterfowl research shows a unique age structure of a large portion of first-year breeding mallards in the Sandhills, suggesting their older colleagues continue to the Prairie Pothole region in the Dakotas and Canada's prairie provinces. These first-time mothers are apparently on a steep learning curve, as only about 3 to 5 percent of mallard nests are successful in the Sandhills, compared to 15 to 20 percent success in more northerly locations.

The temporary sheets of water provided by spring rains and snowmelt across meadows in the Sandhills are perfect foraging areas for shorebirds such as white-faced ibis, Wilson's snipe, and lesser and greater yellowlegs. Two shorebird species that stay in the Sandhills for breeding are also a favorite of birders: upland sandpipers often pose for photographs atop fenceposts, and American avocets nest near wetlands in the western Sandhills. Avocets use their unique curved bills to filter invertebrates from the shallows of wetlands and may frequent wetlands with alkaline waters that have high levels of invertebrates.

Wilson's Phalarope

Larkin Powell

During spring migration, Wilson's phalarope can be found in groups in small ponds and wetlands in the plains. The birds are often seen spinning in the water as if one of their paddling legs was broken. The spinning is purposeful, as it is a way for the birds to concentrate aquatic insects and forage more efficiently. However, there is more to know about phalaropes than their funky spinning behavior! Wilson's phalarope is one of the few species in which the traditional male and female roles are switched. The females lay eggs for at least one male and then disappear while the males guard and incubate each nest for her. This mating system is called polyandry, Greek for "many men," the opposite of polygyny, "many women." A careful observer will notice that the female phalarope is more colorful than the male—again, the opposite coloration pattern of most bird species. What are the advantages of this mating system? Sitting on a nest is dangerous business with predators lurking in the landscape, and it is energetically demanding to produce eggs and care for young. The female phalarope spreads her risk among many nests. She spends energy on eggs, while the males spend their energy caring for the nests and young. The males do not need to be colorful as they are not competing for females.

This female Wilson's phalarope swims through water, searching for invertebrates; these birds often whirl, alone or in groups, stirring up larvae and other food sources. Photograph by Tom White. Used with permission.

Concerns for the Future

Conservation planning for birds in the Sandhills is focused on details of land use, such as dynamics of cattle grazing, management and drainage of meadows for haying, and management of lakes. Birds are benefiting from current projects such as restoration of fens that had been previously drained and removal of common carp from lakes. Removing a fish to benefit birds may seem odd, but the non-native carp stir up sediments as they feed in lakes, which reduces the amount of light that can reach into the water column and support the growth of submerged vegetation on which waterfowl feed during migration. One small change in the system can have cascading effects.

Like humans, birds choose homes based on location. Sandhills birds are first attracted to the region for its expansive grasslands and wetlands. Next, birds seek a portion of landscape that provides what they need for survival and reproduction. Last, their focus is on a specific type of clump of grass, shrub, or tree that is

Eared grebe pairs mate on their own nesting platforms. This one is in Grant County.

best for supporting and protecting their nest. Therefore, the region must retain its breadth, its unique grasslands and wetlands, and its diverse types of microhabitat that appeal to breeding birds. Horned larks, for example, are found in areas with sparse vegetation and bare soil. In an ironic twist of fate, as ranchers have worked to "heal" disturbed blowout areas of bare sand in their pastures and graze in a conservative manner that does not result in overgrazed condition, horned lark sightings on routes of the Breeding Bird Survey in the Sandhills have declined from approximately thirty sightings per route in the 1970s and 1980s to five to ten sightings per route in the last two decades. Despite the large grassland landscape, the specific type of habitat needed by horned larks has declined.

Bird communities constantly change in structure, for a variety of reasons. The fossil remains in south-central Nebraska, for example, contained remains of a ptarmigan, now found in Alaska, and passenger pigeons, now extinct. The Ice Age conditions present when the ptarmigan was found here and a whole-out slaughter of a species during the market-hunting era explain those two changes in our bird community. More recently, only the chestnut-collared longspur has disappeared from annual surveys in the last two decades, while eleven species have appeared during the same period. The increases in tree cover in the Sandhills probably pushed the red-bellied woodpecker and tree swallow into the region, while house finches and Eurasian collared-doves are invasive species that have swept through the plains. Bald eagles have appeared on surveys in recent years, which is a happy story of conservation success following declines from shooting and the ill effect of DDT. It is now possible to spot a massive nest of our national bird in a large cottonwood tree at many locations in the Sandhills.

Larkin Powell is a professor of wildlife ecology and director of the School of Natural Resources at the University of Nebraska–Lincoln.

Long-Billed Curlew

Larkin Powell

Native American myths suggested the bill of the curlew was stretched by a man-god creature during an argument. Certainly, the curlew is known for its unique facial feature, which may be most useful on the wintering grounds where they forage for invertebrates in the mud of wetlands along Mexico's coast. In the Sandhills, ranchers know curlews for dive-bombing anything that comes near their nest site, and their aggression is usually effective with interlopers. Curlews arrive early to the plains in the spring and leave for their wintering grounds in June or early July while other species are only halfway through their breeding season. The curlew is North America's largest shorebird—large enough for a meal. Commercial hunters often sought them to ship to restaurants as a delicacy before protection from the Migratory Bird Treaty Act in the early 1900s.

On the plains, long-billed curlews are camouflaged in sparsely vegetated short-grass prairie. This photo was taken near Crescent Lake National Wildlife Refuge in Garden County. Photograph by Tom White. Used with permission.

Sharp-tailed grouse perform their spring mating rituals on a lek in Thomas County.

Adult burrowing owl atop a burrow in Garden County just after sunrise. Photographed by Tom White. Used with permission.

Nematodes of the Sandhills

Thomas Powers

The most abundant animals in the Nebraska Sandhills are also one of the most seldom seen. Nematodes are microscopic roundworms found in every Sandhills habitat, from the soils, streams, lakes, and rivers to the interior cavities of plants and animals. They are aquatic animals, moving through the water-filled spaces among soil particles. Their size, generally around 1mm in length and 50 microns in width, allows them to navigate through soil pores without disrupting soil structure. A handful of soil may contain thousands of nematodes and 40 to 50 different species.

Nematodes are renowned for their ability to withstand extreme habitats. In the hot springs of Yellowstone National Park they are found eating thermophilic bacteria. They can be thawed from the frozen soils of Antarctica's Dry Valleys, often considered the harshest climate on earth. In Nebraska, nematodes can live in the alkaline lakes of the western Sandhills, in sediments with pH levels exceeding 10.0. The sandy composition of Sandhills dunes requires that water-loving nematodes cope with potentially lethal extremes of drying. They rely on the water in soil pores for movement, respiration, and the ability to sense their environment. Nematodes are too small to move to greater depths as soils dry out. Instead, they replace the water in their cells with sugars and antioxidants that allow them to survive extreme desiccation in a state of suspended animation for years. This same physiological process also enables nematodes to survive in frozen soils without cell damage.

The different species of nematodes play many roles in the Sandhills. Most prominent are the microbial feeders, that graze on microbes and microflora. Bacterial feeders have funnel-like mouthparts and a muscular pharynx equipped with a pulsating bulb that creates sufficient suction power to vacuum up bacteria. Fungal feeding nematodes use a fine, hypodermal needle-like modification of their mouthparts to pierce fungal mycelia to suck out cellular contents.

Nematodes have always been Sandhills residents and probably thrived in the tundra during the two million years of Ice Ages that preceded the Sandhills' formation. They likely were among the first microinvertebrate colonizers of the Sandhills, distributed by winds. One theory of nematode distribution is the "Buffalo wallows" theory proposed by Gerald Thorne, who suggested that bison would drop mud and nematodes along their migration route after visiting a wet wallow site. Underlying the dune systems and their nematode communities are the Sandhill fens that include plants considered to be glacial relicts. These plant communities likely have relict nematodes, whose characterization could provide a window into Ice Age soil fauna.

Thomas Powers is a professor in Plant Pathology at the University of Nebraska–Lincoln.

Two species of plant-feeding nematodes from the Alkaline Lakes region. Images by Peter Mullin and Rebecca Higgins. Used with permission.

Sandhills Inconspicuous Mammals Make the Region Unique

Shaun Dunn

A lone bull elk wanders through fog at Fort Niobrara National Wildlife Refuge in Cherry County.

The first time I ever saw the Sandhills, I was mesmerized by the rolling green hills dotted with various wildflowers. Like the diverse blend of plants that make up the Sandhills of Nebraska, the ecoregion also hosts a large variety of mammal species typically found in both the mesic (moister) tallgrass prairie and the more xeric (drier) shortgrass prairie. Historically the most conspicuous mammal species was the American bison (Bison bison), which currently are found only in managed herds in Nebraska. Now the most visible large grazers are domesticated cattle (Bos taurus) and four species of wild ungulates: pronghorn (Antilocarpa americana), elk (Cervus canadensis), mule deer (Odocoileus hemionus), and white-tailed deer (O. virginianus).

But it's the inconspicuous mammals that help make the Sandhills such a unique ecoregion. A great example of a rarely seen mammal is the least shrew (Cryptotis parva). The scientific name of this species means "hidden ear, small," an apt name given the shrew is rarely longer than 3.5 inches and weighs about 5 grams, the same as a nickel. As for those "hidden ears"? These shrews have two small ear holes, but they are well hidden beneath their short but dense fur. Despite its small size, the least shrew adds immense ecological value to the Sandhills by engaging in "nutrient cycling"—digging burrows, consuming invertebrates (e.g., insects, worms, spiders, etc.), and moving organic and inorganic matter throughout its range. Nutrient cycling is necessary for any ecosystem to maintain itself because it allows species to survive within that ecosystem.

A slightly easier nutrient cycler to see is the charismatic (in my opinion), nocturnal sand-loving rat called Ord's kangaroo rat (Dipodomys ordii). Where there's open sandy soil you'll find these rats hiding in their burrows during the heat of the day and foraging for seeds in the cool evenings. Ord's kangaroo rat (and several species of mice in the Sandhills) belong to the family of rodents

Long-tailed weasel at a Cherry County ranch.

called Heteromyidae (different mouse); likely named so because this group of rodents has evolved several physical and physiological adaptations to survive in drier climates. The most obvious of these adaptations is the fur-lined external cheek pouches in which they carry seeds back to their burrow. Having external cheek pouches likely prevents unnecessary moisture loss as the seeds are being taken in and out of the pouch. Kangaroo rats are so well adapted to life in hot, dry climates that they don't drink water; all the water their body needs comes from the seeds they collect. And their highly efficient kidneys concentrate their urine so no bit of water is wasted. A more common Heteromyidae in the Sandhills is the plains pocket mouse (Perognathus flavescens), a small nocturnal mouse that is thought to be very common in the region, but in a casual visit to this ecoregion you're not likely to see either species unless you know to look for them.

The northern grasshopper mouse (Onychomys leucogaster) is also a common Sandhills rodent. These mice are more commonly found in disturbed areas, short-grass prairie, or grazed rangelands where there are plenty of insects, lizards, snakes, and other small mice for them to eat. Unlike the previously mentioned species, the northern grasshopper mouse's diet is largely carnivorous, and depending on the season only about 25 percent of their diet is plant material. Some authors have noted an association between this mouse and the black-tailed prairie dog (*Cynomys ludovicianus*, another once-common species in the Sandhills) as they both like areas with short vegetation so they can see predators on the approach.

The thirteen-lined ground squirrel (*Ictidomys tridecemlineatus*) also prefers shorter vegetation; however, two other species of ground squirrel occupy the Sandhills from opposite sides of the ecoregion. The spotted ground squirrel (*Xerospermophilus spilosoma*) is found in dry, sandy soils with sparse vegetation and ranges all the way from Mexico to southeastern Wyoming; its

Northern river otter in a small pond near Brea, Box Butte County.

most northeastern range is the Sandhills of Nebraska. This species is well adapted to the xeric environments it inhabits, unlike the third species of ground squirrel found in the Sandhills: Franklin's ground squirrel (*Poliocitellus franklinii*). Franklin's range from Illinois and Wisconsin east to the Nebraska Sandhills and then north into Canada. Contrasting the previous two species of ground squirrel, Franklin's prefers the ungrazed areas of mixed-grass and tallgrass prairie where there is plenty of vegetative cover for eating and hiding from predators. And yet all three of these ground squirrels are able to find suitable habitat within the Sandhills not only because of the region's size but because of the wonderful variation within the ecoregion.

The Sandhills also contain wetlands and forested riparian areas that attract species different from those who inhabit open grasslands. These include many of the common species you'll find all over the Great Plains, like beavers (*Castor canadensis*), white-footed and deer mice (*Peromyscus leucopus* and *P. maniculatus*, respectively),

The sheer quantity of pocket gopher mounds is exposed by a prescribed burn at the Nebraska National Forest at Halsey. Photograph by Mark Harris. Used with permission.

Pronghorn in Dawes County.

opossums (*Didelphis virginiana*), and of course the only mammals capable of true flight: bats. Common bat species include the big brown bat (*Eptesicus fuscus*), eastern red bat (*Lasiurus borealis*), hoary bat (*L. cinereus*), and the silver-haired bat (*Lasionycteris noctivagans*).

All these smaller mammals also play a role as food for the carnivores that call the Sandhills home. Again, there are several species that are common throughout the Great Plains, and you've likely heard of them before, like badgers (*Taxidea taxus*), bobcats (*Lynx rufus*), coyotes (*Canis latrans*), red foxes (*Vulpes vulpes*), and

Badgers build their dens in rangeland and short-grass prairies where their dens are marked by mounds of soil at the burrow entrances. Photograph by Tom White. Used with permission.

striped skunks (*Mephitis mephitis*). But there are also a few species you don't hear about as much, like the long-tailed weasel (*Mustela frenata*). These powerful hunters only weigh about a third of a pound but are known to kill prey larger than themselves by giving them a strong bite on the neck, right at the base of the skull.

A final mammal that is likely still found in the Sandhills is the eastern spotted skunk (*Spilogale putorius*). Much smaller than their striped counterparts, eastern spotted skunks once inhabited much of the eastern United States, but in the 1950s their populations declined sharply across their entire range. One place we occasionally still see this species in Nebraska is the Sandhills, but we don't know for how much longer.

The Sandhills is such a distinctive ecosystem and contains a truly unique combination of mammals—all of which should be experienced and appreciated by everyone.

Shaun Dunn is natural heritage zoologist for Nebraska Game and Parks Commission.

A curious winter coyote is wary of intruders at Blue Creek in Garden County. Photograph by Michael Forsberg. Used with permission.

Kangaroo Rats' Habits Enhance Plant Diversity

Keith Geluso and Jeremy A. White

Ord's kangaroo rats (*Dipodomys ordii*) are conspicuous Sandhills rodents. Their large hind feet and long tails, and similar but much smaller body shape, prompted the name "kangaroo," although they are unrelated. Kangaroo rats commonly hop across roadways on moonless nights (and never moonlit nights), using their long tails for balance. Their horizontally oriented burrow openings, with runways leading to and from, are abundant in open sandy areas with sparse vegetation. Footprints and tail drags are visible early in the morning, evidence of their nighttime activities. These seed-loving rodents have strong ecological connections to other organisms in the Sandhills.

Kangaroo rats collect seeds as food resources, storing them either in deep burrows (larder hordes) or shallower dispersals (scatter hordes). Ord's kangaroo rats switch caching patterns seasonally in the Sandhills. They scatter-hoard seeds in warmer months when sand is loose, but in winter when the sand freezes, they become larder hoarders.

With their scatter hoards, kangaroo rats promote germination of many plant species, both grasses and forbs, dispersing seeds at optimal depths for germination. Kangaroo rats recover some of their own scatter hoards but also raid caches of others, stealing their stored seeds. Many seeds are uneaten, and eventually they germinate and emerge as new forage for cattle and native herbivores.

Although their large, round, conspicuous burrow openings are abundant throughout the Sandhills, kangaroo rats actually live in small, inconspicuous burrows. They plug these small burrows, disguising them from predators. The larger burrows have several openings and appear to function as escape tunnels to avoid predators. Although kangaroo rats do not live inside them, the open underground systems are homes for other local species such as box turtles, lizards, snakes, beetles, bees, crickets, and arachnids.

Keith Geluso is a professor of biology at the University of Nebraska at Kearney.

Jeremy A. White is a lecturer in biology at the University of Nebraska at Omaha.

An Ord's kangaroo rat on sandy ground.

Sandhills Sweet Water Lakes Are Productive Fisheries

Daryl Bauer

I was born on the western edge of Nebraska's Sandhills and am a descendant of homesteaders, farmers, and ranchers. If you believed the presettlement maps, the Sandhills was considered the "great American desert." It was and still is an arid place, where grasses stabilize sand dunes. Aside from some hay fields, my ancestors learned the region was best for raising cattle—too dry to farm.

Surprisingly, numerous wetlands and lakes lie in the valleys and flats between those grassy sand dunes. We had a lake on our place. It was a great spot for paddling a homemade kayak, hunting ducks and geese, or skating in the winter. I enjoyed those activities, but fish run in my blood. I was always more interested in what was swimming beneath the surface of our Sandhills lake.

Daryl Bauer fishing in a Sandhills lake. Photo by Daryl Bauer. Used with permission.

I have been peering into the water trying to make contact with what swims in those Sandhills waters ever since. Oh, what treasures I have found.

Nebraska is a place where north meets south and east meets west. The state lies in the middle of not only a country but a continent, with great diversity in geography and climate from one corner of Nebraska to the other. Some would argue that Nebraska is nothing but a transitional zone between varieties of landscapes. Except for the Sandhills; they are uniquely Nebraska.

The most well-known standing waters in Nebraska are human-made reservoirs, whereas almost all the state's natural lakes are in the Sandhills. Especially in the western Sandhills, the lakes are either too shallow or contain too many minerals to support fish. Fortunately, others are fed by the abundant groundwater that percolates through and beneath the sandy soils. What the cowboys called "sweet water" lakes are some of the most productive fisheries in the Great Plains.

Sandhills lakes contain fish more commonly found in places to the north, south, east, and west. These fish likely found their way to the region during periods when the climate was much different than today's. Even now during wet years, lakes can become connected as water fills the valleys and low spots. Although records are sparse back in time, no doubt human activities have moved and stocked many fish throughout the Sandhills.

Flowing Waters

The headwaters of Sandhills streams and rivers start in marshy, wet meadows. In places groundwater can be seen percolating up through the sand. Some of the state's rarest and prettiest fish can be found in those pure headwater streams. A variety of dace, pearl, finescale, and northern redbelly are found nowhere else in Nebraska; in fact, they are commonly found in places far north of Nebraska. The disjunct populations here are testament to a time when the climate was much colder. These fish persist in Sandhills headwaters only because they found refuges of clean, cool spring water.

Plains topminnows can be found in rivers and streams throughout Nebraska but are particularly abundant in slow-flowing Sandhills streams. These colorful fish, usually found hovering near the surface, are probably more abundant there than anywhere in the world.

If you look closely, down on the gravel where you might expect a fish without a swim-bladder, colorful Iowa, and in some cases, orangethroat darters can be found zipping about.

Flowing downstream, streams become rivers; habitat and fish communities change. In most cases Sandhills rivers possess species that are common in flowing waters throughout Nebraska. A variety of minnows that thrive in sandy, prairie streams are typical. Red, sand, and bigmouth shiners are common, as are central stonerollers and longnose dace. Flathead and creek chubs are prevalent, as well as western silvery and plains minnows. The diversity of relatively small minnows may not seem like much to anglers, but they are important to the ecosystem and provide tasty meals for a variety of mammals, reptiles, and birds.

Indeed, Sandhills streams and rivers are brimming with fish, but recreational fishing on those waters is limited. Stretches that support introduced brown or rainbow trout are of special importance to Nebraska anglers.

Unfortunately, barriers, some natural but mostly human-made dams, prevent upstream migration of channel catfish and other species that could provide additional recreational fishing opportunity on Sandhills

Black crappie by C.G. "Bud" Pritchard.

Plains killifish by C.G. "Bud" Pritchard.

White bass by C.G. "Bud" Pritchard.

Northern pike by
C.G. "Bud" Pritchard

rivers. As a result, large fish found in many stretches of Sandhills rivers are limited to white and other suckers and carp. Gar can be found in the lower reaches of rivers, such as the Loup.

Standing Waters

Wet meadows can be found throughout the Sandhills. During wet periods those meadows expand by acres and acres. A variety of pioneer fish species can be found in the wet meadows, marshes, and even flooded road ditches. Fathead minnows, green sunfish, black bullheads, and grass pickerel are quick to take advantage of newly flooded habitats.

Larger lakes and more perennial standing waters commonly have those same species of fish present and are home to many others. Sandhills lakes with enough depth to support fish year-round and with relatively low alkalinities are incredibly productive. These lakes are shallow, twenty feet or less, and are essentially food shelves. They support a diversity of aquatic vegetation and an incredible number of aquatic insects, amphibians, crustaceans, aquatic worms and leeches, snails, and a variety of other small creatures that provide an abundant buffet of fish food.

Some of the fish species that thrive in the Sandhills lake habitats include northern pike, which are believed to be a native species; the Sandhills appear to be the northern pike's southernmost range. Yellow perch are another cool-water species that reach their peak abundance in Sandhills lakes.

Sandhills lakes produce some of the fastest growing and largest bluegills and black crappies in the Great Plains. Largemouth bass also thrive in the expanses of aquatic vegetation. Walleye and even hybrid saugeye (sauger × walleye) have been introduced to some Sandhills lakes;

they are most successful in lakes with less submerged aquatic vegetation and harder sand substrates.

Research shows Sandhills lakes are so productive that fish communities function differently in them. Unlike other standing waters, interspecific competition is seldom a limiting factor because there is enough food for all. Environmental factors, weather, and amount of precipitation are more likely to limit reproduction and numbers of fish. When present, northern pike are the apex predator and influence the size distribution of panfish populations. Other animals, such as turtles, mammals, fish-eating birds, and waterfowl, thrive in the Sandhills because of the productivity of the waters and the fish they produce.

In the Great Plains, where water is limited, every waterbody can be an important fishery. This has been especially true for generations of Nebraska anglers who have fished the Sandhills lakes. Historical black-and-white photos of homesteaders show smiling faces and stringers of fish. Maybe somewhat surprisingly, with the abundance of aquatic vegetation in the summer, ice fishing has been particularly popular on Sandhills lakes.

Fortunately, the Sandhills are made of sand. Farming and irrigation have made minimal marks on the Sandhills and its waters. While human presence can be seen in the barbed wire fences and windmills, for the most part, the Sandhills are relatively untouched. As long as grass holds the dunes and water percolates through the sand, the waters will flow and supply productive habitats for an abundance of fish—treasures waiting to be discovered by future generations of Nebraskans.

Daryl Bauer is a fisheries biologist for the Nebraska Game and Parks Commission.

Common Carp
Invasive Scourge

Daryl Bauer

It seemed like a good idea at the time. After all, as the land was settled people would need readily accessible and inexpensive protein. What could be better than another import, one with fins and scales? So a number of state and federal agencies brought the common carp to the shores of America and throughout Nebraska.

Common carp were the first of the invasive carp to hit North America's shores, imported more than a hundred years ago. All invasive carp, such as silver and bighead carp, derived from Asia, but common carp have been present for so long that many do not think of them as non-native, invasive species. Their impact on water quality and aquatic habitat leaves no doubt that they are one of the worst aquatic nuisance species with which we have been cursed.

Unfortunately, common carp are very successful in the waters of the Nebraska Sandhills. They readily take advantage of newly flooded habitats, and they are particularly prosperous in relatively shallow, productive waters. Some Sandhills waters have been dominated by common carp almost to the exclusion of other species, especially more desirable sport fish species.

Common carp feed by rooting around in bottom sediments. Their activities eliminate submerged aquatic vegetation and result in poor water quality dominated by algal blooms. Habitat suitability for sport fish, waterfowl, and other wildlife is severely degraded when common carp dominate Sandhills lake fish communities.

Stewardship of Sandhills lakes has for decades included management of common carp populations. This is

A fisherman lands a white bass at Merritt Reservoir State Recreation Area in Cherry County.

accomplished by removing or even eliminating them where possible. Preventing their movements into new waters or reinvasion of waters where they have been removed is another important management strategy. These activities will probably always be needed on Nebraska's Sandhills lakes.

Herpetofauna Adapt to Sandhills Idiosyncratic Landscapes

Dennis Ferraro

The species of amphibians, turtles, and reptiles (known as herpetofauna) of the Sandhills region are similar to other areas of Nebraska and the upper Great Plains. Twenty-seven of Nebraska's sixty-three species are found there. Yet the individual assemblages of many of these common species have adapted in unique ways to the idiosyncratic landscape called the Sandhills.

I was first introduced to the Sandhills in the mid-1980s as a young man from the woodland forests of New England; I was enthralled with the vastness. I began to search the ecosystem and was soon rewarded with the lizard species commonly found in the Sandhills. Northern prairie lizards were the most abundant, scurrying among the sparse native grasses and diving into the cover of yucca plants. The faster and sleeker six-lined racerunners were amid more dense grasses on the shaded, moister north-facing slopes of the hills. I found the lesser earless lizards in the near naked blowouts and was astonished by the way they would quickly disappear into the fine sand when threatened. A fourth lizard, the many-lined skink, is more common on the southwestern edge of the Sandhills and only found under cover.

Soon after, I discovered one of the eight snake species I frequently encounter gliding across the sand, the North American racer, a slender, smooth-scaled speed demon. I've captured hundreds of racers across Nebraska and the eastern U.S. Those found in the Sandhills are gorgeous, possessing a bright velvety green on top with a stunning yellow underside; most others have a drab olive or blue-green coloration. Something about the Sandhills makes these lizard-eating snakes stand out like no other racer. As a curious herpetologist in a new ecosystem, I customarily would begin by lifting rocks, logs, and stumps to find my secretive targets. When I landed in the Sandhills I gazed north, east, south, and west, and all I could see was a vast breadth of spectacular landscape with nothing to flip and look beneath. After searching for a few hours and turning over about a dozen pieces of lumber and old tires, I exposed a western milksnake. It was only about eighteen inches long, and unlike any milksnake I had ever caught before, it had diminished reds and wishy-washy white bands. It was the obscure pale milksnake, a subspecies, or morph, primarily found in the Sandhills. Milksnakes are small-lizard eaters. In years to come I would find dozens of them and learn that in the absence of human-made cover they would be found under dead yucca plant roots.

The plains hognose snake is a short, stocky, light-colored lizard feeder. I usually locate them at dawn or dusk when they are rooting at the base of forbs and trying to pop up an unsuspecting lizard before the heat of the day makes lizards impossible to catch. Likely the utmost lizard eater and most reclusive snake of the Sandhills is the glossy snake (*Arizona elegans*), a secretive snake that remains under the loose sand and generally emerges before dawn to hunt down cooled lizards. While

Northern earless lizard.

commonly found in extreme southwestern Nebraska (Dundy County), only two have been revealed in the Sandhills, one by Joe Gubanyi in Thomas County (1987) and a second in Hooker County (2016) that I verified. I consider the glossy snake populations of the Sandhills my personal holy grail.

I consider the bullsnake preeminent of all Nebraska's snakes. Growing to more than eight feet in length, it has mastered the art of rodent predation, feeding on pocket gophers, kangaroo rats, prairie dogs, and small rabbits. They are so efficient a predator that they outcompete other snakes, forcing them to relocate. This action

Ornate box turtle in the Sandhills. Photograph by Chris Helzer. Used with permission.

triggered the false lore that bullsnakes eat rattlesnakes. The bullsnakes of the Sandhills are generally lighter in color and possess more sandy yellow markings. Prairie rattlesnakes, the region's only venomous snake, were purportedly as common as bullsnakes a couple hundred years ago before the dramatic decline of prairie dog towns. The majority of Sandhill prairie rattlesnakes hibernate, give birth, and mate in the prairie dog towns. They are noted to travel upward of a mile searching for summer feeding grounds. Their fidelity to prairie dog towns renders rattlesnakes habitually to be found closer to the lower clay soil features of the Sandhills. Prairie rattlesnakes are one of my most beloved snakes; after capturing and releasing hundreds over the years, I have nothing but respect and admiration for these diminishing members of the biodiversity of the Sandhills.

The Sandhills is home to six species of turtles and can be considered the epicenter of three special species: Blanding's, ornate box, and yellow-mud turtles. The semi-aquatic Blanding's turtle is a lover of fens and pothole ponds. Data indicate there are more of these endangered turtles in the Sandhills of Nebraska than any other location. A terrestrial turtle, the ornate box turtle is commonly sighted crossing roads and trails. These omnivorous creatures feed on insects, grubs, and baby mice by burrowing under dried cow patties and humps of grass; I suspect they used bison dung piles in the past. Before hibernation they switch their diet to the vitamin C–packed rose hips and prickly pear cactus fruit numerous on the ground in autumn. Yellow mud turtles have one of their two isolated populations in the Sandhills aquatic

Prairie rattlesnakes are an icon of the West. Detested and feared by many, they provide a wide array of ecosystem services that go largely unnoticed. Photograph by Dakota Altman, Platte Basin Timelapse. Used with permission.

areas (the other is in southwest Nebraska). This small (less than 6 inches), oval, long-lived turtle deposits just one or two eggs annually, a factor in its small population numbers; another is that their eggs are a favorite of the plains hognose snake.

While deemed a dry location, the Sandhills' artesian weeping groundwater creates an unusual haven for several amphibians. The western tiger salamander is the only salamander species in the Sandhills, and its larvae are extremely prevalent in the interim sloughs, fens, ranch ponds, and cattle tanks. This long-lived amphibian spends decades in moist mammal burrows, only emerging during spring rains to trek to temporary bodies of water for reproduction. Additionally, I have encountered sexually mature larval forms, known as neotenic, in permanent water situations. My research indicates this species is especially adapted to the alkalinity of Sandhills water; its cousins, the eastern tiger salamanders, spotted salamanders, and small-mouth salamanders, cannot tolerate such high alkalinity levels.

Of the eight frogs and toads found in the Sandhills, the Great Plains toad and the plains spadefoot are especially well adapted. Both toad species are well-suited for sandy short-grass prairie that receives precipitation in a few massive events. Explosive reproducers, these toads emerge from their sand grottos during spring and summer thunderstorms to sing, mate, and lay eggs. Their eggs will hatch, and larvae will transform into miniature adults all within a week's time. I'm especially fond of the imaginative characteristics of the plains spadefoot: their ability to stare at you with wide eyes while slowly disappearing backward into the sand, the male's sheep-like bellowing call, and the larvae's tendency to become cannibalistic.

The rivers and lakes of the Sandhills are haunts for the micro-sized chorus frogs and leopard frogs. These permanent waters have also been invaded and occupied by bullfrogs. Invasive bullfrogs are devouring native frogs, baby turtles, and young waterfowl. My plea is to initiate programs to stop these intruders from changing the biodiversity of the Sandhills.

In a short time, the Sandhills developed into my nirvana. In the summer of 2020 I conducted my data collection solo, spending a week at a time camping in the Sandhills, not seeing another human the entire duration. Just me and the astonishing biodiversity of the Sandhills, it was magnificent as I was in my happy place.

Dennis Ferraro is professor of conservation biology and herpetology in the School of Biological Sciences at the University of Nebraska–Lincoln.

Jeffrey Lang and Alan Bartels studying Blanding's turtles at Valentine National Wildlife Refuge.

Blanding's Turtles: Sandhills Smileys

Ashley Forrester

Within the Sandhills wetlands lives a colorful steward with an Oscar-winning smile. Although this docile, ancient treasure makes no more than a hissing sound when threatened, they speak loudly about the health of Sandhills ecosystems. They are Blanding's turtles.

Blanding's are unlike any turtle in terms of beauty and behavior. I recognize them by the bright yellow coloration on their chin and neck. This profile is reminiscent of a brachiosaurus: long, with a clublike head. The curvature of their mouth mimics a smile, earning them the nickname "smileys" by some locals. Like other turtles, Blanding's bask upon muskrat structures but in a more regal fashion. They periscope along wetland edges with caution and move through submerged with the secrecy of 007. Their large hazel eyes are humanlike and, I believe, hold an ancient wisdom of the Sandhills.

I have had the chance to meet several Blanding's turtles and follow the lives of over a dozen adults in my work as a graduate student at the University of Nebraska at Kearney. With colleagues, this research extended the distributional range northeast. The range of Blanding's turtles is limited to parts of Ontario and Nova Scotia, New York, Massachusetts, New Hampshire, Pennsylvania, Maine, the Great Lakes region, Minnesota, Iowa, and Nebraska. Blanding's turtles are listed as a species of conservation concern throughout their range. Nebraska is the only state that lists the species as secure.

The largest population of Blanding's was found at Valentine National Wildlife Refuge in the early 2000s. My research adds to what we know about Blanding's and informs management practices. Threats to turtle surviv-

Blanding's turtles like this one are numerous in the Sandhills. Photography by Mariah Lundgren. Used with permission.

al are many, but alteration and destruction of habitats are primary contributors to declines elsewhere. The Sandhills remain relatively unaltered and sparsely populated and apart from roads, provide suitable habitats that are still connected. The life cycle of a Blanding's turtle, from soft-shelled egg to football-sized adult, is interconnected to the mosaic of Sandhills wetlands and upland sand dune habitats. This makes the Sandhills the last stronghold for Blanding's. As an indicator species, this means that the Sandhills are likely doing well too. May we protect our smileys.

Ashley Forrester earned her master's in biology in 2022 from the University of Nebraska at Kearney.

Diverse Landscapes Enrich Insect Diversity and Numbers

Jeffrey Bradshaw

Just as insects have evolved to fill numerous niches throughout the world, so, too, have they taken advantage of the Nebraska Sandhills. The diversity of habitats and landscapes across the Sandhills can be seen in the unique communities of insects found in these varied grasslands. Aquatic or semiaquatic insect communities are more common in the subirrigated meadows, and

xeric or desert-loving species are more common on the dry dune tops. What makes the Sandhills unique is that these communities can change in a short 800-foot distance from the foot to the crest of a dune.

The habitats within the Sandhills to which insects have adapted can be surprising. Sand blowouts, while some-

Dung beetles on bison manure. Photograph by Chris Helzer. Used with permission.

times viewed negatively, are actually important habitat for several unique insect species. The sandy tiger beetle, *Cincindela limbata*, is specifically found in these habitats and stream banks nearly exclusively within the Sandhills. Other tiger beetle species also take advantage of these habitats, where they are key insect predators as adults and larvae. The complexity of coadaptation between species is remarkable within these systems. Insect decomposers, such as burying beetles and dung beetles, play crucial and diverse roles. While American burying beetles may work to decompose a prairie dog corpse, some dung beetle species have adapted to take advantage of prairie dog dung. These decomposers work in concert to restore nutrients to the soil to produce more grass that can then be consumed by herbivores. While habitat diversity over such short distances is impressive, the Sandhills ecoregion also varies at large scales. Longer growing seasons with more moisture are found to the east, with drier, shorter growing seasons to the west.

Insects take advantage of the plants that have adapted to the Sandhills' diverse soil, water, and wind conditions. The yucca is an example of a plant that becomes more common as you move from east to west across the Sandhills. And it provides an example of the diversity and unique adaptation of Sandhills insects. Four yucca species are common to Nebraska: *Yucca glauca, Y. aloifolia, Y. recurvifolia*, and *Y. filamentosa*. Although high densities of these plants can be problematic for ranchers, they do support an interesting and diverse insect life. Several species of insects thrive on yucca. Giant skipper butterflies feed on the stems as caterpillars and pollinate the flowers as adults. Meanwhile, Cole's bush cicadas (*Megatibicen tremulus*) call for mates on yucca stalks, and the female lays her eggs on the plant. The nymphs then live out their lives underground, feeding on sap from the yucca root. This cicada is particularly interesting as the species is referred to as a "cryptic" species, meaning *M. tremulus* looks exactly like another cicada, *Tibicen dorsatus*.

American Burying Beetle

Steve Spomer

The American burying beetle, *Nicrophorus americanus*, is an endangered species found especially in the Sandhills and Dissected Loess Hills. Formerly occurring over the eastern half of the United States, the beetle is now found predominantly in Nebraska and Oklahoma. Reasons for its demise are only speculative. It is undoubtedly the largest and most beautiful of the carrion beetles, being black with four large orange spots on its wing covers and with an orange pronotum (the area between the head and wing covers). Burying beetles bury carrion that we would otherwise have to smell. These nocturnal beetles detect the carrion, then work to bury it, pulling fur, feathers, or scales away and secreting fluids that help preserve the corpse. Eggs are laid beneath the corpse, and the parents take care of the young larvae, feeding them until they are old enough to feed themselves. This behavior is quite rare in insects and is usually confined to social insects like bees and ants. Research is underway to identify and preserve their habitat in the state, and there are efforts to reintroduce these beetles into areas where they once occurred.

Steve Spomer is a retired research technologist for the Department of Entomology at the University of Nebraska–Lincoln.

Painted grasshopper, aka barber pole grasshopper. Photograph by Chris Helzer. Used with permission.

Researchers were able to identify the species as separate when they analyzed their distinctive calls.

Although much attention has been given to insects as pests, only a small number have negative economic or societal impacts. The majority of insects serve critical roles, providing ecosystem services from decomposition to pollination.

Grasshoppers have a notorious reputation in Nebraska and throughout western rangelands for competing with cattle for grass. Indeed, there are three to five species of grasshopper common to grasslands that are commonly referred to as "outbreak species." Climatic and environ-mental cycles can lead to very high densities of some grasshoppers and when combined with drought can be very destructive to rangeland if left unmanaged. However, there are around a hundred species of grass-hoppers that are common to Nebraska. Similar to insect species overall, most grasshoppers are not pests. In fact, Russian thistle grasshopper (*Aeoloplides turnbulli*) might be considered beneficial as it feeds on Russian thistle and lambsquarters, while snakeweed grasshopper *(Hes-perotettix viridis)* preferentially feeds on snakeweeds, which are toxic to cattle. Some species of grasshopper, such as painted grasshopper (*Dactylotum bicolor*), have a striking appearance and specific hosts preferences.

Insects in the Sandhills can also serve as a food source for other animals. The clean, clear ephemeral ponds and streams in the Sandhills can support extremely high populations of mayflies (Ephemeroptera) for example. Immature mayflies (nymphs) feed off algae and detritus along the stream or pond bottom. Mayflies may live up to two years in this immature, aquatic stage. However, adults might only live a day or two following emergence from their aquatic stage, primarily in the spring. Mayfly hatches can reach very high densities and are weak flyers; bats, birds, amphibians, and fish all take advantage of the adults as food sources.

Western bush cicada, aka Cole's cicada, on yucca. Photograph by Chris Helzer. Used with permission.

Giant Skipper

Steve Spomer

Many know of the close relationship between the yucca plant and the yucca moth. But a charismatic butterfly in the Sandhills also has a relationship with yucca plants. Strecker's giant skipper, *Megathymus streckeri*, is the largest butterfly (by weight) in Nebraska. In early June when the yucca begins to bloom, the butterfly emerges from its underground pupa, and the territorial males patrol the stands of yucca, searching for females. Males patrol in wide circles, occasionally landing on the dead yucca stems, where they resemble the old seedpods. One can actually hear their wingbeats as they patrol. The egg-laden females are more secretive, hiding in the yucca foliage and only flying from plant to plant to lay a single egg. However, if frightened, the female can fly off at an incredible speed. The egg hatches in about ten days, and the larva burrows into the base of the plant, eating, tunneling, and growing until eventually reaching the root. The larva spends the winter in the root, finishes its growth in the spring, and constructs a tube made of silk and its own excrement leading to the surface. Males emerge in late May or early June, with females emerging about a week later. A good place to see these "giants" is Valentine National Wildlife Refuge, especially in the hills between Dewey and Clear Lakes.

Steve Spomer is a retired research technologist for the Department of Entomology at the University of Nebraska–Lincoln.

Robber fly with a captured sandy tiger beetle. Photograph by Chris Helzer. Used with permission.

Cutworm species (Noctuidae) overwinter in Sandhills soils and some, such as the army cutworm (*Euxoa auxillaris*), can reach very high densities on Nebraska grasslands. While outbreak populations can denude large areas of grass, many ground-nesting birds depend on foraging for cutworms in the spring as they provide the protein needed to support egg production and nesting chicks. The surviving caterpillars of the army cutworm become a moth that migrates west in late spring to early summer and will oversummer high in the Rocky Mountains. These moths become critical protein sources for grizzly bears as they forage among the scree fields in the high mountains. It's interesting to reflect on the impact of the Sandhills ecosystems even across the continent.

Insects are the most species-rich group of animals on Earth. Their size, mobility, and life strategies have afforded them the ability to adapt to nearly every terrestrial and freshwater niche on the planet. The precise number of insect species is a topic for some debate—there could be as many as thirty million insect species—yet only about nine hundred thousand living species have been described.

Nebraska's Sandhills represent an ecoregion ripe for research into the roles and numbers of insect inhabitants. The overwhelming number of insect species has yet to be studied sufficiently to fully understand their roles within ecosystems. This is especially true for unique, hard-to-find species, many of which can be found in the Nebraska Sandhills. They provide important ecosystem services in their aesthetic beauty, maintaining natural cycles that pollinate flowers, recycling nutrients back into the soil, and providing food for other wildlife in Nebraska ecosystems and beyond.

Jeffrey Bradshaw is an entomologist and extension specialist at the University of Nebraska Panhandle Research and Extension Center in Scottsbluff, Nebraska.

Sandy Tiger Beetle

Steve Spomer

A master of camouflage, the sandy tiger beetle, *Cicindela limbata*, is found in stabilized dunes and blowouts. Originally named from specimens collected in Nebraska in the nineteenth century, the sandy tiger beetle's range barely extends into neighboring states. The wing covers are white, with some light markings of copper, green, or blue, which match the color of the sand. Although adapted to live on the hot sand, adults may hide in the shadows of plants or dig burrows to escape extreme temperatures. Adults are found from April until June and then again in late August into September. Eggs are laid in the spring, and the larva lives its entire life in a burrow, feeding on anything that comes near its entrance. Larvae probably spend two years in burrows, then they pupate in a side chamber and emerge in late August of the third year. Tiger beetles are predators and considered beneficial insects. Their large eyes allow them to detect small movements, and their short bursts of speed make them one of the fastest known insects. There are thirty-one species of tiger beetles in Nebraska, including the federally endangered Salt Creek tiger beetle.

Steve Spomer is a retired research technologist for the Department of Entomology at the University of Nebraska–Lincoln.

RANCHIN

G

Calves being separated from their mothers before a branding, Hooker County. Photograph by Joe McDaniel. Used with permission.

Ranching through the Seasons
Planned for the Worst, Hoped for the Best

Sarah Sortum

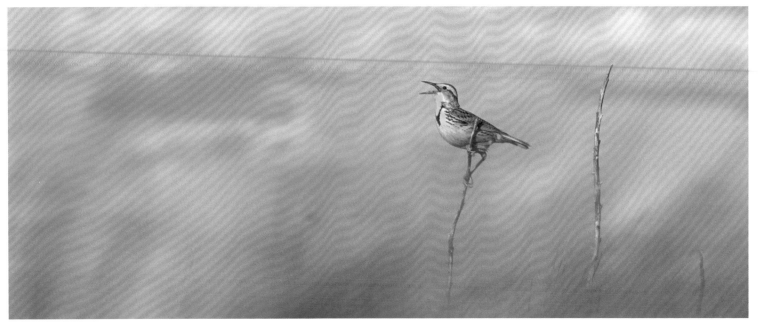

Nebraska's state bird, the western meadowlark, sings its distinctive song on a Sandhills prairie in Grant County. Photograph by Michael Forsberg. Used with permission.

The line between optimism and despair is grass-blade thin. Ranchers live within this narrow gap day to day, season to season. As contradictory as the Sandhills themselves, ranchers are a paradox. Stubborn in purpose, yielding to progress. Dreamers and optimists all, despite the grumblings. Their character is proven by action. Year in and year out, moving through the seasons. Facing setbacks, barely trusting small victories, they keep going. Keep trying. Planning for the worst, hoping for the best.

While each ranch is singular in detail, there is commonality in environment that creates a shared backdrop. There are straightforward reasons, repeated by plain-dealing people, to ride the dips and swells of this land and life. But the most powerful draw, the tugging force that anchors ranchers to this sandy country, is not easily or logically defined. The push and pull of survival can rarely be planned or properly recounted. It can only be played out over time.

This chapter recounts one ranch's experiences. It does not, and should not, represent the story of every ranch in the Sandhills. Each ranch, each family, has equally important tales to tell. But across this common stage, there are patterns that connect. Here, in the sand, are impressions of determination, joy, heartache, beauty, courage. These, and more, make up the seasons of the Sandhills.

Calving Season

A quick cup of coffee and it's time to head out to check again. The hills reflect a pink glow for a few minutes as the sun fully rises on this brisk morning. Following the familiar route in the calving pasture everything seems calm, with cows spread out grazing or laying down chewing their cud. Being sure to check the spots that cows often choose to calve (sometimes for reasons only known to the bovine mind) the age-old process is starting. The water bag is out, I back away to give her time and privacy.

After checking the rest of the pasture I wait on a small hill before revisiting the calving cow. The breeze starts to stir while the meadowlarks call out all around me. I tilt my ear toward the boom of the prairie-chickens I know are a few ranges over. I look the other way wondering about the sharp-tails . . . but movement catches my eye. A young muley buck is sidling up the opposite hill, on the trot. He freezes to look at me, broadside and beautiful. In an instant he's gone over the crest without a sound or second look. Time for me to go, too.

When I come over the small rise I see the sun glint off the wet newborn calf, wobblily raising his head from the flattened grass, while the cow turns in a circle to smell him. I notice one eye is surrounded by a patch of black on his otherwise white face, with a black body and a hint of white on his stomach. The cow senses me and sends a true mother dragon stare accompanied by a warning

Moving cattle on the Switzer Ranch in Loup County. Photograph by Michael Forsberg. Used with permission.

snort. "Good Mama," I whisper and once again back away. We'll come back later to make sure the newborn is up and able to nurse before ear tagging him and sorting them into an adjoining pasture with the other pairs of cows and newborn calves.

Every calving season has its ups and downs. With "spring" calving usually taking place anywhere between February and June, the metaphorical start of the rancher's fiscal year encompasses extreme highs and lows. From blizzards to pleasant warm days, weather is often the adversary or advantage.

Regardless of weather extremes, diligent round-the-clock care is given. The work only increases as the season wanes on, with more calves on the ground. Human patience and endurance are tested while toiling in a stark world that is just awakening from winter's stillness. As each calf drops to the ground to rise, hope does as well. Slowly, new life begins to emerge and resurrect. Internalizing those moments helps motivate goals and aspirations. But reality whispers; without a successful calving season, there will be fewer calves to sell in the months ahead. Less income against rising costs. No matter how strong the dream or pull of the lifestyle, ranching is a business like any other. If only perseverance could be bottled.

Returning to the corrals to do barn chores, I notice the tiny shoots of green poking out from last year's growth. We've had a lot of moisture the past couple of years, soaking deep into the hills, until being pushed back out through seeps and springs. It's hard to watch water go away. I wish I could hold onto it for the dry spell. Because it will be dry again someday. But now, the grass will have a good start to the growing season, which offers a promising year and one less worry.

Growing healthy calves on healthy grass. That's a good start.

Growing Season

The fledging life of spring blooms under the warm sun. Fawns follow close, butterflies graze, grass stretches up toward the sky. The ground moves with life. Ants and beetles frantically traverse the grainy particles, dodging the mounded excavations of pocket gophers. Working, strengthening for what's coming next. Above, up in the cottonwood, the eagles labor as well. Daily tending the huge nest that houses their own future. Life between these two spheres also finds ways to thrive amid the privations of a sandy country. Using this season to repair, revive, spread, and prepare. So do we.

The growing season is a season of hope, as long as it rains. Witnessing life taking its due course is thrilling in its glory and terrifying in its fragility. The best we can do is allow the hills to swell with life as they were intended, offering a helping hand when we can, patiently bearing any losses. The growing season always seems too short, but we're in it for the long haul.

When the summer pastures have grown enough to support grazing, we trail the newly branded baby calves with their mommas to the hills. After feeling closed in through winter and spring, it feels heavenly to ride out in the open. Greenup has come timely and is slowly overtaking the muted hues of last year's remaining growth. I breathe in the smell of soft, damp earth as it slowly warms underneath my horse's hard feet. The breeze rustles the puccoons on the hillsides, drawing my eye to the sharp yellow flowers. I've missed the colors of the growing season and am excited to greet all the prairie plants again in their brief turn.

Perhaps the unsung heroes of calving season are the mounts used to aid the rancher in this endeavor. Much more than a mode of transportation, ranch horses assist in nearly every facet of the day. Like all companions, they learn their partners and roles well. They aid in checking, sorting, and doctoring cattle and drag calves to the fire at branding time. Some even become quite the physical protectors of their riders, using their own bodies as shields if necessary. There are many memorable moments made during calving season, but the fondest ones usually involve a horse.

The cows and calves we're taking to summer pasture may not feel the same sentiments exactly as I do, but they are happy too. The old cows know what's up. They lead the way to fresh grass with a determined stride, snatching a mouthful of tender green along the way. The calves run and buck, relishing the chance to stretch their legs and bluff their bravado. The calf with the patch of black around his eye catches my attention before dashing ahead. Like his herd mates, he's slick and shiny with bright eyes. Everything is fresh and clean under a gentle May sun, full of promise and potential.

We arrive at the pasture these pairs will call home for the next months. As with the other pastures, the fence has been gone around and fixed in preparation. The windmills have been turned on and serviced to ensure water. A grazing plan has been made and modified to aid us in harnessing the natural process of grazing to forward our stewardship goals. Soon, the bulls will be turned out, beginning the cycle of life once again.

But all that fades to the background as I take another breath of sweet Sandhills air under a baby blue sky and revel in the simple pleasures of the day. We stop at the windmill and settle the herd. While mothers and babies reunite, we listen to the whine of the fan and soft clatter of the rods that draw water up from the ground. Slowly we sort off the pairs until we're sure every calf has found its momma. After seeing the calf with the circle of black around his eye a few more times, I start calling him Patch in my head. Not real original, but easy and fitting. We turn around to ride home in the dimming light. The evening brings a flash of coolness, making my shoulders tense. But I know it's only temporary, because tomorrow I'll feel the warmth of joy again as we go back to summer pasture.

We'll continue to check the pastures throughout the season, a chore that will need to be done a couple times a week, more if it's hot or the wind doesn't blow enough to keep water in the tanks. The growing season requires keen observation and monitoring. It offers the greatest potential of influence from management. Reading the cattle for health and the pastures for growth and grazing response takes a practiced eye and confidence in decision-making. Short-term adjustments contribute to long-term trends that the land will reflect. Balancing the best interests and needs of ourselves, the livestock, the wildlife, the prairie, and the future is a constant give-and-take that becomes embedded in our daily choices.

A ladybug finds sanctuary in a Rocky Mountain bee plant in Loup County. Photograph by Michael Forsberg. Used with permission.

June watches the puccoons give way to penstemon and larkspur, adding a touch of grace amid the needleand-thread grass. Dickcissels join the meadowlarks to serenade us as we rotate cattle through the pastures with grasshopper sparrows buzzing in the background. The calves take advantage of good eats and mother's milk, growing in frame, muscle, and attitude. The colts find their legs as well, flying down the soft hills, leaving their mothers trailing patiently behind. And the timely rains and warm sun promise that a nice hay crop is on its way.

The heat of mid- and late summer pushes the warm season grasses on the hilltops to thrive. The late afternoon clouds pass in front of the sun making a swift moving patchwork of shadows over the varying shades of green. Watching the patterns disappear across the hills reminds me time is fleeting and spurs us to work quickly to make hay while the sun shines. On the meadow, bobolinks sway with the tall grass at the edge of the hayfield while a harrier soars low over the adjacent hills. We push to make every day count, finishing in the light of a broad Sandhills sunset, knowing our fatigue has made a difference.

As the growing season tapers, the pressure of preparedness niggles into our conscience. Although the days are still sweat soaked, winter is beginning to whisper in our minds. There's much to be done to get ready. Harvesting the hay that will help feed the livestock is paramount. It won't be long before we bring the cattle home from summer pasture, making a whole new set of chores.

But there's still time. So for now, I count my blessings. Working with my family and kids every day is at the top of that list. Multiple generations, side by side, building upon a grounded and visible history. Providing a very real sense of place and purpose. Playing in the rodeo arena at night, finding reasons to laugh together every day, no matter the circumstances. Teaching each other to echo our surroundings by living brightly in our limited time.

Weaning season

Autumn is heavy. The air on a flushed fall day feels saturated above the still-warm sand. Seed heads droop with their bounty, shimmering across the hills. The undulating grass entices the wind to help spread the last of their lifeblood until the sowing is done and winter stills the ground again. The cows walk slowly out of summer pasture with burgeoning bellies, full of summer's richness, with calves at their side and new life growing inside. The colors on the animals turn strong and deep, perhaps in defiance of the upcoming gray months. The prairie stems shift to a brindle palette ranging from umber to crimson, mirroring the robust tones of the season's sunrises.

My signal that fall has arrived is when an ancient trill turns my eyes up to the sky. The sandhill cranes marching south again settles it. They lead the way to a warmer promise while our resident prairie-chickens and grouse flock up to stay put. Now winter is not just around the corner, it's on our doorstep, and it looks hungry.

If the growing season is a time of hope, weaning season is a time of optimistic uneasiness. Weaning the calves from their mothers is much more than physical separation. It's a harvest of our living product but more than just an animal. It's a reflection of the countless hours of care, years of planning, and improvement of the land and herd, our sweat and tears imprinted into each individual calf. A representation of what's come before us, our stubborn diligence and future hopes. But rarely do we solely determine what our hard-won product is worth. Like many facets of ranching, several variables out of our control will decide what our income is for the year.

Instead of focusing on the gambles involved, it's best to zero in on factors we can control. So we do our best to

Sarah Sortum and her family ride horseback in the evening on the Switzer Ranch in Loup County. Photograph by Mariah Lundgren, Platte Basin Timelapse. Used with permission.

help wean the year's calf crop in ways to reduce stress and optimize health, setting them up for success in preparation for their next step. The calf I call Patch is part of that process, learning how to navigate on his own. He reminds me of a teenager: portraying a tough guy image but missing momma underneath. Blowing snot at me to impress but a little scared of all the new changes. I chuckle at his antics and tell him we'll help him through.

The weaned calves can be marketed in a variety of ways. Whether via private treaty or public auction, seeing the calves leave the ranch is often bittersweet. A strange mix of emotion stirs. From pride of product, loss of animals you enjoy and care about, nerves regarding selling price to gratefulness for the necessary business income. But focus is soon returned by looking forward. A snapshot of the future is "preg checking" the cows. Finding out how

many cows will be producing a calf next spring is another pivotal day that has the power to determine fiscal success or struggle for another year.

We prepare for winter by buttoning up the growing season. Bulls have already been pulled from the herd, windmills will need to be shut off, and hay still needs to be hauled. Cattle are brought into pastures a little closer to the home place where they can be taken care of easier if the weather turns bad. We lay the groundwork for cold weather, thankful for every pleasant day of fall.

Winter

This is where the bluff is called. Winter weeds out the weak, promising rest only for the well-prepared while demanding patience and fortitude. It forces us to acknowledge our own strengths and limitations, hopefully enabling us to accept ourselves in the grander scheme of Time. Unyielding as cold leather, it's a time of waiting and persevering. But also a time for planning what the next year can be.

Patch, the now almost-yearling, is part of a group of calves that were not sold in the fall but retained to sell later. His winter hair has come in thick and a bit shaggy with a healthy sheen, protecting him from the elements. Even so, I marvel at how well he does, along with all of the animals in this now hard and unforgiving environment. Their capability to do well in the extremes of our climate, recycle nutrients from the land that are otherwise mostly unusable, and turn that into a benefit for themselves and us is an often-overlooked wonder. But all Patch is concerned with is what the tractor is bringing him today as he (somewhat un-athletically, I must admit) runs and kicks up in an exuberant celebration of feeding time.

I've never heard winter referred to as the feeding season, but that pretty much sums it up. The once strengthening grass has become dormant, losing its nutrition. While still valuable forage, some type of protein supplement helps keep the ranch livestock in optimal health. Of course, if the grass becomes covered up in white, hay will need to be fed to meet their needs as well.

Heading out to "cake the cows," feeding them protein cubes on pasture, is an enjoyable chore. The cows are eagerly summoned by the honk of the horn or whine of the siren to gather for the beneficial treat. It's a good time to play with the tamest or bravest of bovines, feeding the cubes by hand while waiting for the laggers to amble out of the hills. That time can also serve as a moment of private reflection and future planning. Something about being alone in the hills encourages an inward conversation. The sand seems to offer a soaking up of cares when you need it.

As enjoyable as caking can be, I have the opposite sentiments for breaking ice. Yet the cattle need to drink, so it's a necessary evil. To be fair, there is something quite satisfying about swinging an axe into a solid chunk of ice to have it break clean. But after the ice is broken, the chunks need to be lifted with a pitchfork and thrown clear. After the third or fourth tank my cold fingers swell up like pickles, struggling to bend around the axe and pitchfork, while my weak back complains. Working on a large tank causes me to sweat under my many layers of clothing. This does not help as I travel to the next stop, muttering scathing remarks to the frigid wind that snakes under my collar.

But discomfort helps punctuate the pleasures. Finding a place out of the wind, warm toes, and the restorative power of a hot meal are among the blessings craved and relished. And while winter can be harsh in the hills, it still shows moments of startling beauty to lift our spirits. I'm reminded there is a time and season for everything when I see the swans gliding through the foggy air or when the stars loom crisp and bright over a snow-covered night. The morning frost climbs up the stiff stems of the grass, encasing each detail in white, waiting for the sun. The rays encourage the sleeping stalks to sparkle in eye-squinting brilliance, reminding us our treasure is where our heart is, leading us on to another day. After all, spring is just around the corner.

Final Musings

Ranching through the seasons always involves risks and rewards. But whatever the gain or loss, there is appreciation. The lifestyle offers a physicality, independence, and immersion in the natural world that a certain type thrives on. I see evidence of this in the old ranchers in the Sandhills, and there are many. Their bodies have broken down over the years as they gave themselves to their work, to the land. They're entering their final season of life here. A place where, as men and women, they could create and be themselves. That trueness to self sounds so simple but remains elusive to many. Here they have kept going, kept trying. Planned for the worst. Hoped for the best. Usually without thought to the world's judgment but with their own harsh determination of self and sacrifice. Putting the best interests of the land before themselves. But every old rancher starts young, and thankfully, the Sandhills also holds present and future stewards that respect the traditions of the Sandhills while breathing new life into their management.

In my own process of becoming an old rancher (for I cannot think of a better thing to be), my feet often lead me to the respite and beauty of the creek at the end of the day. No matter the season, the prairie stream seeps and bubbles vitality from the ground that reinvigorates land, man, and beast. The clear water is lively inside the quiet banks and draws my eye to the bottom. The soft ridges of sand on the creek bed mimic the shapes

of the hills around me. The elemental force is different, but the results are similar. Nature repeating itself, just like the seasons from year to year and the souls who live through them. Grand rhythms of complexity and detail that coalesce into what we simply call life. It makes me feel quite small yet flooded with gratitude because I've been afforded the chance to experience this shared journey. It can be challenging, but there's solace in knowing this land always holds to the truth amid an uncertain world. It can belittle you into acknowledgment of a higher order but also offers a gentle raising up. Not on firm ground, mind you. Just a sandy firmament that reminds you a slip is only a prideful moment away. Tread with care, respect, and tireless devotion; it may just hold you up.

Sarah Sortum is a fourth-generation member of a family of that operates the Switzer Ranch in Loup County, Nebraska.

Trumpeter swans fly low over the Calamus Reservoir in Loup County at dawn on a winter's day.
Photograph by Michael Forsberg. Used with permission.

Leopold Conservation Award Winners

Douglas A. Norby

The ranchers who manage the nearly 20,000 square miles of grass-covered dunes that are home to some five hundred thousand cattle have a special knowledge of the Nebraska Sandhills. Like the Indigenous people who occupied the area before them, the most successful ranchers have respect for the land and its ecosystems. This respectful land ethic is a hallmark of the Sand County Foundation. Based in Madison, Wisconsin, the foundation honors Aldo Leopold, considered the father of wildlife ecology and the United States' wilderness system. Leopold's famous 1949 work, *A Sand County Almanac*, is a landmark in the American conservation movement. He believed contact with the natural world shapes our ability to extend our ethics beyond self-interest to include care for waters, soils, animals, and plants. Leopold believed humans have a moral responsibility to the natural world, and that the future of American wildlife lay largely in the attitudes and decisions of American farmers and landowners on private lands.

In 2003 the foundation created the Leopold Conservation Awards to honor those dedicated to the land ethic and to inspire others to adopt similar conservation stewardship practices. Criteria include conservation ethic, resilience, leadership and communication, innovation and adaptability, and ecological community.

Eight Sandhills ranches, along with eight other Nebraska farms and ranches, have been honored with the Leopold Award since 2006. Sandhills ranchers have been recognized for practices that maintain the integrity of the land for cattle and using conservation tactics like prescribed burns and rotational grazing to ensure the future of their ranches.

2006: Wilson Ranch

The fifteen-thousand-acre Wilson Ranch, located northeast of Lakeside, is owned by fifth-generation ranchers and brothers Blaine and Brian Wilson. The Wilsons' development of a "wildlife pasture" strictly for habitat protection included a drip system and windbreaks. They also created a wetland area that has attracted several species of birds back to the area.

2008: Four Bar O Ranches

Run by the Cox family for more than a century, the Four Bar O ranch is operated by A.B. Cox and his daughter Scout. Using rotational grazing over their twenty-three thousand acres reduces the need to harvest hay for feed. When they do harvest, they mow in a unique mosaic pattern that provides habitat for wildlife. Cox also is dedicated to helping educate others about the importance of maintaining the land; he has been involved with conservation groups and community outreach programs, hosting workshops, clinics, and tours.

2012: Shovel Dot Ranch

The Shovel Dot Ranch in Bassett was founded by Benjamin Franklin Buell in 1882. On a move from

Raindrop collects on a barbed wire fence in Grant County. Photograph by Michael Forsberg. Used by permission.

Michigan to Washington State, Benjamin fell in love with the Sandhills and settled there. The ranch is run by his great-grandchildren Larry and Homer, and their wives Nickie and Darla.

While adopting common conservation techniques, such as fencing for effective cattle distribution and installing 50 miles of water pipeline, the Buell family also has developed several human-made lakes on their property that are fenced to ensure habitat for deer, turkey, swans, ducks, and geese. Two creeks provide diverse natural habitat for many other types of wildlife. The Buells provide tours to visitors from all over the world and are active in many community groups.

2013: Beel Ranch

Henry C. Beel bought the twenty-two-thousand-acre ranch near Johnstown in 1937 and seven years later began filing conservation plans. Today the ranch is run by his grandchildren: brothers Frank, Henry, and Adam, and their wives Jennifer, Mary, and Jenny.

The Beels expanded their conservation efforts by increasing their water supply to ensure plentiful water for their rotational grazing system and provide habitat for wildlife. They have designed and coordinated the installation of 32 miles of pipeline, with eighty-nine hydrants, six wells, and forty-five new tanks to go along with the existing sixty-seven windmills.

2014: Pelster Ranch

The Pelster Ranch near Ericson is known as one of the early developers of rotational grazing. Its original owner, the late Duane Pelster, said his guiding principle was "Be good to the land, and the land will be good to you."

The rotational grazing that Pelster implemented enables plants to thrive, even during extended drought. Cedar and weed control have led to healthier grass and in-creased wildlife, including prairie-chickens, deer, ducks, geese, and even a family of otters living in a pond on the land. The ranch also uses limited sustainable hunting to keep the deer population in check.

2016: Plum Thicket Farm

Plum Thicket Farm, located near Gordon, is a diverse crop farm and cattle ranch owned by Rex and Dr. Nancy Peterson, their son Patrick and his wife, Krista. When they purchased the property in 1998, they knew their twenty-three hundred acres were vulnerable to drought and blizzards, so they adopted no till practices to improve water retention and reduce erosion. The Petersons rotate their corn, pinto beans, field peas, and wheat crops to improve soil quality, provide better grazing for cattle, and create natural habitat for pollinators. Moving their calving season to May and letting the cattle feed on cereal rye enables cattle to graze sorghum in the winter and saves the labor of baling it.

2019: Broken Box Ranch

Using prescribed burning techniques, Russ Sundstrom, his wife, Angela, daughter Cheyenne, and his brother Neil, have helped their land in the Loess Canyons flourish. The Sundstroms have brought the hilly landscape back to health through rotational grazing, making the ranch productive for cattle, and giving 250 different species of birds a home. Russ has cleared hundreds of acres of invasive cedar trees and uses aggressive grazing methods to clear other unwanted vegetation.

The Sundstroms are active in the community, and the Broken Box Ranch was accepted as a Rangeland Health Demonstration Ranch in 2019. Russ collects data and monitors different conservation and management methods and their impact on the land and wildlife. The ranch is also enrolled in the Nebraska Game and Parks Commission Open Fields and Waters Program, which allows public hunting on the ranch to help manage turkey, deer, quail, and elk, while also offering protection to endangered species.

2021: Switzer Ranch

Fourth-generation ranchers and siblings Adam Switzer and Sarah Sortum of the Switzer Ranch run a cow-calf operation on their twelve thousand acres and began to move toward biodiversity goals in 2009. Part of this change was developing Calamus Outfitters, providing customers with river float trips, eco-tours, and lodging and event space.

The business not only ensures that the ranch will stay in the family, but it has brought attention to the little-known prairie grouse and its dwindling habitat. "At the time we didn't realize the plight that grassland birds were in," Sortum recalled upon receiving the award. "If this is their last stronghold, we have got to step up and make sure we provide what they need to survive."

Using conservation methods, such as prescribed burning and conservation, the Switzer Ranch has provided a habitat where the birds can thrive. The ranch hosts guided tours of the birds' habitat and a yearly prairie-chicken fest.

Douglas A. Norby is an editorial assistant for *The Nebraska Sandhills*.

LEOPOLD CONSERVATION AWARD®

PRESENTED BY SAND COUNTY FOUNDATION

Irrigation in the Sandhills

Jerry Volesky

The Nebraska Sandhills is well known as extensive native grasslands, but the abundance of groundwater in the underlying aquifer and development of center pivot irrigation systems led to interest in the potential for crop production in the Sandhills. The expansion of center pivot use was substantial during the 1960s and 1970s and included irrigation development in the Sandhills. Currently, there are about 331,000 acres that are irrigated within the geographic area of the Sandhills. Whereas every Sandhills county has at least some irrigated acres, most of these acres are in the peripheral areas of the Sandhills, where land is more level, and the soils are somewhat less erosive. This includes significant portions of Holt, Wheeler, Brown, Rock, and Antelope Counties. Center pivot irrigation also can be found in scattered locations within interior Sandhills counties, such as Grant, Hooker, Thomas, Blaine, Arthur, and McPherson, with anywhere from two thousand to thirteen thousand irrigated acres.

In the 1970s, faculty from the University of Nebraska–Lincoln West Central Research and Extension Center in North Platte conducted research at a facility called the Sandhills Agricultural Laboratory, located near Tryon. This research focused on several aspects of corn and grain sorghum production, including irrigation and nutrient management, variety testing, and cropping systems for sandy soils. Another important area of research at this facility concerned irrigated perennial grasses and provided a basis for recommendations pertaining to selection of species and variety, fertilizer, irrigation, and grazing management.

Whereas corn and soybeans are the primary crops grown on the more contiguous irrigated acres of the eastern or peripheral Sandhills areas, alfalfa, perennial cool-season grasses, and annual forages are more common on the scattered center pivot acres located elsewhere within the Sandhills. These scattered center pivot acres can be a valuable resource for forage production, particularly if a ranch does not have any, or limited, subirrigated meadow acres. Additionally, the irrigated forage production provides a means to reduce some of the negative impacts associated with drought.

With annual forage production under irrigation, a double-cropping approach is typically used. This often includes seeding a cool-season species, such as rye or triticale, in early fall. The following spring (May or early June) that crop can be grazed or harvested for hay. Immediately following that harvest, a warm-season annual species, such as Sudan grass, forage sorghum, sorghum–Sudan grass hybrids, pearl millet, or foxtail millet is planted. This warm-season forage crop is grazed or harvested in mid- to late summer. The sequence is repeated, with the planting of the cool-season annual again in the fall. Instead of the winter-hardy rye or triticale, spring-planted oats can be another cool-season option. Although the oat growing period is typically not finished until later June, there is still adequate time for growing a warm-season annual forage crop. Total production for both the cool- and warm-season forage crops can range from seven to ten tons per acre.

Center pivot irrigation in the Nebraska Sandhills using water conserving technologies. Copyright Valmont Industries, Inc. Used with permission.

Alfalfa or cool-season perennial grass production on irrigated acres is another viable option that can benefit a ranching operation. Alfalfa alone, or as the dominant part in a mixture with grass, will provide a high-protein hay source. The use of introduced cool-season perennial grasses is generally favored over warm-season grasses (e.g., big bluestem, switchgrass, Indian grass), because of their greater response to irrigation, fertilizer, and longer growing season potential. A mixture of several species is most often used in these irrigated stands. There are numerous species available, but mixtures that include orchard grass, smooth bromegrass, meadow bromegrass, creeping foxtail, or intermediate wheatgrasses have been found to be well adapted for use on sandy soils and in the Sandhills climate. Adding a legume, such as alfalfa or clover, to the mixture is a common practice.

Similar to a subirrigated meadow, many producers like the flexibility of irrigated cool-season grasses, where they have the option of either grazing or haying or using a combination of haying and grazing on that forage resource. Whereas subirrigated meadows are generally hayed once in midsummer and have some regrowth for fall or winter grazing, irrigated cool-season grasses can be harvested anywhere from two to four times depending on the fertilizer and irrigation management. The cool-season grasses complement the warm-season dominated native Sandhills range, allowing grazing to take place earlier in the spring before native range is ready. There are several grazing and haying combination strategies that can be used, including spring grazing, a summer haying, and then grazing again in fall; or two or three hay harvests and then fall grazing. When strictly hayed, production potential from the irrigated grasses might range from four to seven tons per acre totaled over multiple harvests. When strictly grazed, carrying capacity may be in the range of five to eight animal unit months (AUM) per acre. Management should include some form of rotational grazing that allows for multiple grazing cycles, with the proper time periods for grazing and grass regrowth.

Jerry Volesky is a range and forage specialist, Nebraska Extension specialist, and interim director of the Center for Grassland Studies at the University of Nebraska–Lincoln.

Rotational Grazing and Sustainable Grasslands

Jim Jenkins

Cattle grazing, Grant County. Photograph by Michael Forsberg. Used with permission.

Beef cattle, and the ranchers who manage them, play a crucial role in maintaining the health of the Sandhills' fragile grassland ecosystem. This grassland includes more than seven hundred plant species and grazing animals such as cattle, deer, elk, bison, goats, and sheep; these plants and animals have evolved together for eons. The Nebraska Sandhills is a largely unadulterated landscape; its miles of windswept grass hills and low-lying meadows contain more cattle (500,000) than humans (23,776 in 2020). With more than eight billion people upon the planet, this relatively untouched landscape is unusual.

Much of our food is raised in a closed-loop monoculture, but Sandhills cattle live on and are key contributors to the rich and diverse prairie landscape they graze. Cattle dung fertilizes the soil and feeds insects and the millions of microbes that live in the sandy soil. Through manure, cattle spread seeds across the prairie landscape, enhancing the longevity of the diverse plant species. Cattle movement and hoof action enhance the nutrient cycle by breaking down plant organic matter so it is more easily integrated into the soil. This same hoof action creates space for raindrops to pool and absorb into the soil instead of running off. Even the biting action of ungulates stimulates plant growth, improving plant health. Grazing also prevents the succession of less desirable woody species, which can fragment grasslands, causing a decline in both flora and fauna.

The miracle cow produces food and milk by consuming forages that are indigestible by humans, while at the same time providing environmental benefits to grassland landscapes. Grazing animals not only contribute food to our world but, when properly managed, contribute to the overall health of the planet, because grasslands make up nearly one-third of the planet's land mass, and properly managed grazing animals equals healthy grasslands, which act as a large-scale carbon sink.

Grasslands comprise about half of Nebraska's agricultural land and are the foundation for one of the most productive beef economies found anywhere in the world. This beef economy is built in large measure upon Sandhills grass owned by private landowners, as there is little public land ownership in Nebraska. Preservation of the Sandhills biome relies almost exclusively on the stewardship of individual ranch families. Essentially, the rancher is in the business of converting grass to beef and therefore has an economic incentive to take care of both the grass and the cattle. A Sandhills cow and her calf live almost exclusively on native forages raised on the ranch, as large-scale mono-cropping is not possible on the sandy and fragile soils found in this area.

The Nebraska Sandhills went through a severe alteration in the 1800s as Native Americans and bison and other wildlife were eliminated from the plains. For nearly forty years, from 1860 to 1900, the Sandhills region of Nebraska was an empty expanse. Reports from that era indicate that without grazing pressure, the Sandhills grasslands began to deteriorate. European settlers viewed the region as largely uninhabitable. By the mid- to late 1860s, railroads reached across the country connecting the new settlements with the growing populations on the East and West Coasts. With the growing demand for protein, cattle operators began to procure wild cattle, principally from Texas, and drive them north to the railroads in Nebraska and Kansas. At some point, cattle from points south were further fattened on the open range of central and western Nebraska. Ranchers began to notice that their cattle did well on Sandhills grass and could even overwinter in the Sandhills.

The passage of the Kinkaid Act in 1904, which provided 640 acres of free land to ranchers willing to settle the less-productive western rangelands, started the settlement of the Sandhills region.

The ecology of the Sandhills dictates that its agricultural economy be built on beef cattle and the grass on which they live. Cropping systems are not a viable option on most Sandhills soils. Forage grows in upland pastures made up of rolling grass-covered dunes and low-lying wetlands with water percolating up from the aquifer, which often lies just a few feet below the ground's surface. In the summer the cattle graze on the upland pastures, and much of the winter feed is harvested from subirrigated meadows.

Beef cattle in Nebraska live principally on grass, stored local forage, and crop residues. According to United Nations data, 86 percent of cattle diets around the world consist of forages and residue that could not otherwise be used by humans.

In Nebraska, calves live at their mothers' sides for six to eight months, until they weigh 450 to 650 pounds, and then are weaned. Some of the heifer (female) calves are retained for breeding, while the balance of the heifer and steer (castrated male) calves move into the backgrounding or stocker phase. Weaned calves gain another 300 to 400 pounds eating principally grass and stored forages, prior to going into feeding pens for the finishing phase. The finishing phase usually takes place in confined feeding pens where cattle eat a diet high in protein and fat for approximately 150 days to bring them to their slaughter weight of 1,300 to 1,500 pounds.

Because grass plays such a critical role in underpinning the first two phases of Nebraska's beef industry, there is plenty of incentive for cattle ranchers and other stakeholders to improve stewardship of the state's grasslands.

Scientists affiliated with the University of Nebraska's Center for Grassland Studies conduct interdisciplinary research, education, and service programs focused on managing livestock and wildlife on Nebraska grasslands.

Since 1998 the center, along with the Nebraska Grazing Lands Coalition, hosts the Nebraska Grazing Conference, a two-day event that serves to educate graziers on the best practices of range management. The university also operates several large-scale research ranches that document the efficacy of different grazing practices. Nebraska Extension hosts numerous workshops and pasture tours designed to assist ranchers in more effectively and sustainably using their grass and forage resources.

A growing number of ranches have implemented advanced practices that rotate cattle through a number of pastures during the grazing season in an attempt to approximate the patterns of large bison herds. The idea is to allow the grass to rest for a period ranging from thirty days to as much as a year, depending upon rainfall and pasture conditions. While there are significant capital costs in the fence and water infrastructure for dividing pastures, ranchers can generally run more cattle per acre by rotating them, while simultaneously improving pasture quality. Prior to the growing season, ranchers put together a plan based on last year's grazing rotation, stocking rates, type and size of animals, and other variables such as soil moisture and weather forecasts. This plan likely goes through a number of iterations as the growing season progresses.

In addition to improving grass management, ranchers, veterinarians, nutritionists, and university researchers have made great strides in developing more productive cattle. Since 1980 the beef cattle herd size has dropped from 132 million cattle head to just over 90 million head. In that time, genetic and herd management protocols have increased the carcass weight by 30 percent, enabling the industry to produce 15 percent more beef with 40 percent fewer cattle. The result of these efforts is a cow herd with the lowest carbon footprint of any cow herd in the world.

As planet Earth exceeds a population of eight billion people, Sandhills ranchers and their cattle herds are leaders in producing high-quality animal protein on one of the most beautiful, largely intact grass-scapes anywhere in the world.

Jim Jenkins is the operating partner for his family's diversified farming, ranching, and cattle-feeding operation near Callaway, Nebraska.

Sandhills landscape featuring small soapweed at Samuel R. McKelvie National Forest, Cherry County.

FUTURE
OF THE
SANDHILL

S

Sunrise at Walgren Lake State Recreation Area, Sheridan County.

Sandhills Task Force

Shelly Kelly

Local ranchers donate panels for penning horses at the 4-H Trail Ride in Halsey. The ranchers also donate Nebraska-certified weed-free hay, which is legally required in the Nebraska National Forest to prevent the introduction of invasive plants.

The Nebraska Sandhills Task Force was formed to apply Sandhills residents' valued virtue of "being a good neighbor" to the conservation world. In the late 1980s and early 1990s, contention and distrust grew between private landowners and the federal government. New wetland protection legislation, passed and implemented by the federal government, placed restrictions on what could be done on private land. Rumors grew that the federal government was trying to buy more land, and the "Cattle Free by '93" sentiment, an idea to remove cattle from large swaths of land in the West, fed private landowners' distrust.

Concurrently, holistic resource management, where ranchers work to improve all facets of their resources, not just their income, was gaining traction; many respected ranchers were attending classes to learn more. Ranchers became more curious about learning ways to improve their stewardship. Some ranchers thought conservation agencies were trying to steal their land or at least place restrictions on them that could cause hardship. Some conservation agency folks thought ranchers intentionally harmed their land or wildlife.

Eventually, some forward-thinking ranchers and conservationists agreed to sit down and have face-to-face conversations about their differences. They found many of their goals and ideas were nearly the same or at least complementary, and very few of their ideas were actually in conflict. The group decided they would be better off if they could work together to find ways to promote private, profitable ranching and conservation of the Sandhills.

The Longhorn Cattle Drive from Fort Niobrara National Wildlife Refuge to Fort Robinson State Park travels through the snowy streets of Valentine in November 2000.

Thus, the Sandhills Task Force was formed in 1993. It is a nonprofit 501(c)3 organization led by a sixteen-member board of directors in which at least nine of the members make their primary livelihood from ranching. The remaining directors represent conservation and government organizations. The overarching theme of the task force is that all groups find a way to work together to enhance the Sandhills' wetland-grassland ecosystem to sustain private, profitable ranching, wildlife and vegetative diversity, and the associated water supplies. The task force's structure, with the board weighted toward working ranchers, lends credibility and assures ranchers that conservation agencies won't have all the power.

Ranchers are the original conservationists as they depend upon a healthy ecosystem to raise a profitable cattle herd. Ranch families make a considerable investment in the land, with hopes that their investment will pay off when they sell their calves. Generally, the only income generated by the land is through cattle ranching, and the cattle do best when the land is in excellent condition; ranching and conservation go hand in hand.

The Sandhills Task Force has helped build partnerships in the conservation community and ensures ranchers' voices are heard when new programs or policies emerge that may impact private lands. The group has also raised funds to help landowners implement conservation practices that not only improve the ecosystem as a whole but also help to ensure that ranches will thrive in the future. All conservation projects are holistically planned to have the widest possible benefits.

The most common ranch improvement practices taken on by the task force include controlling invasive eastern redcedar (*Juniperus virginiana*) and other invasive woody species, adding infrastructure to improve grazing systems, repairing or restoring wetlands and streams, and renovating the shallow Sandhills lakes to remove invasive carp. These projects are completed on private lands with willing landowners and typically in conjunction with two to four additional funding partners. Project design includes the landowner and all partners to ensure it is improving the ecosystem in the desired way. Bids are sought, and when the cost is determined, an agreement is written and reviewed by all parties. Once the practice is completed, everyone reviews it to make sure it meets their expectations. The paperwork is minimal, so the focus can be on building a solid relationship with the landowner, which greatly improves the quality of the conservation projects.

Having a grassroots, rancher-led nonprofit in the Sandhills has improved the natural resources and the ranching community by building trust and maintaining transparency through all its efforts. The task force has been able to bring considerable money to the Sandhills region to improve the ecosystem upon which ranchers, wildlife, birds, and neighboring communities all depend. From 2016 to 2020, the task force spent $3,019,000 in cost-share on conservation projects covering 207,600 acres. Those funds were leveraged, so for every dollar the Sandhills Task Force spent, an additional $3 was contributed by other partners. That means improvements neared $1 billion in a five-year period.

Invasive narrow-leaved cattails ignite under the heat of a controlled burn in a Sandhills grassland. Burns help to reduce encroachment of nondesirable vegetation and provide space and nutrients for native plants to flourish. Photograph by Dakota Altman, Platte Basin Timelapse. Used with permission.

Smoke rises as a controlled burn moves across a Sandhills grassland. Two people on the burn crew keep a close eye on the fire line. Photograph by Dakota Altman, Platte Basin Timelapse. Used with permission.

In 2020 the task force hired two new employees and in 2021 launched a new program, the Sandhills Stewards, designed to help ranchers improve business practices.

As we look to the future, the task force maintains partnerships with conservation organizations and agencies and is seeking to build new partnerships with organizations having interests in the Sandhills. Efforts focused on education are an important part of outreach. These include workshops and ranch tours held throughout the year, where information is shared between fellow ranchers and professionals and the communities. To teach the coming generations about rangeland management and progressive ranching practices, the task force has participated in the Nebraska Youth Range Camp, which predates the task force by twenty years. The five-day camp attracts high school students from across the state, who experience hands-on learning and activities and meet like-minded peers.

The Sandhills of Nebraska is a special place, full of unique and determined people who enjoy and respect the rolling native prairie, the solitude, and the creatures that call it home. Groups like the Sandhills Task Force are dedicated to maintaining the grassland-wetland ecosystem and the ranching way of life.

Shelly Kelly is executive director of the Sandhills Task Force in Broken Bow, Nebraska.

Eastern Redcedar

Shelly Kelly

Eastern redcedar is arguably the biggest threat to the native Sandhills grassland. Cattle do not eat cedars, grass doesn't grow under cedars, and cedars grow and spread quickly in a pasture. At one time, intense wildfires regularly occurred, either sparked by lightning or set by Native Americans; the highly flammable cedar trees were killed on the open prairie. As the Sandhills were settled by Europeans and equipment improved, wildfire suppression enabled cedars to spread. Additionally, cedars were planted throughout the region as windbreaks and for "wildlife habitat." However, we now know that cedars do far more damage to wildlife habitat than the small benefit they provide.

As a result of the suppression of wildfire and the increased seed source present from cedar plantings, grassland acres are being taken over by invasive cedar. This is an awful scenario for a rancher. With education and financial assistance provided by the Sandhills Task Force and its partners, ranchers are learning how to control cedar through cutting and burning. Pasture is cleared by mechanical means, with a follow-up treatment of a prescribed burn two to three years after the mechanical treatment to control the seedlings that come back after the disturbance.

The net result is that cattle will have more grass to graze, the grassland birds will have the tree-free habitat they need, and the entire ecosystem will thrive with a diversity of plants, insects, and wildlife. This is a win-win-win outcome.

Economy, Ranching, and Ecotourism in the Sandhills

Richard K. Edwards and Katie Nieland

The central question for the future of the Sandhills is this: How can the region develop an economy that helps its residents thrive while preserving its unique grassland environment? The Sandhills comprise about 25 percent of the land area of Nebraska, but its residents constitute only 1.2 percent of Nebraska's population and generate about 1.4 percent of the state's gross domestic product. Our answer to the question of the Sandhills' future is that its residents should build an economy powered by two primary export industries, ranching and ecotourism, supported by the numerous secondary industries that assist them and sustain the region's residents.

The Sandhills are widely acknowledged to be a special and precious place. But the very attributes that make it unique and treasured—its remoteness, its fragile ecology, its low population density, its lack of a dense

The Longhorn Cattle Drive from Fort Niobrara National Wildlife Refuge to Fort Robinson State Historical Park in November 2000.

built infrastructure—make it problematical for attracting industries that employ large numbers of workers, need easy transportation in and out, and have other typical industrial requirements. Ranching and ecotourism build upon the Sandhills' special character, turning its attributes into strengths, rather than attempting to remedy perceived deficits.

Ranching

Ranching has been the region's dominant economic activity since Euro-American settlement began in the nineteenth century. Most common is raising cattle, but there was significant sheep ranching and raising of horses between 1900 and 1930, and since about 2000, bison ranching has been added. The region has seen only minimal farming; in Cherry County, for example, less than 2 percent of the land is used for row crops, virtually all of it irrigated.

Ranching—whether cattle, bison, or something else—is recommended because of its historical and heritage roots, its present economic vitality, and its crucial role in sustaining the grassland. Range scientists tell us that the grasslands evolved with major ungulates and that maintaining a healthy grassland requires grazing. Current owners of most land in the Sandhills are thus simultaneously ranchers and environmental stewards, and both by their own history and current preferences wish to continue. Their deep knowledge of and care for the land is one of the Sandhills' greatest resources, and their future involvement will be essential for preserving the Sandhills.

Cattle production is vulnerable to a boom-and-bust cycle, and new factors, such as climate change and shifting consumer preferences, may force significant adaptations in traditional cattle ranching. Many producers respond to these forces by seeking ever-lower-cost production methods, but some are exploring more high-profit and

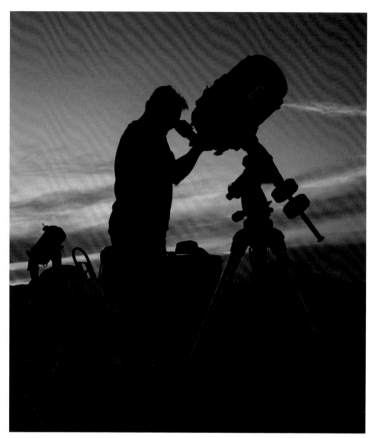

A Celestron 11-inch high-definition telescope is used to observe the night sky during a Nebraska Star Party at Merritt Reservoir State Recreation Area

environmentally supportive production. Such production may involve niche grazers, such as high-end (e.g., wagyu) and grass-fed cattle, bison, other grazers for specialty markets, and more direct rancher-to-consumer sales.

Ranching, like all occupations, can be done well—that is, sustainably, based on long-term vision—or poorly, with insufficient care for the consequences of short-term, careless, and destructive techniques. Fortunately, many area ranchers have a growing interest in grazing innovations that support grassland health and even devote special attention to preserving wildlife habitat.

Ecotourism

Ecotourism—travel that deepens the visitor's engagement with nature, conserves the environment, and improves the

Canoers on the Calamus River.

well-being of local communities—offers landowners the opportunity to gain a second revenue source (after grazing) that is compatible with ranching and profits from the ranchers' biggest existing asset, their land. In effect, it creates a second "crop" each year on the same land.

Ecotourism in the Sandhills is a promising business opportunity because of the region's incredible natural endowment. Hiking to the top of a grassy dune in the heart of the Sandhills to see rolling hills stretching out for miles instills a sense of awe. Catching a glimpse of a pronghorn, taking in the dark night sky, or watching a prairie-chicken dance shows us a landscape that is alive and vital. The region provides critical habitat to some two-hundred-plus species of birds. Jane Goodall,

a frequent visitor to see the sandhill crane migration, calls it "one of the seven wonders of the natural world." The Sandhills are filled with biodiversity, crucial habitats, and exceptional opportunities for visitors to have fun while deeply engaging with nature.

Tourists travel for many reasons, and even before the founding of national parks, people traveled to the Sandhills to immerse themselves in its nature. Today, many of us lead most of our lives indoors, yet somewhere deep in our psyches we know that being outside in the open air brings many benefits—physical, mental, and spiritual. And as concern for the health of our planet increases, people often want their travel to have deeper ecological meaning. Ecotourism is today's version of following John Muir into the High Sierra or John Wesley Powell down the Colorado River. But unlike Muir or Powell, most of us come from walks of life where we cannot devote months and years to nature. Ecotourism offers a way into their world.

How ecotourism promotes conservation is simple but sometimes overlooked: If ranchers and other landowners want to attract ecotourists, they must provide protected habitat and sufficient wildlife to create memorable environmental experiences. Ecotourists arrive and spend money for access, lodging, food, guides, tours, and other services offered by landowners and others in the nearby communities. And the cycle is completed when ranchers

and landowners see they have an economic incentive and reap an economic reward for maintaining habitat and protecting the wildlife that attracted the ecotourists.

We can already see the growth of this nascent industry throughout the Sandhills. On the region's southern edge, the annual sandhill crane migration demonstrates what is possible. Upon reaching Kearney, visitors are greeted by a sign reading "Sandhill Crane Capital of the World." Kearney and the nearby communities of Gibbon and Wood River have constructed viewing sites, hospitality facilities, and support services, which accommodate the crowds streaming in from across the country.

Hereford cattle at Bowring Ranch State Historical Park, Cherry County.

A bit farther to the north, deeper into the Sandhills, Calamus Outfitters is a great example in showing how cattle and ecotourism work together to sustain multiple generations on the Switzer Ranch. The family business offers engaging educational tours of the landscape, often centered on the springtime mating dance of the prairie-chickens and sharp-tailed grouse. At the same time, visitors get to see and learn about the cattle operation and relax on the beautiful landscape.

In another example, the annual Nebraska Star Party gathers hundreds of amateur astronomers in the Sandhills. They take advantage of some of the darkest night skies in the country to gain a clearer view of stars, planets, and the Milky Way. The local community takes steps to ensure light pollution is minimized to keep these groups coming back. The vast landscape is accompanied by a dazzling night sky.

Ecotourism operations draw upon a wide range of ancillary services, creating a "multiplier effect" of business opportunities. We have already seen Valentine, Chadron, Alliance, and other towns develop hotels, restaurants, guiding services, booking agencies, catering firms, bus and other transport companies, and additional enterprises to serve the growing trade. These businesses create local jobs.

For Sandhills residents to thrive, ecotourism and other nature-dependent activities must aim to provide high-quality, transformative environmental experiences rather than just a low-cost place to recreate. It does little to promote regional prosperity (nor does it typically enhance environmental awareness) when travelers gas up their vehicles in Denver or Omaha, bring food and supplies with them, and spend few dollars in the area. Visitors who arrive from afar, whether from California, Chicago, or Frankfurt, tend to stay the longest and spend the most money. Just as in ranching, where the most innovative operations are

Ice fishing at Pelican Lake on the Valentine National Wildlife Refuge, Cherry County.

moving toward high-value-added activities rather than lowest cost commodity production, so too in ecotourism, the better strategy is to provide visitors with memorable, even life-changing experiences, for which they are happy to pay a premium price.

Other Nature-Based or Nature-Related Industries

Ecotourism is not the only way the region's residents can take advantage of its unique nature resources, and we see business and employment growth in related pursuits as well. While not necessarily as environmentally sup-

portive as ecotourism, these activities when developed responsibly can also be consistent with a long-term, sustainable vision for the region.

Some of these related activities add further attractions for visitors, enhancing the Sandhills as a tourist destination. Offering different kinds of activities is critical for attracting high-value visitors coming from a great distance. Having made a long trip, they often seek more than one type of experience. Recently developed high-end golf courses use the region's sand dunes to mimic links courses. Many ranches offer hunting and fishing,

Duck hunters in a boat camouflaged by a stand of cattails, Cherry County.

activities that generate substantial income in the area. Other enterprises, such as Sandhill River Trips in Thedford, Glidden Canoe Rental in Mullen, and the annual Burwell Rodeo offer recreational opportunities. Visitors interested in the region's culture and history can visit the Museum of the Fur Trade in Chadron and the Knight Museum and Sandhills Center in Alliance, or for a short drive outside the region, Pioneer Village in Minden or the internationally famous Willa Cather Foundation in Red Cloud. These and other varied enterprises work together to create a rich portfolio from which visitors can choose their activities and experiences, greatly enhancing the Sandhills' attraction to tourists.

Another category of potential nature-based economic opportunities grows out of the environmental services that the Sandhills do or could provide to the state and nation. If federal or state legislation recognized and paid for the value of these services, the region would gain additional revenue flows. The Sandhills are already a crucial link in providing high-quality water to Lincoln and Omaha, for example. So, too, as climate change grows more damaging, carbon sequestration in grasslands may become more pressing and a social benefit the rest of society may find worth paying for. These are environmental services currently supplied by the Sandhills for which the region is not compensated. Whether they can become significant sources of revenue flowing into the region is unclear.

We lack detailed data on the current structure of the Sandhills economy, including the economic impact of nature-based tourism in the region. There are, however, a few numbers that might provide some insight. A recent study found that the economic impact of the 2017 sandhill crane migration was $14.7 million. More generally, tourism is still just a small portion of the area's current total economic activity, especially compared to cattle production.

Regarding the potential for growth, ecotourism appears to offer greater opportunities for future growth, due to societal trend toward services rather than goods and toward more engagement-intensive tourism. By contrast, cattle production would appear to have more limited growth potential, given the societal trend away from red meat. Cattle ranching in the Sandhills will remain very significant but likely with limited growth potential. National and international market demand for Sandhills beef, ecotourism services, and other exportable goods and services will determine the region's future development. But it is an extremely fortunate circumstance for Sandhills residents that their current largest industry and their best future-growth industry are so highly compatible in their operations. The two may even work together to smooth out each other's cyclical fluctuations.

The Sandhills region is blessed with a unique and precious grassland environment and dedicated, hard-working, and talented residents. Its major occupation, reaching back to the earliest days of white settlement and continuing to the present, has been raising cattle. Ranching is a pursuit deeply entrenched in the residents' skills, identity, and culture. That will continue. Already we see those residents discovering new and innovative pursuits, such as ecotourism, which both protect the environment they are so proud of and add new revenue streams to bolster their ability to thrive economically. Realizing this vision will call on the best of the Sandhills' local leadership.

Richard K. Edwards is director emeritus of the Center for Great Plains Studies at the University of Nebraska–Lincoln. He is co-editor of *Homesteading the Plains: Toward a New History* (2017).

Katie Nieland is associate director of the Center for Great Plains Studies at the University of Nebraska–Lincoln.

Despite the name, Sandhill cranes are rarely found in the Nebraska Sandhills. Cranes congregate by the hundreds of thousands in early spring along the Platte River in Central Nebraska on their annual migration north to Canada and beyond to breed. Each year, over 40,000 visitors come from outside the state to view the cranes on the Platte and in the surrounding fields. This image was made on the Central Platte. Photograph by Tom White. Used with permission.

World-Class Golf Courses

Douglas A. Norby

The Nebraska Sandhills is home to a wealth of recreational activities, but a growing draw for tourists from out of state and abroad is its world-class golf courses. With vast rolling hills and endless acres of natural beauty, the Sandhills make a perfect venue for golfers seeking a variety of courses not intruded upon by man-made structures.

When private Sandhills golf courses were first being developed in the mid-1990s, they were available only to those seeking high-end experiences at exclusive clubs. Today, the Sandhills has become a destination for all golfers, offering excellent municipal courses and exclusive club courses, many designed by world-famous golf architects.

Golfing provides a growing source of tourism revenue, while striving to conserve the unique beauty of the Sandhills. Golf legend Jack Nicklaus once compared the area to the Scottish Highlands, where the game of golf was invented. Designers have focused on adapting courses to the landscape—one where sand bunkers occur naturally, native grasses provide the rough, and clear, flowing rivers act as the water hazards.

The Sand Hills Golf Club in Mullen, built in 1999, led the development of high-end links-style courses in the Sandhills. It is one of the most exclusive courses in the country, ranked in the top ten U.S. courses by Golf Digest magazine from 2011 to 2021. A private club open only eight months of the year, this course is one of the most high-end options in the country for hitting the links.

The Dismal River Club, a few miles of south of Mullen, is another exclusive club that draws members from abroad. It offers not only a fantastic course but also hunting, fishing, and other outdoor adventures.

For those planning a golf-based vacation, the Prairie Club in Valentine offers three courses, with some holes running along the Snake River canyon. The Dune, Pine, and Horse courses each offer a unique experience and also have been nationally recognized by golf publications. The Prairie Club offers packages that include dining and lodging, encouraging those looking for a getaway to come and stay and play at this unique golf destination.

The Sandhills is also home to some of the finest public courses in the country. The Wild Horse Golf Club in Gothenburg was ranked as the seventy-seventh best public course in America by *Golf Digest* in 2019. The Bayside Golf Club in Brule is a public course designed by top golf architects that offers the natural beauty of the Sandhills without the restrictive membership required by some clubs.

Douglas A. Norby is an editorial assistant for *The Nebraska Sandhills*.

Demographics of the Sandhills Over Time

Dennis Bauer

Many factors have influenced the population of the Sandhills over the past 120 years. The 1929 economic crash, followed by the severe drought of the 1930s, caused a major population decrease in almost all counties in the Sandhills. From the 1950s to the present, economics has been the biggest driver of the region's population decreases. Profit margins have remained almost constant over the last forty years while the costs of producing a calf, the region's main cash crop, have increased dramatically. This, coupled with the ever-increasing cost of living, is making it difficult to achieve the same life that people in the region have enjoyed in the past.

The population in the Sandhills has been declining since the 1920s and is projected to continue the downward trend into the year 2050 (table 1). For example, Brown County has lost more than 70 percent of its population since the 1920s and is projected to lose 45 percent of its population between 2010 and 2050. There are many reasons for the population decline, including a more mobile society and the opportunity for youth to see and choose a different way of life through exposure to higher education and technology. Yet the main driver is still economics, which has affected the number and size of ranches in the Sandhills region, as shown in table 2.

Table 1. Population totals of select Sandhills counties based on U.S. Census data

County	1890	1920	1950	2010	2050
Brown	4,539	6,749	5,164	3,145	1,748
Cherry	6,429	11,753	8,379	5,713	3,398
Grant	458	1,456	1,057	614	328
Hooker	426	1,378	1,051	736	481
Rock	3,703	3,083	3,026	1,526	803
Thomas	517	1,773	1,206	647	355
Wheeler	1,683	2,531	1,526	818	485

Note: 2050 estimates come from a study done by the Center for Public Affairs Research, University of Nebraska at Omaha.

Table 2. Number of farms and ranches in select Sandhills counties based on U.S. Census data

County	1900	1950	1987	2002	2017
Brown	513	538	344	311	268
Cherry	1,082	866	745	557	567
Grant	110	75	92	73	64
Hooker	51	79	78	81	97
Wheeler	269	297	213	194	215

The number of farms and ranches has continued to decline. The remaining ranches have expanded their operations, a necessity to maintain their standard of living. Data from the Nebraska Farm Business Association indicate that in the early 1980s, the annual cost of living for a family of four was $20,000 to $25,000. In 2020 the cost of living was $100,000 (figures are not indexed for inflation). Expenses continue to spiral upward over time, while cattle prices fluctuate. These numbers illustrate the need for ranches to get bigger or for the owners/operators to supplement their incomes with off-farm enterprises to keep up with the cost of living.

One expense that continues to increase steadily is property taxes. For example, in Brown County the tax for Sandhills upland range was $3.59 per acre in 2006. The 2020 rate on the same parcel was $7.64 per acre. Another way to look at this is on a per-calf-sold basis. Assuming thirteen acres per cow per year and a 90 percent calf crop, in 2006 the cost was $53 per calf in taxes. In 2020 the cost per calf was $112.86. That is $59.86 more per calf, cutting into the net profit of the operation. Other costs also have continued to rise, including feed, labor, veterinary services, fuel, equipment, and medical supplies for cattle (vaccines and health products).

According to FINBIN, one of the largest and most accessible sources of farm financial and production benchmark information, in 2000 the average livestock operation in Nebraska realized a net return of $111 per cow, with total direct and overhead cost of $349 per cow. Compare this to a net return in 2020 of $8.04 per cow, with total direct and overhead costs of $794 per cow. Costs have continued to rise, while cattle prices fluctuate from year to year, making it almost impossible to predict the future profitability of most ranches. The result is some ranches going out of business and other ranchers buying the smaller ones, creating larger operations out of necessity.

An interesting part of this story is that for those reporting weaning weights, weights have remained the same, from 588 pounds in 2000 to 587 pounds in 2020, showing that producers are not selling more pounds of calf per cow over the last twenty years. With input costs doubling in the last twenty years, ranchers can only make more money if cattle prices are considerably higher today than they were in 2000.

Another demographic affecting the Sandhills is the amount of land in absentee ownership. Data from the Brown County Assessor shows that more than 38 percent of the land in the county is owned by persons or entities that do not live in the county. This has led to operations getting larger, as absentee owners are more likely to sell the properties and invest in ventures with greater returns. People who have been off the ranch for years sometimes lose their connection with the land and are more likely to sell. This in turn creates fewer operations in the area.

Changes in land ownership in the Sandhills could have far-reaching effects. The median age of ranch owners/operators is sixty-plus. As these individuals retire, who will buy these operations? Ranches may continue to get bigger and bigger at an even faster rate. This does not mean it will be detrimental to the Sandhills, but it may paint the region in a different light.

What do these changes mean for the future of the Sandhills? The good news is that the Sandhills will endure no matter how the population demographics change. Ranchers using best management practices that have been adopted by most operations will ensure the conservation and preservation of this resource. Almost all producers today put a high value on the resources entrusted to them and strive to leave their operations in better condition than when they started.

One almost certain change is that the population will be less than it is today. This places a greater burden on small rural communities to maintain their infrastructure of health care, schools, roads, grocery stores, and other critical services. Where will people go to obtain these services? Will ranching operations become so large that supplies and services will be transported in from outside the area, making it more difficult for local businesses to survive? What impact will that have on local communities?

Despite these potential changes, Sandhills ranchers and residents have a history of resilience and the ability to adapt to change, and the Sandhills will continue to be the land of wide-open spaces, with a sea of grass waving in the breeze through the rolling hills. Future generations will undoubtedly feel as past and present residents do, that there is no better place to live than the Sandhills of Nebraska.

Dennis Dauer is an emeritus extension educator with University of Nebraska Extension in Ainsworth, Nebraska.

Sunrise at Cottonwood-Steverson Wildlife Management Area, Cherry County.

Local Knowledge and the Future of the Sandhills

Mary Ann Vinton and Jay Leighter

Roundup of cows and calves before a branding, Hooker County. Photograph by Joe McDaniel. Used with permission.

The Aunt Mary, a pasture in the central Sandhills, lies along the north fork of the headwaters of the Dismal River. Mary Crouch filed the Kinkaid patent in 1915, and her relative, George Swiggart (great-great-grandfather to Mary Ann, co-author of this chapter), took it off her hands when it was proved up. Since then, this parcel has been known as the "Aunt Mary" and has been run as one of the most distant winter pastures, receiving the older calves and their mothers after close monitoring at birth near the ranch house. It's also one of the closest summer pastures, where grass-fattened yearlings amble from the low river ground up into choppy hills searching out swales of nutritious grama grasses, avoiding the coarse bunches of little bluestem dominating the dunes. The Aunt Mary is distinctive for being used in both seasons, but for different purposes.

Blue grama, hairy grama, and side-oats grama are species of grass belonging to the genus *Bouteloua*. They tend to be short in stature and high in nitrogen content. Ranchers call them "hard." Hard is something you can depend on. Mary Ann's rancher brother, one of the first ranchers Jay interviewed in our research, calls them grandma grasses and says things like, "It's a good year for grandma grasses."

Since 2018, the two of us have been putting our feet on the ground in the Sandhills, often in the Aunt Mary. Mary Ann, the biologist, shifts between recalling memories of her deep family history in this place, introducing family and neighbors to our team, and leading a small army of students and colleagues into the field to fly drones, take photos, and collect and identify species. This work paints a picture about patterns and variability from dune top to meadow. Jay, the ethnographer, benefits from Mary Ann's relationships, spending time bumping around in trucks, hanging out at the squeeze chute, and sitting at kitchen tables recording the stories, thoughts, and concerns of ranching families. Family memories of

Paul Vinton, Hooker County rancher, driving. Photograph by John O'Keefe. Used with permission.

Clara Schmid with her daughter confers with her father, Paul Vinton, in the alleyway of a cattle chute on a Sandhills ranch. Photograph by John O'Keefe. Used with permission.

haying, blizzards, droughts, bull sales, and calf weights are analyzed to locate patterned ways people talk about life in the Sandhills.

What bolsters our friendship and research collaboration is that we are both concerned with a singular question: What is the potential long-term stability of the Sandhills in the face of increased stress on natural and social systems?

It is a complicated question that neither of us can answer alone. Ecologically, winds, water, and time have shaped the Nebraska Sandhills into grass-covered upland dune

Rounding up cows and calves on a four-wheeler, Hooker County. Photograph by Joe McDaniel. Used with permission.

tops and lowland valleys where surface water gathers, creating wet meadows. The central North America climate enables a unique combination of plant cover, including both cool and warm season grasses. The interaction of soil type, topography, and weather makes understanding the ecology of this place quite difficult. Culturally, the people of the Sandhills are deeply connected to the land.

It would be impossible to come to terms with who they are, what concerns them, and how they understand the past, present, or future without some sense for the local ecology and agricultural practice.

Early homesteaders tried and failed to grow crops, settling instead through mistakes, luck, and triumph on ranching as the most profitable and productive use

spersed with wet meadows brimming with groundwater. The proportion of non-native species remains low. Surviving in the Sandhills involves knowledge and practices developed with deference and humility by the people who live there.

Our impulse has been to meaningfully combine personal history, expertise in grasslands, and new research on the Aunt Mary with ethnographic observation and rancher interviews to try to understand the place, the people, and the deeply intertwined relationship between the two.

Mary Ann has worked in all kinds of grasslands: short-grass steppe, desert grassland, tallgrass prairie, and mixed-grass prairie. In each, there is something that explains where and how much vegetation grows; often, this is water—the amount and timing of rainfall or even complex soil water dynamics like "root hydraulic lift." In the tallgrass prairie, it often involves fire or nutrients like nitrogen or phosphorus and the rate that they cycle from dead grass to soil to plants and back, sometimes passing through herbivores first.

Ranchers have their own way of thinking about and talking through these things. Their knowledge of the land—knowing when, where, and how often to graze their cattle—is critical to maintaining the productivity of the land and their livelihoods.

Mary Ann emailed this story to Jay early on in our work:

> I had 45 minutes until my next class, time to call my brother and tell him we were planning to visit the ranch to do field work. It is early October, and we start talking about the Aunt Mary. He has cows further east, in the "summer range," and is thinking aloud about when to bring them back for the winter. September has been wet.
>
> "The Grandma grasses are greening up again, even though they are warm-season. Maybe they should

of the land. But cattle ranching here is not like cattle ranching anywhere else. Ecological evidence suggests that most residents have learned to coexist on the land in a way that minimizes ecological diminishment. "Go back" fields, still apparent on some level areas, date from failed attempts at farming by Kinkaid settlers. Apart from those areas, the Sandhills landscape is still largely dune after dune of grass-stabilized sand, inter-

stay on summer range for a few more weeks. I just don't know what to do," he muses. "I've never seen a September like this, so wet, you know the water is coming up in the valleys earlier than ever. Those Grandma grasses head out, and you'd think they are done, but they are still growing. Plenty of forage, especially in the heavier soils, where the Grandma grasses grow."

I have 5 minutes before class, but I want to be patient in letting him work out this puzzle, plus I am learning. I have never worked in a grassland with so many time and landscape-based contingencies on forage. My academic colleagues don't meander through stories about where and when the grass grows.

The next summer, a drought has set in, and Jay is speaking to a rancher in the bunkhouse, cold beers on the table and the recorder going. The rancher offers an assessment of the grass, along with his concern and desire to act:

> I don't like the way some of them pastures look. I feel kinda bad, kind of a drought. Feel like I need to do something. Cut down on numbers or do something.

Later that summer, while enjoying a little "windshield time," a rancher explains to Jay the value of flying over the Sandhills:

> It's what you see. You learn to look and see how much sand there is, how much white there is when you're looking down. It will not lie to you from the air, the grass won't.

Our goal is to make a record and analyze as many instances of ranchers talking about ranching in the Sandhills as we can. We want to understand the local logic of things, how ranchers come to know what they know, how they think things work or don't, and how people in the

Sandhills make sense of who they are and what should be done. To do so is to describe the culture through communication, what gets said, and what is significant. More technically, this work describes a system of significant terms and meanings that have the potential to reveal beliefs about action, emotion, and identity. Grass is a symbol that, from the local point of view, requires constant monitoring; the health of the grass impacts how ranchers feel day to day and season to season; "taking care of your grass" defines a rancher's purpose.

The hard part is learning something about cultural communication and then draw connections and develop insights with what we understand about precipitation, sandy soils, topography, and biodiversity. The goal is to make a record of a place that people revere, hold close to their hearts, worry about, want to protect, take ownership in, are moved by, have become attached to, or is part of them. It has a long natural history, and a relatively stable but not unproblematic human history. Questions about the future of the Sandhills are riddled with emotions and wonder, derived from diverse fields of knowledge and understandings of identity, and include the motivation to protect, even if the nature of protection is contested and nuanced. Key questions that motivate our research loom:

> How does a rural place rich in groundwater, wind, and sun fare in an increasingly connected economy, where regional urban areas face dwindling freshwater supplies and increased demand for renewable energy?

> How do family ranches survive in the face of "outside" capital? What is the impact of "absentee" landowners?

> How does the advent of "lab grown" meat and the shift to more plant-based diets impact a region where production of beef cattle is likely the most sustainable use of the land? Can high quality, humanely raised, "grass-fed" meat find a market?

What are the implications of a changing climate and more extreme conditions in this fragile system?

It is necessary to learn from those whose knowledge of the Sandhills is based in looking carefully every day. Ranchers notice the slightest variations by recalling experience or oral histories. They communicate those changes to one another, are mindful of daily and seasonal impacts, and have the patience and humility to adapt to ecological forces they do not control. The future of the Sandhills largely depends on those who live there, as it has for 150 years. Sandhillers will be the first to notice the most subtle changes in climate and dune stability.

The people and this place are inextricably bound. Questions about the future of the Sandhills are largely dependent upon embracing and celebrating this bond as the foundation for finding answers.

Mary Ann Vinton is a professor and program director of environmental science at Creighton University in Omaha.

Jay Leighter is an associate professor of communication studies and director of the Sustainability Studies Program at Creighton University in Omaha.

Fence line and lake north of Crescent Lake National Wildlife Refuge, Garden County. Photograph by John O'Keefe. Used with permission.

Alternative Futures of the Sandhills

Craig Allen and Caleb Roberts

"A Public Domain, once a velvet carpet of rich Buffalo-grass and grama, now an illimitable waste of rattlesnake-bush and tumbleweed, too impoverished to be accepted as a gift by the states within which it lies. Why? Because the ecology of the Southwest happened to be set on a hair trigger." Aldo Leopold, author of *A Sand County Almanac* and champion of land ethics, made this observation of rangeland in New Mexico in 1935. He recognized that some landscapes are fragile and, given enough disturbance, can suddenly lose productivity. Ranchers in the Nebraska Sandhills, too, recognize the potential fragility of their landscape.

The Sandhills have changed from sea to desert to forest to grassland, and they can—and will at some point—change again. No ecosystem is stable for all time. Ecosystems contract and expand like lungs; they collapse and emerge as completely new ecologies. These are not new phenomena. They have been occurring for millennia. What is new is the rate at which they are occurring and our understanding of humanity's role in causing them.

Early Sandhills' pioneers experienced devastating prairie fires and sand blowouts, often caused by railroads and by overgrazing, respectively. Both blowouts and fires are forces that can push a landscape beyond an ecological threshold, causing it to change fundamentally. Blowouts could spread and turn the Sandhills into a moving dune field, as they were less than a thousand years ago. Fires, too, remove vegetation, potentially leading to moving sands and the change of the Sandhills from productive rangeland to sand dunes.

What does this uncertainty mean for the Sandhills? It means there are alternative futures the Sandhills could have. Without the hundred-thousand-acre fires and millions of bison refreshing, fertilizing, stirring, and replanting the grasses and pushing back the tide of trees, what could happen to the Sandhills? And with the new influences of climate change, more people, more fences and cattle, and more fragmentation from roads and human land use, what new paths could the Sandhills take? Will the Sandhills be recognizable in a hundred years or even ten or twenty years?

One way to grapple with these questions is to consider all the paths the Sandhills may take given these changes and how to keep or make the Sandhills resilient to them. History, current trends, and imagination can be used explore these alternative futures, then stakeholders can use this knowledge to guide the Sandhills to the place they want it to be.

CURRENT

Future 1: The Sand-Woods

A prairie is only a prairie if it burns. If a prairie does not burn, it becomes something else. Globally, human fire suppression coupled with human actions, like tree planting, and human-caused problems, like climate change, are leading to a phenomenon called "afforestation." During afforestation, trees and shrubs begin peppering grasslands, congeal into patches of woodlands, and then sometimes completely coat the landscape and become forests. The Great Plains, where the Sandhills are nestled, are collapsing under the weight of trees, and evidence is mounting that the Sandhills are not immune to this threat. Satellite imagery and artificial intelligence are tracking tendrils of trees spreading westward along roads and rivers, sprouting from shelterbelts and nurseries. American robins—woodland birds—are pushing westward into the Sandhills where they historically did not occur. It is not clear how long the afforestation process would take, but given the rate of afforestation over the last several decades, the Sandhills prairie could shift to sand woods in less than a hundred years.

SAND-WOODS
Afforestation + Fire Suppression + Climate Change

FULL FOREST
Afforestation + Climate Change

Future 2: Dune Sea

Historically, the biggest fear in the Sandhills was a catastrophic loss of grass cover and a return to mobilized sand dunes. Although experiments suggest that the Sandhills can experience blowouts without blowouts spreading, that could change, for example with prolonged drought or drought coinciding with catastrophic wildfire. This is not an improbable future—Sandhills sand dunes were largely free of grass and mobile in very recent geologic history. This future would benefit few. Sand dunes are not productive rangeland, and few wildlife species would inhabit the Sandhills transformed to a dune sea. Currently careful land stewardship has been successful in keeping this undesirable alternative future at bay.

DUNE SEA
Overgrazing + Climate Change

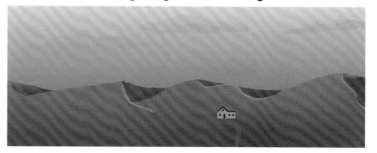

Future 3: A Shadow of the Past

If fires burned a hundred thousand acres in a day, if fences no longer broke the blanket of prairie into a homogenized tilework, if cedar waxwings no longer spread juniper seeds with their droppings, and if humans no longer planted trees that bore thousands of seeds each year, the Sandhills could, potentially, return to a state similar to pre-European colonization. The amount of change this would take is staggering—it would require change in not only the ecology but the society of the Sandhills. It would require a culture that thrives with fire instead of fearing it. It would require a culture that sees fences and boundaries but also sees past them to the larger landscape they all share. Groups such as the Sandhills Task Force, The

Nature Conservancy at the Niobrara Valley Preserve, the Nebraska Prescribed Burn Council, and many others are working to make this alternative future of rolling prairie, unbroken by trees, and united by stewardship a reality.

SHADOW OF THE PAST
Widespread Fire Usage + Grazing Without Borders

Future 4: Dead Man Walking

Perhaps the most obvious future for the Sandhills is exactly like today's Sandhills: mostly intact prairie, fences carving up the grass like cookie cutters, cattle sleeping under the cottonwoods by the river, sparse ranches, little towns, some ranches cracking into ranchettes when the kids don't come back, center pivots in the swales, sharp-tailed grouse dancing on the hills, old cedars standing in clean shelterbelts, and younger cedars creeping out of the river valleys and peeking above the prairie grass. These are beautiful and familiar images to many. But keeping this status quo does not mean doing nothing. All the pressures the Sandhills are facing will only increase over time, meaning maintaining today's Sandhills will become harder and harder. The tides of trees will pile higher, the droughts will get longer and deeper, more people will want a little

piece of the wide-open spaces, and stakeholders will be left fighting for shrinking scraps of a memory of the Sandhills. Soon, the Sandhills could become a "dead man walking," still alive, but shuffling toward its end.

Future 5: Suburban Sandhills

Pandemics and remote work have limited the desirability of city living and increased the benefits of rural living. The Sandhills, with low population density, beautiful vistas, lakes, and proximity to the Front Range of the Rocky Mountains, is attractive for acreage developments, both for full time and vacation living. This future has ranching forced out by increasing land values and taxation rates and ultimately destroys the amenities that made it attractive in the first place.

Stranger (Less Likely?) Futures

Alternative: Potato Fields

Exploding human populations globally and diminished fresh water supplies increase the attractiveness of the Sandhills for row crop agriculture. The Great Plains Aquifer provides plenty of irrigation water, and crops, such as potatoes, thrive in sandy soils. Because row crops are more profitable than rangeland, the entire Sandhills becomes cropped. This leads to fragmentation, loss of grass and wildlife, depletion of the aquifer, and flattening of the landscape to better enable center pivot irrigation. Although ranching is no longer viable, former ranchers are economically benefited by this transition.

DEAD MAN WALKING
Afforestation + Fire Suppression + Urbanization

DRY LAND AGRICULTURE
Human Population Growth + Climate Change

Alternative: Back to the Future

By 2050 humans are producing laboratory-raised meat, and real meat consumption has plummeted, in tandem with the increasing global population. To maintain their livelihoods, ranchers have embraced the idea of a buffalo commons and profit from the Sandhills National Park. The Sandhills becomes a global tourism hotspot, featuring wild landscapes and snippets of "life in the twentieth century," where ranching activities are reenacted by paid actors.

Alternative: Fueling the World

Currently, cattle production feeds the world. Decreasing demand for beef and increasing demand for clean energy leads to the development of the Sandhills for energy production. Ranching is relegated to largely hobby farms, as the sale of solar and wind energy drives economic productivity in the Sandhills. Rolling dune vistas are lost to seas of solar panels and the architecture of tens of thousands of wind turbines. From all, a network of aboveground electric transmission cables spiders the landscape, and extensive road systems scar the landscape.

ENERGY DEVELOPMENT
Economic Transformation + Climate Change

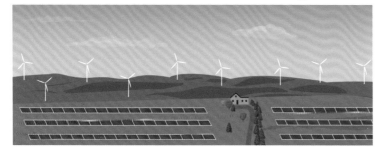

Potential futures for the Nebraska Sandhills. Graphics by Abigail Snyder, School of Natural Resources, University of Nebraska–Lincoln. Used with permission.

Conclusion

How do stakeholders respond to these alternative futures? Continue with business as usual and hope for the best, or take proactive steps to predict changes and reverse the problems?

Determining alternative futures can be helpful in guiding management to ensure that desirable futures are likely and undesirable futures avoided. Some of our scenarios may seem far-fetched, but ecological surprises are common. While Sandhills ranchers have been extremely successful in avoiding blowouts and fires, the focus on these has led to a new, unforeseen enemy in the form of invading redcedar, which threatens ranching livelihoods in a different way. Recognizing and acknowledging this and other problems is needed for action to prevent undesired change over large landscapes. This has happened, and many ranchers in the Sandhills have joined forces to help manage and continue to steer the Sandhills to a desirable, sustainable, future.

Craig Allen is a professor in the School of Natural Resources and director of the Center for Resilience in Agricultural Working Landscapes at the University of Nebraska–Lincoln.

Caleb Roberts is assistant unit leader, U.S. Geological Survey, Arkansas Cooperative Unit.

Windmill on a Sandhills farm at sunset.

Acknowledgments

The editorial team of *The Nebraska Sandhills* owes gratitude and thanks to a number of individuals. We especially thank Michael Boehm, Harlan Vice Chancellor for the Institute of Agriculture and Natural Resources at the University of Nebraska–Lincoln. He was a project champion from the start, envisioning it as part of the fiftieth anniversary of IANR's founding in 2023. Others on the IANR leadership team who deserve kudos are Jeff Bassford, Cara Pesek, and Sheryl May. We also thank Walt Schacht, Emeritus Sunkist Fiesta Bowl Professor of Agronomy and director emeritus of the Center for Grasslands Studies at UNL; and Richard K. Edwards, director emeritus of the Center for Great Plains Studies at UNL. Both offered invaluable ideas, sources, and leads as early planning was underway in 2019 and 2020, as did Margaret Jacobs, current director of the Center for Great Plains Studies.

Scientists, writers, and photography archivists, especially archivist Jaclyn Vogt at the Nebraska Game and Parks Commission, were great contributors. Thanks as well to the members of UNL's Platte Basin Timelapse, including Mariah Lundgren and Dakota Altman. We also thank Lindsey Hillgartner at History Nebraska and Mary Ellen Ducey and Josh Caster at UNL Libraries for their assistance.

Others who did not provide essays but contributed expertise include Angie Fox, University of Nebraska State Museum; Virginia "Ginny" L. McGuire, hydrologist, U.S. Geological Survey, Nebraska Water Science Center; Alan B. Bond, emeritus professor, School of Biological Sciences; David Wedin, professor, School of Natural Resources; and Abigail Snyder, web designer in the School of Natural Resources.

We thank the many scholars, journalists, historians, property owners, and State of Nebraska scientists who contributed articles and ideas. Thanks much to those who donated the use of their photographs: Phil Schoenberger, Chris Helzer, Platte Basin Timelapse, Michael Forsberg, and Tom White. We also thank Catherine E. Blount for permission to use photographs from her collection regarding DeWitty. Thank you, Daniele Hunter, assistant literary agent, McIntosh & Otis Inc. Thank you, Richard Berkland of Valmont Industries.

Thanks to Donna Shear, director emerita of the University of Nebraska Press, for greenlighting the project, and to the entire Press team, including Ann Baker and Bridget Barry. Kudos to the University of Nebraska Foundation team led by Josh Egley and Marcia White, for fundraising; a special thanks to our very first (and continuing) underwriter, Tom Farrell.

Thank you to the incredible group of faculty and nonfaculty scientists and scholars at UNL and other universities for their contributions. Finally, thank you to Judy Diamond for stepping in when Monica Norby had to pull back due to a health concern. To know that our bench at the University of Nebraska is deep and filled with experts willing and able to help is greatly appreciated.

Further Reading about the Sandhills

Agee, Jonis. *The Bones of Paradise*. New York: William Morrow Paperbacks, 2017.

Bleed, Ann S., and Charles A. Flowerday, eds. *An Atlas of the Sand Hills*. 3rd ed. Omaha: World-Herald Foundation, 1998.

Harrison, Jim. *The Road Home*. New York: Washington Square, 1998.

Janovy, John J., Jr. *Keith County Journal*. Lincoln, NE: Bison Books, 1996.

Joern, Pamela Carter. *The Floor of the Sky*. Lincoln, NE: Bison Books, 1996.

Johnsgard, Paul A. The Niobrara: *A River Running through Time*. Lincoln, NE: Bison Books, 2007.

——. *This Fragile Land: A Natural History of the Nebraska Sandhills*. Lincoln: University of Nebraska Press, 1995.

Jones, Bryan L. *North of the Platte, South of the Niobrara: A Little Further into the Nebraska Sand Hills*. Nacogdoches, TX: Stephen F. Austin University Press, 2018.

Jones, Stephen R. *The Last Prairie: A Sandhills Journey*. New York: Ragged Mountain, 2000.

——. *Nourishing Waters, Comforting Sky: Thirty-Five Years at a Sandhills Oasis*. Lincoln: University of Nebraska Press, 2022.

McIntosh, Charles B. *The Nebraska Sand Hills—The Human Landscape*. Lincoln: University of Nebraska Press, 1996.

Owen, David A. *Like No Other Place: The Sandhills of Nebraska*. Lincoln, NE: Bison Books, 2012.

Powell, Larkin A. *Great Plains Birds*. Lincoln: University of Nebraska Press, 2019.

Randolph, Ladette. *A Sandhills Ballad*. Lincoln, NE: Bison Books, 2011.

Sandoz, Mari. *Old Jules*. Lincoln: University of Nebraska Press, 1962.

Snyder, Grace, and Nellie Snyder Yost. *No Time on My Hands*. Lincoln: University of Nebraska Press, 1986.

Contributors

Craig Allen is a professor in the School of Natural Resources and director of the Center for Resilience in Agricultural Working Landscapes at the University of Nebraska–Lincoln.

Daryl Bauer is a fisheries biologist for Nebraska Game and Parks Commission.

Dennis Bauer is an emeritus extension educator with University of Nebraska Extension in Ainsworth, Nebraska.

Michael J. Boehm is University of Nebraska Vice President and the Harlan Vice Chancellor for the Institute of Agriculture and Natural Resources at the University of Nebraska–Lincoln.

John R. "Rob" Bozell retired as Nebraska State Archaeologist in 2021 and remains active in archaeological research and consulting.

Jeffrey Bradshaw is an entomologist and extension specialist at the University of Nebraska Panhandle Research and Extension Center in Scottsbluff, Nebraska.

Jessica Corman is an associate professor in the School of Natural Resources at the University of Nebraska–Lincoln.

Judy Diamond is a professor of libraries at the University of Nebraska–Lincoln and curator at the University of Nebraska State Museum. She is a co-editor of *The Nebraska Sandhills*.

David D. Dunigan is a research professor in the Nebraska Center for Virology at the University of Nebraska–Lincoln.

Cheryl Dunn is research manager and herbarium coordinator for the Department of Agronomy and Horticulture at the University of Nebraska–Lincoln.

Shaun Dunn is natural heritage zoologist for Nebraska Game and Parks Commission.

Martha Durr is a professor in the School of Natural Resources at the University of Nebraska–Lincoln, state climatologist, and director of the Nebraska State Climate Office.

Roger Echo-Hawk is a writer and artist who studies Pawnee history.

Richard K. Edwards is director emeritus of the Center for Great Plains Studies at the University of Nebraska–Lincoln. He is co-editor of *Homesteading the Plains: Toward a New History* (2017).

Michael Farrell is a photographer, filmmaker, and co-founder of Platte Basin Timelapse.

Dennis Ferraro is a professor of conservation biology and herpetology in the School of Biological Sciences at the University of Nebraska–Lincoln.

Ashley Forrester earned her master's in biology in 2022 from the University of Nebraska at Kearney.

Michael Forsberg is a conservation photographer and research assistant professor in the School of Natural Resources at the University of Nebraska–Lincoln. He is a co-founder of Platte Basin Timelapse and a co-editor of *The Nebraska Sandhills*.

Sherilyn C. Fritz is George Holmes University Professor in Earth and Atmospheric Sciences and Biological Sciences at the University of Nebraska–Lincoln. She is a co-editor of *The Nebraska Sandhills*.

Keith Geluso is a professor of biology at the University of Nebraska at Kearney.

Troy Gilmore is an associate professor in the School of Natural Resources at the University of Nebraska–Lincoln.

Erin Haacker is an assistant professor of Earth and Atmospheric Sciences at the University of Nebraska–Lincoln.

Kim Hachiya is a retired communications specialist for the University of Nebraska–Lincoln and author of *Dear Old Nebraska U* (2019). She is a co-editor of *The Nebraska Sandhills*.

Paul R. Hanson is a professor in the School of Natural Resources at the University of Nebraska–Lincoln.

Mary Harner is a professor of communication and biology at the University of Nebraska at Kearney.

Mark Harris is a former associate director of the University of Nebraska State Museum and a freelance photographer and author of *Rodeo Nebraska* (2015).

Chris Helzer is a prairie ecologist and The Nature Conservancy's director of science in Nebraska.

Adam Houston is a professor of Earth and Atmospheric Sciences at the University of Nebraska–Lincoln and director of the Severe Storms Research Group.

Jim Jenkins is the operating partner for his family's diversified farming, ranching, and cattle-feeding operation near Callaway, Nebraska.

R. Matthew Joeckel is senior associate director of the School of Natural Resources, director of Conservation and Survey Division at the University of Nebraska–Lincoln, and Nebraska State Geologist.

Bethany Johnston is a University of Nebraska Extension educator at the Central Sandhills Extension Office in Burwell, Nebraska.

Shelly Kelly is executive director of the Sandhills Task Force in Broken Bow, Nebraska.

Ted Kooser is the former Poet Laureate Consultant in Poetry to the Library of Congress, serving from 2004 to 2006. He is Presidential Professor Emeritus at the University of Nebraska, where he taught poetry writing.

Jesse T. Korus is an associate professor in the School of Natural Resources at the University of Nebraska–Lincoln.

Ted LaGrange is wetland program manager for Nebraska Game and Parks Commission.

Jay Leighter is an associate professor of communication studies and director of the Sustainability Studies Program at Creighton University in Omaha.

Emily Levine is an independent scholar of the Great Plains focusing on Indigenous history and culture.

David Loope is professor emeritus of Earth and Atmospheric Sciences at the University of Nebraska–Lincoln.

Martha Mamo is John E. Weaver Professor and Chair of Agronomy and Horticulture at the University of Nebraska–Lincoln.

Joe Mason is a professor of geography at the University of Wisconsin–Madison.

Katie Nieland is associate director of the Center for Great Plains Studies at the University of Nebraska–Lincoln.

Douglas A. Norby is an editorial assistant for *The Nebraska Sandhills*.

Monica Norby retired as assistant vice chancellor for Research and Economic Development at the University of Nebraska–Lincoln. She is editor in chief of *The Nebraska Sandhills*.

Andrew S. Pollock is a partner with Rembolt Ludtke law firm. He grew up in Keith County, Nebraska.

Larkin Powell is a professor of wildlife ecology and director of the School of Natural Resources at the University of Nebraska–Lincoln.

Thomas Powers is a professor in Plant Pathology at the University of Nebraska–Lincoln.

Clayton L. Reinier is a GIS research specialist for the School of Natural Resources at the University of Nebraska–Lincoln.

Caleb Roberts is assistant unit leader, U.S. Geological Survey, Arkansas Cooperative Unit.

Walt Schacht is Emeritus Sunkist Fiesta Bowl Professor of Agronomy and director emeritus of the Center for Grasslands Studies at the University of Nebraska–Lincoln.

Sarah Sortum is a fourth-generation member of a family of that operates the Switzer Ranch in Loup County, Nebraska.

Steve Spomer is a retired research technologist for the Department of Entomology at the University of Nebraska–Lincoln.

Gerry Steinauer is a botanist-ecologist for Nebraska Game and Parks Commission.

Al Steuter is a landowner and rancher in Johnstown, Nebraska.

Aaron Sutherlen is an associate professor of graphic design at the University of Nebraska–Lincoln. He is a co-editor and chief designer of *The Nebraska Sandhills*.

James Swinehart is an emeritus research geologist in the Conservation and Survey Division of the University of Nebraska–Lincoln.

Carson Vaughan is a freelance journalist and author of *Zoo Nebraska: The Dismantling of an American Dream* (2019).

Mary Ann Vinton is a professor and program director of environmental science at Creighton University in Omaha.

Jerry Volesky is a range and forage specialist, Nebraska Extension specialist, and interim director of the Center for Grassland Studies at the University of Nebraska–Lincoln.

Jeremy A. White is a lecturer in biology at the University of Nebraska at Omaha.

Chris Widga is a vertebrate paleontologist, head curator, and adjunct faculty member in geosciences at East Tennessee State University.

Aaron R. Young is a geologist in the School of Natural Resources at the University of Nebraska–Lincoln.

Courtney L.C. Ziska is an archaeologist and national environmental policy act specialist at the Nebraska Department of Transportation.